SEARCHING FOR MY FAITH

*A Cop's Struggle
with Good and Evil
and the Question:
"Is God Real?"*

FREDERICK MUNCH

outskirts
press

Table of Contents

Introduction

GOD DOES NOT punish- He just steps back, away from your sin, and lets life unfold without His guidance. The Almighty lets our free will and sin tear us down, because only then can we experience despair and begin the process of repentance and pull ourselves up. A magical transformation will take place and faith building will begin. Once we realize how much God loves and cares for us, and that He has been with us even before the womb, we will experience a serenity and contentment that cannot be put into words.

This is a true story. Except for immediate family members, all of the names have been changed to protect people's privacy. Parts of it are very raw. I have opened my soul to the reader and am making public some of my most personal private thoughts and experiences, hopefully in an attempt to help you not make the same mistakes. How sweet life could have been if I had been a true believer much earlier in age. A journey that was always full of doubt. A sickly daily struggle with the question of faith, good and evil, and does God really exist?

Witness how the truth finally wins out, and the suffering, apathy, and desperation are overcome, and it all becomes the down payment for hopefully everlasting life.

We all have a cross to carry. God hung His only Son on a cross to pay for our sins. Can we expect not to experience adversity and trial in traveling the road to eternity?

In the field of public service, the realities and emotions of encountering people's strife can begin to take a toll on the psyche. The onset of depression if not managed can lead to apathy, despair, and behavior that is inexcusable. You can become very cynical and be a passionate "Doubting Thomas." The guilt that goes along with the doubt is debilitating.

The question of God or higher power becomes a question asked by many policemen as they witness the worst in people, and the tragedies that cannot be explained. Why does God permit evil? Why do good people suffer?

These questions were answered and struggles eventually overcome for me after reaching a low point that was incomprehensible. For some reason I never blamed God for the setbacks that happened to me. I blamed me, because in reality I didn't believe there was a God. I never asked why? I knew why- because it was my doing.

The early chapters outline and explain the relationship with family and friends, and with God, and describes the morals instilled in me. I explain the desire and drive to want to help people, and the obsession with keeping a promise I made to my Dad. I go in depth about the police hiring processes at a time when "Affirmative Action" was prevalent.

The "Academy" is described in detail and relates its day to day and minute to minute challenges. A lot of it funny and some of it sad. The Academy sorts out those that shouldn't be there and is always stressful. Anyone aspiring to be a policeman, or wondering how a police academy should be structured, will learn much from those chapters.

The middle chapters describe the actual job, from the first day getting into that 1976 Plymouth Fury and pulling out of the Post parking lot for the first time by myself, and feeling my heart beating out of my chest. I relate many experiences, most hard to re-live and re-hash. Some may make you laugh, and I promise a couple are going to make you cry. All with my continual questioning of my doubt for the existence of God.

There are family tragedies. There are family victories. There are personal setbacks. There are personal triumphs. Always asking myself, "Was God with me?"

There is an injury that changes my entire life, and the subsequent chain of events that lead down a destructive path and tragically the "Accident."

The last chapters I will leave for your imagination as I do not want to ruin an ending. They contain my most personal thoughts on life, religion, family, and most importantly, God. I'm hoping the mistakes I made may prevent even just one person from steering the same course. I'll leave you with what was the most important thing I've learned in my twenty-nine years on the street, and subsequent years until today, and has brought me much peace:

"We know that ALL things work for the good, for those who love God and are willing to work for His purpose." (Romans 8:28).

My hope is after reading this book you may understand the hidden meaning of that scripture from St.Paul. If you love God, ALL things, even bad things, will work for your good. It is amazingly true.

I have written about some raw accounts of things that happened in prison. It is a very scary place. There are no "bad asses" in prison. Everyone eventually catches a beating. And for me, I met an angel there:

"For His angels will take charge over you, and they will lift you up in their hand's, lest you strike your foot against a stone." (Psalm 91).

Please, believe and receive. The transformation is very real. Read the Bible daily. My angel nurtured me and taught me how to pray. God wants the best for us, but we must turn it all over to Him. Tear the rear-view mirror off your car and throw it away. Never look back and hand Christ your keys. Let Him drive. Just get in the back seat and enjoy the ride-enjoy the day-believe and receive. Praise God.

Much of the proceeds from the sale of this book will benefit selected charities.

CHAPTER 1

The Beginning

IT WAS THE spring of 1967 on a Saturday morning and as usual, God had joined us for breakfast. Although no one at the table was aware He was present, we went about the normal Saturday routine. I sat in our kitchen with my Dad and my brother eating cereal. My Mom and sister Marianne were upstairs cleaning and vacuuming.

I didn't know much of anything pertaining to God at that time in my life. I was not even sure if God existed, but as the years passed, and after a lifetime of doubt, that all changed. And the journey from doubt to belief was terrifying, exciting, heartbreaking, and eventually glorious.

> The Almighty will step back from your sin, and that will force you to your knees, and you will cry out. I eventually realized His love is overwhelming for those who truly believe. Through life's adversities, He puts you in the fire to refine you like gold. I came to learn the purpose of life, and the truth that God is real.

We were the typical American middle-class family as far as I knew. We lived within the city limits in a residential neighborhood in Erie, Pa. Neighbors tried to get along back then, and most people wanted to display a general concern for one another. The moral fiber of the country for the most part was righteous and strong. Children were raised with some discipline, and they learned the meaning of respecting others.

My Dad had served in WW II like almost all men his age. He left

High School early to enlist in the Navy during the spring of 1944, and six weeks later found himself on a Destroyer fighting the Japanese in the Pacific.

He served in three notable campaigns, two of which were at Iwo Jima and Okinawa. During the Okinawa battle his Destroyer shot down a Kamikaze. The plane crashed within a few feet of the hull and exploded. It tore a hole in the ship and killed most of the young sailors that were assigned to the engine room.

My Dad at General Quarters (battle stations) was assigned to the rear magazine loading shells in the rear five-inch gun. When they weren't at General Quarters, he was assigned to the engine room as a first-class Fireman. He knew all the men killed that day, and several were his best friends. Even worse, he was on the recovery team, and had to recover, and then help prepare the bodies of the men killed for burial at sea.

He didn't like to talk about the war much, but I would press him sometimes with questions about his experiences. Most kids my age were mesmerized about the war and wanted to hear every story. He very rarely talked about that day, and how he had to scrape a lot of his friends bodies off the steel bulkheads, and those who had been melted to the ladder while trying to escape the fire after the explosion. I always thought at his age, being eighteen at the time, how I would have reacted. I often wondered how that must have changed him. My Dad was my hero. He was more than my hero; he was my Dad.

After the war he worked for my Grandfather who owned a successful construction business in the 1920's. The depression ruined the business and my grandfather started over in the 30's, but never attained the success he once had. My Grandfather moved to Florida in the late 50's, and my Dad worked as a Union carpenter and stayed in Erie. He was a staunch Democrat, a union man, and a quiet, humble, and proud individual. He usually had little to say, but when he spoke, my brother and I learned we better be tuned in. He loved my Mom and his children deeply, and he took pride in being a disciplinarian. I respected his rules and structure. I didn't have much of a choice!

As we ate our cereal things were very quiet. If there was one place you didn't screw around was at the kitchen table. My brother was three years younger than me and was smart enough to observe and learn from my mistakes. Because he was the younger brother and had the craftiness to draw sympathy when the two of us screwed up, I would get the blame, and he would usually skate from any fury dealt out by my Dad. I learned when you're the oldest you draw the heat.

Suddenly my Dad looked up at me raising his head from the cereal bowl and asked, "What's your plans for what you want to be when you get older?"

I was a bit taken back by the question. Basically unprepared, because I really hadn't given it a lot of thought at thirteen years old. I looked into his steel blue eyes and felt anxious. "I don't know," I replied.

He shot back with a bit more intensity in his voice, "Well you should start thinking about it."

I replied quickly, and it was all I could come up with, "I wanted to be a Priest for a few years."

"Forget that. You'll need to learn a trade or go to college for something," he said. "Your Grandfather talked me into working for him after the war. He had big plans, but they didn't work out. I always wanted to be a State Trooper, but I stayed with your Grandfather and I got too old for that."

That was the first time I had ever heard that story as I contemplated its meaning. I realized he was showing remorse and regret, and it surprised me. I sat there for about a minute or so, and kind of just to make him feel better I said, "Ok. I'll be a cop! Yea. I've thought about that before. That's what I'm gonna do Dad! I'll be a State Trooper!"

Dad managed a smirk and a glance but said nothing. Wow, he almost smiled, I thought. I'll have to remember I said that. I wonder what it would be like to be a cop?

Eventually we finished breakfast and began the Saturday routine. My brother and I would get dressed and meet Dad in the garage where he assigned whatever yard work had to be done. I hated lawn work, and my brother was good at playing the "I'm the younger brother and I don't know how to do that yet" bullshit, which would get him out of work. The good thing was when we were done, we were usually allowed to do whatever. Hanging out with friends or watching TV were the main choices of entertainment. There were no video games or computers back then. Spending time with my friends in the neighborhood became my priority.

By age fifteen I started High School. Strong Vincent High School was a city school located on the north west side of Erie. It was old but functional. I never liked school, and I was a B, C student at best. I made up my mind that I was going to be a cop, and I guess my ambition was to enter college and get a degree in Criminal Justice. The rumor was back then that by the time I reached the age to apply, a degree would likely be required for employment. The Criminal Justice degree had become popular, so most of us figured the degree would be important.

There were two schools in the area that offered that degree, Edinboro College, and Mercyhurst College. So, I decided in my 10th grade year the mission was to obtain a degree in Criminal Justice. I knew I didn't have to be class valedictorian to get into college for that major, so my efforts academically really took a back seat to my social life. Also finding a job was a priority if I wanted to have the money for a car when the time came.

On the home front things were great. My parents were totally devoted to one another and to us kids. My brother was three years younger than me, and Marianne, the baby of the family, was nine years younger. Marianne was a late baby in my parent's lives. My Mom was thirty-four when she had Marianne, and she tells the story about her needing a daughter to make her feel the family was complete. Apparently, my parents had decided years before that two children were enough, but Mom made a covenant with the Holy Mother to ask her son Jesus for a little girl. They would name the baby Marianne in honor of Mary and Mary's mother Anne. Well, Marianne was born on August 15th, which is the Assumption, the holy day that Mary was taken into heaven by the Almighty. Go figure. The first time she told me that story I got chills.

My Mom had a special connection with the Man upstairs, although I wouldn't realize that until I got much older and wiser. She was of full-blooded Italian descent. A beautiful person inside and out, and she loved me more than can be put in words. Mom grew up on a farm along with her six brothers and sisters. Papa Pete, my grandfather, came over from Italy in the late 19th century, and farmed. He also had a cement construction business. Mom said they always had enough to eat, and their family was very close, but it was tough growing up. She was born in 1929 the year the stock market crashed, and the terrible depression began.

By High School one of the issues I was dealing with was the meaning of God, religion, and spirituality. I had attended Catholic grade school, and at the age of 10 or 11 I was pretty sure I wanted to become a Priest. I had talked with my family about it, and I felt a need to serve and repay God for all he had done for me and my family. I loved God, or at least I thought I did, but something happened over a three-year period. I think the change began when I discovered females. That revelation will change a 15-year old's mind on just about anything.

Most concerning to me was I began to doubt. Did God really exist? How could God let bad things happen? Was He really watching over us? Does He punish bad people? If He's real, why would He permit sin? All this was very confusing for me. I didn't dwell on trying to find these answers, but being a doubter made me feel guilt. I knew that I needed more than blind faith in accepting His existence. My Mom was so spiritual, and I admired her so for that, but when I heard her talk about God as often as she did, it would frustrate me because I couldn't be more like her. I always hoped someday I would get answers to these questions.

More importantly at the time was the new interest in girls. None of us guys in the hood had girlfriends to speak of. The only experience I had with female's were a couple of crushes I had in junior high school.

Then there was one-night in the hood when my buddy Tom brought this girl over to a friend's back yard where we were all hanging out. There was about four or five of us there on the porch in the back yard.

Tom walked into the back yard and announced he had a girl out front and said, "She likes to make out."

"Make out"? my friend Terry questioned. " With whom?"

"All of us," Tom said. "She wants to walk around the block with one guy and make out," Tom explained as he laughed out loud.

"Which guy?" I asked.

"All of us." Tom said. So, one by one we each took a turn walking this girl around the block, and about every 50 feet or so stopped and kissed. Yea, it was weird, and a good thing it was dark out. I have no idea who the girl was or what ever happened to her. That was my experience with women to that point in my life.

One day my friend Walt who lived across the street, told me he had met a girl at school, and she had invited him over to her house. He had gone over, and really liked her. He was meeting her tonight and asked if I was interested in meeting her friend. Girlfriend? I thought. "Yea I guess," I said to Walt. "What does she look like?"

"I don't know." Walt said.

"What's her name," I asked.

"Cindy. We're meeting tonight at seven thirty on the corner of 27th and Hampton."

"On a street corner?" I asked.

"Yea. It's no big deal. We'll just talk to them for a while and walk them home."

"OK," I said. "But if she's a skeef (That's a 60's word for really ugly) I'm only staying for a minute and then I'm saying I gotta be somewhere."

At seven thirty Walt picked me up and we walked the two blocks to 27th and Hampton. We were late so the two girls were already standing there. I felt my heart start to race a bit as we got closer. Cathy, Walt's girlfriend, introduced herself to me and introduced Cindy. "Hi," I said.

"Hi," she said back.

I felt like I was supposed to be talking but I couldn't think of much to say. It was very tense or so it seemed. After stumbling through the next half hour or so with small talk we walked the two of them home.

On the way back I said to Walt, "She's pretty and built kind of nice but she's only thirteen!"

"What"?

"Yea. She told me she was thirteen. She looks like she's about eighteen. Doesn't she?" I asked.

"We can't get in any trouble. We're just going to see them once in a while over at Cathy's house. So, no biggie," Walt responded.

"Ok" I said. "No biggie."

Yeah, no biggie. Little did I know I had just met my wife, mother of my children, and soulmate for the next forty-one years.

CHAPTER 2

Affirmative Action

THE MONTHS PASSED and High School dragged on. When I turned 16, I got a job at McDonalds along with Walt. I tried to take the job seriously. It was better than the paper route I had for three years. I worked about 10 hrs. a week, usually two school nights for a couple of hours, and 5 or 6 hrs. on Saturday or Sunday. It gave me a little financial freedom and I started saving for a car.

Cindy and I developed a friendship and I saw her a couple times a week usually over at Cathy's house along with Walt. On nights I didn't work Walt and I would walk to Cathy's and spend an hour or two in their basement where Cathy's mom had a couple of chairs and a couch set up for us. Cindy would tell her Dad she was going over to visit Cathy, but obviously there was no mention of boys. Her father was a big stocky Hungarian. I had no intention of meeting him any time soon.

By the end of my senior year at Strong Vincent I had been accepted on a probationary status to Mercyhurst College. Mom was happy that I had been admitted. Dad was pretty skeptical and wasn't happy about coming up with most of the tuition. College loans back then didn't exist as far as I knew. Mom had taken a job at a clothing store as a sales associate. Cindy and I had stepped up our relationship and I had met her parents that year and was allowed to pick her up in the car. She had plenty of guys interested in her, but most knew we were "going steady," which was the big thing to do back then.

Cindy had gotten to know my family quite well and my Mom really thought the world of her. Also, my senior year I had been moved up to 2nd assistant manager at McDonalds. Starting college was overwhelming. Most of these professors I learned were Liberal types and I thought most of them had twisted opinions. They had spent their entire lives in school, and I didn't think they had many life experiences. It seemed to me that they thought the world was just a bed of flowers and we were supposed to go through life holding hands with one another. I ignored their dissertations for the most part and struggled through my first year. I was working about 20 hrs. a week and had bought a car.

Regarding Cindy we had hit some rough waters because of my school and working. Not a lot of time to spend with her. We had a few short breakups and the longest was about six months. I dated a little during the breakups as did she, but it always seemed that we would re-unite. It was becoming apparent to me that we couldn't stay away from one another.

College seemed to fly by. I had carried a 3.8 GPA in my Major and a 2.2 in other studies. Certainly not a scholar, but the mission of graduating I had set for myself years before was near completion. Christmas of 1975 Cindy and I got engaged. I respected her and felt that I loved her, and figured she'd be a good Mom. I knew 1976 would be the year for marriage. I really had no more excuses, and kids got married real young at that time. I was set to graduate the upcoming June and not surprisingly she set the wedding up for August. I graduated from Mercyhurst in June of 1976; mission completed. It was the first thing in my life I had accomplished after setting a goal, and it was a great feeling. We got married August 28th. 1976. I was 22 years old, and Cindy was 20.

I had applied to the State Police as soon as I turned 21 and applied to local departments. I was scoring well on the tests, but Veterans points and Affirmative Action was killing me. I'd be in the top third on these lists and by the time the Feds awarded points I'd be knocked down to the middle or lower third. The Veterans points I had no problem with because I felt those guys deserved special consideration for what they had done for our Country. Dad had shot down the idea of me enlisting in the military out of high school. He wanted me to get an education and besides there was a war going on and I don't think he wanted the stress of having a son in the military during war time. My draft numbers were always high and never got close to being drafted. What upset me was this Affirmative Action, which required hiring two minorities for one white. I don't mind losing a job to someone who is better than me as far as scores, but why should I lose a chance at a job just because my skin is white?

I was never prejudice towards minorities. My Mom had taught me to discern everyone individually, and that all people are children of God, and we were to respect that. My High School was integrated, and I had friends that were minorities, so I was pretty open minded when it came to race. Actually, the whole group of kids I had hung with were never bitterly prejudice because that was the way we were raised. I always felt prejudice was just uncontrolled fear of something unknown.

Moms philosophy had worked for me not to judge a group of people as all the same. This was then my first experience of being discriminated against. To say the least by the fall of 1976 I was a frustrated man.

CHAPTER 3

Personality Test

THINGS HAD GONE well with me working at McDonalds after college, and we were now into the spring of 1977. The owner who was a great guy and savvy businessman, had promoted me to a Store Managers position. It wasn't the career field I had hoped for, but for the time being it was a great job to learn about dealing with people, and it afforded me a lot of responsibility which was invaluable experience.

One day while working I saw a buddy of mine from college in the front lobby. I went out to say hello and talk for a while. He too wasn't having much luck landing a police job. Departments just weren't hiring because the economy was in the tank. My friend told me during our conversation that he was going to apply to the Ohio Highway Patrol. He learned through the placement office that they would be testing soon. I was happy to hear that, but there was a part of me that was kind of happy with what I had fallen into here at McDonalds. I got the info from him and told him I'd give him a call soon

Running into my friend the previous week stimulated my interests again, so I made application and arrangements to take the Ohio Highway Patrol Exam. I had contacted my friend Bob and we agreed to ride together to the testing. It was a Saturday morning and I had taken the day off from work which was a feat in itself. Bob drove his Volkswagen Beetle and we headed west towards Warren Ohio. The test was going to be given at Champion High School.

It was about an hour and a half drive and upon arrival we were greeted by about two hundred other hungry applicants. I felt frustrated. How would I get picked from over 200 other people, most of them being native Ohioan's? I had almost given up before it even got started. I guess I became very relaxed due to the apathy I was experiencing.

They took roll call and were explaining the procedures of the test taking. We were seated in a large auditorium occupying every other seat. Suddenly two Troopers stomped into the auditorium interrupting the Trooper that was giving instructions. Both of them looked like they were on a mission. Stoned face, with Stetsons on, they stomped up the center aisle. They were scary guys. Two sets of shifty eyes scanned the audience as one of the Troopers yelled, "Sutton, Roger Sutton." Whoever Sutton was I didn't want to know him. Poor Roger who was seated several rows off to my right chokingly yelled, "Here sir!"

The tallest of the two Troopers said, "Are you Roger Sutton?"

Roger again reluctantly answered, "Yes sir!"

"Up against the west wall," barked the Trooper. The auditorium was like a morgue. I wondered if I was about to witness an execution. Once over against the wall the Trooper ordered Roger to take his shoes off. Rogers face turned three shades of red as he kicked off his Penney loafers. I couldn't believe what I saw. Stacked cut up newspapers taped to the bottom of his socks. It looked like about three quarters of an inch thick on both heels. Roger was trying to cheat them on the height requirement. Both Troopers grabbed Roger by each arm and marched him out through the auditorium doors and down the hall and out of sight. Most of us were looking around at one another in disbelief with our mouths hanging open. "How did they know?" asked the guy sitting next to me on my left side. I just shrugged my shoulders.

A couple minutes later the two Troopers returned, but now they had two more Troopers with them. One of them stepped forward as I notice the Sergeant's chevrons on his sleeves. "What you have just witnessed," he said. "is an attempted act of dishonesty. The Highway Patrol hires only the highest integrity, and moral applicants. We do not tolerate liars. If there is anyone else in this auditorium who feels he cannot live up to these high standards, or has changed their mind about joining our organization, please feel free to leave now."

Surprisingly two guys in the front row closest to the door stood up. It only took them about two seconds to get through the door. One other braver soul stood up in the center of one of the isles and made his way along and down to the front and out through the door.

A few minutes went by, and after the drama subsided, they passed out the test. I can guarantee you that no one was going to attempt to cheat on that test.

Four hours later the written test was over. Sarge and his boys walked the isle way the entire time. We were all afraid to turn our heads even to check the wall clock for fear of being hair dragged into the isle way. I can remember thinking that I didn't care how I did on the test I just wanted out of there. Storm Troopers for policeman, I thought. This could be pretty cool.

After the test we were all told to go outside and wait while they electronically graded them. Once outside the usual conversations took place like, "What did you put down for this one?" or "I didn't under-stand this one?"

The test was unique in the fact that it was Math and English com-position which all of them are, but only one segment lasting about an hour. The remaining three hours was like a personality test asking ques-tions ranging from; What is your favorite sport? To; what's your wildest fantasy? One question that stuck in my mind was: Underline the state-ment that is most like you. I would rather: 1. Read a book. 2. Kiss a girl. 3. Watch TV. 4. Steal a car.

Well, thinking back to test taking in my college days we were always taught one of the answers is obviously wrong. So, I don't think they'd like to see you answer, steal a car. Now the three remaining answers usually would be pretty close, although there was always some hidden meaning in the question. Let's see, what phrase is most like me? I would rather? Honesty! If I had just learned anything from poor Roger and the speech from Sgt. Slaughter, it was honesty! What true blue red blooded 23-year-old male wouldn't answer, 2. Kiss a girl? But maybe they would think I was a pervert? We all like to watch TV, and I was never much for reading books. Honesty! Honesty! I had to answer kiss a girl. What the hell, after what I had just witnessed, I wasn't sure if I wanted to live in this state anyway (Haa). I checked the box,2. Kiss a girl. I remained consistent and honest in my answers. But I could see this test would tempt you to manipulate your answers to look like you were perfect. The test continued in that format for the remainder.

After mulling around outside for about fifteen minutes, Sarge appeared in the doorway with a clipboard in his hand. Sarge stated he was going to call out names, and these people were to go back inside and have a seat in the auditorium. Ok, I thought, sit back inside? Must be if you passed, go back inside.

Sarge began calling out names one by one very quickly. I guess others thought the same way I did because a couple guys who got their names called out kind of acted like they had won a prize. A couple guys even high fived each other when their names got called. It seemed like forever as I heard each of these names called and I hadn't heard mine. I had been standing with my back against the outside wall about six feet away from the entranceway. I could see the faces of everyone that entered after their name was called. One guy as he approached the doorway looked at me with a cocky smirk, like to say, they called me and not you-ha. I was getting more frustrated as he called nearly all the names, and it had gotten down to about only 25 of us still outside.

Sarge promptly stopped and turned and went inside. There had been another Trooper outside with us. Bob walked over towards me and said, "Let's go." I looked in his eyes and I could see the dejection. A couple other guys started walking towards the parking lot. The Trooper spoke up, "Where are you going?" The two stopped and didn't answer. "You just passed the test. You can't go home now," he said with a smile.

"What did he say?" I asked as I turned towards Bob.

"We passed," Bob said as he laughed out loud.

The Trooper continued, "You guys passed and will be called in after the Sergeant dismisses the group inside." Haa, I thought, hey I passed!

After about five minutes the door opened and the fellows inside started to file out very slowly. It was easy to see the disappointment on their faces. Oh, the guy that dissed me when he was called in. Where is he? I thought. I watched for him as I made my way near the area where I had been standing earlier. I saw him about four or five guys back filing towards the door. I stood back at an angle where he had to see me when he came through the doorway. Our eyes met and I said, "Take care now," as I forced a smirk similar to the one he had given me. He walked by saying nothing. Normally I'm not like that, but he had set himself up for some bad Karma.

We got inside and sat down in the auditorium seats. Sarge stepped up in front and congratulated us for passing the first phase of testing that day. He explained that the State Patrol anticipated testing 13,000 applicants statewide that day. He said that eventually they would pair that down to hiring around three to three hundred and fifty Troopers over the next cycle.

Wow, I thought, 13,000 and only hiring 300. What are the odds of actually getting hired?

The next couple hours went by quickly. We had to pass a depth perception test, eye test, hearing exam, blood pressure etc. It was very thorough. Of the twenty or so of us that passed the written, at the end of the day there were about thirteen of us left.

Before dismissing us Sarge explained what was coming next. First, he said we were very unique to get through that written test, and that its more focused on the personality the Highway Patrol is looking for. He said in the next few weeks a background investigation would be initiated. They would be contacting everyone we ever knew etc.

Shit, I thought. I hope they don't spend too much time with my neighborhood buddies, I almost chuckled out loud. Sarge continued saying in the next couple of weeks we would be scheduled to take a physical agility test that would be given at the Highway Patrol Academy in Columbus. Sarge basically went over some paperwork he had given us explaining the agility test, and what was to follow. He then thanked us, and we were dismissed.

The ride home with Bob was pretty cool. I was glad and amazed that we both passed the testing. It would have been a long ride home if just one of us would have passed. Bob and I talked the whole way home about how squared away those Troopers were, and the intensity of the testing. We were both happy and thankful.

I silently asked myself as I looked out the passenger window at the beautiful blue sky, is God with me on this? I said a few prayers of thanks just in case He's there and listening.

CHAPTER 4

Agility

ABOUT TWO WEEKS passed and I received a letter to report to the Ohio Highway Patrol Training Academy located in Columbus. I had been reviewing the agility requirements over the last couple weeks and had been doing a lot of running. One of the requirements was a mile and a half run to be completed within a certain time limit. As I recall I think it was thirteen minutes. Any time over that was a fail. The other requirements you couldn't really practice for. You either were strong enough or you weren't, and there was no real time to weightlift to increase strength. I really wasn't that concerned except for the run. I was never much of a long-distance runner, and a mile and a half to me was an eternity. After all, at age 23, I'd better be in good enough shape to pass an agility test, or I have no business even thinking about being a cop.

Bob called me that night to see if I had gotten the letter. We compared notes and were both scheduled on the same day and time. As I recall the day was a Wednesday, and it was another miracle to get the day off from work. We had to be in Columbus at nine am. It's about a five-hour drive, so we left from Erie at about three thirty in the morning. It took us the whole five hours to get there. The speed limit was fifty-five, and Bob's ride I don't think could go much faster than that.

We got checked in and changed into gym clothes and were escorted to the gymnasium. The Academy was impressive. The gym was huge and had been set up for the testing. They had a seven-foot chain link fence set up at one end. The other end had a body dummy lying on the floor. Beside that was a couple balance obstacles, and there was also a 1976 Plymouth Grand Fury Highway Patrol car parked at the other end of the gym. Man, I thought, that is a big car to push.

There were about thirty of us seated in the bleachers. A gym instructor approached us and introduced himself as Lieutenant Vassar of the Academy staff. He also introduced a couple other instructors. He then asked if we had any questions on the events. There were a couple questions that he answered, and we lined up at his direction. I was about tenth in line. We were lined up behind the chain link fence. One at a time the instructor blew a whistle and you had to negotiate the course. I watched intently as the guys in front of me went one at a time. First you had to get over the seven-foot fence. Then run the length of the gym jumping a couple hurdles on the way to the body dummy lying on the floor. Pick up the dummy and drag it about thirty feet while stepping around some cones. There were a couple other short obstacles on the way, but the whole course was about two minutes long. Passing was determined by the time it took to complete. After that we had to do a standing jump up against a wall where they marked how high you could get off the ground.

Then we stood in line to push the car. The instructor stood outside the car and walked along side of it with a hand brake. He would blow the whistle and the event would begin. I watched a couple guys in front of me do it. It looked like the best way was to start the car moving by putting your back against the rear bumper and push backwards with your legs until the car reached a couple miles an hour. Then spin around and push forward with your hands on the trunk area. The length of the push was about forty feet or so, and you had to do it in under a specified time.

My turn came with the car and I set my back against the bumper and trunk area. The whistle blew, and with all my strength I got the car moving quickly, but I felt a popping sensation in my lower back. It didn't hurt, but I felt something move. Maybe some vertebrae or tendons in there shifted? I got the car to the finish line in good time. What the hell did I do to my back?

We were given about fifteen minutes to rest prior to starting the run. I could feel my back starting to tighten up like a hard knot was forming. Geez, I thought, let's get this run over with before my back gets too bad to move. I had never really hurt my back seriously before. I fell hard one time on my tailbone which laid me up for a couple days when I was a kid. So, this back-injury stuff was new to me. It slowly started to hurt and was getting worse.

The instructors broke us up into groups of five. We were instructed that we had to complete the event by running 34 laps around the gym, that measured a mile and a half.

My group of five lined up and the whistle blew. It hurt as I ran but I still had good range of motion. I finished the event in under the time limit, but just barely. I was happy, but not proud. I finished fourth in my group. The guy behind me had ten seconds to spare. That's cutting it close, I thought. Wow, glad it's over with.

My back was pulsing with pain now and I really was struggling not to show the pain. I just wanted to get out of there soon. Lt. Vassar congratulated us on our passing the agility and advised we would be contacted soon regarding the starting of our background investigations. With that we were dismissed.

Bob and I both passed. I think there was only five or six guys out of the group of thirty that didn't make it. We got into his "bug" and headed north. It was going to be a fun ride home.

CHAPTER **5**

Background

A COUPLE WEEKS had passed, my back slowly got better, but I was having trouble concentrating on anything. I had the Highway Patrol on my mind constantly. I wondered why I hadn't heard anything. I even called Bob a couple of times asking if he had any news. Then while at work a few days later the call came. "Mr. Munch, this is Tpr. Martz from PSP Lawerence Park. I'll be doing your background investigation at the request of OSP," he stated. Wow, I thought, the Pennsylvania State Police.

"Great'" I responded. "I've been constantly thinking about when I was going to hear something."

"I've been doing your background for about a week. We're going to need to get together" Tpr. Martz said.

"Sure," I excitedly said, "Anytime you want."

Tpr. Martz and I spoke briefly, and he said he'd be getting in touch with a lot of my friends and family and was there anything I needed to tell him. I told him there was nothing I could think of, and I inquired as to when an Academy class might start. Martz explained he knew no details other than he was told to assist Ohio in doing my background. With that our conversation ended, and I thought I was going to do cartwheels across the front lobby of the store!

Of course, I told my Dad and a couple of close friends what was going on. I told my friends if they were contacted not to lie about anything. I was confident anything he found wasn't going to hurt me. I had led a pretty straight and narrow life. I had a couple experiences of being drunk, but I really wasn't much of a drinker. I knew the worst thing was to get caught in a lie, so that wasn't going to happen. I was going to be totally honest. Kind of a boring life, but it looked like all that might be going to pay off.

About a week went by and then I received another call while at work from Tpr. Martz. He explained that he wanted to get together. I told him anytime was good, but I needed a bit of notice to get off work. He said he'd call me again in a few days to set that up because right now he was busy, and his schedule was changing day to day. He also asked me about a couple of people I had known in high school. That really surprised me because I never hung out with them much and hadn't seen either of them in years. I didn't press him on why he was asking about me knowing them. I was going to just keep my mouth shut during this process, and if he told me to run naked down the middle of State St. at high noon, I wasn't going to ask "why?" I was going to do anything necessary to get through this background and hopefully on to Columbus.

A few days past and Tpr. Martz stopped at my apartment. He explained briefly that he was done with the background investigation, and he would be finalizing it and sending it through channels to Columbus within a week. He spent a few minutes explaining he found nothing earthshattering for which he felt would disqualify me, but stated that was up to Columbus to decide.

I shook his hand and he said, "I probably won't be seeing you again so good luck. OSP is a great organization. I wish we were getting you."

Wow I thought. What a nice thing to say.

"Thanks, Tpr. Martz," I said. "I wish I was going to PSP but the Affirmative Action is killing me."

"Yea," he replied. "it's a shame."

With that he left, and I breathed a sigh of relief.

Good day? It wasn't over yet. Cindy had something to tell me. Oh-I thought. What more? We were still standing in the kitchen. Cindy calmly, and very as a matter of fact said she was pregnant.

"That's great," I said as I began to hug her. "When did you find out?" I asked.

Cindy explained she had gone to the doctors that morning and wanted to keep it from me until she was sure. We'd been trying for a couple months so it hadn't taken long. She would be due sometime in mid to late July of next year. We were both very excited and made plans to tell the rest of the family. No, it wasn't a good day, it was a great day!

A couple weeks went by and I had been talking with Bob on the phone every few days. His background was completed also about the same time as mine. So, it began a wait and see, and wait and see, and wait and see time.

The Holidays came and went. It was 1978. Frustrations were high, but there was nothing I had any control over. So why worry? My father had said many times to look at something more in a negative way. Because when it turns out bad, your prepared. And if it turns out good, then your pleasantly surprised. (Ha) My Dad. No one like him. Very disciplined. Very structured. Very much a realist. That's ok, but that's a little depressing in the long term? Isn't it? I liked to be more like my Mom. An optimist, expecting good things to happen. Don't be a worrier. "Have Faith," she would always say. But that's the key, I would think to myself, Faith. Faith in God. My Mom was a true believer. No doubt about that. I admired that in my mother. I was even envious of her strong faith. I wanted to have faith like hers.

It was late January and I came home from work at the usual time, around six thirty. The apartment was dark, so I figured Cindy had gone out shopping. I turned on the lights in the kitchen and on the table was a letter. I walked towards the kitchen table and saw the "Flying Wheel" insignia on the return address. Yeah!! It was form OSP!! I picked it up and at the same time I had to sit down in the chair. I slowly opened it. I could feel my heart pounding in my chest and my mind had gone totally blank. I kept tearing the top open and pulled the letter out. I opened the folds and began to read; "Dear Mr. Munch, we are happy to inform you that you will be offered a position as a Cadet Trooper in an upcoming Academy class. Unfortunately, at the present time we are under a hiring freeze for out of state residents. This freeze is lifted from time to time. We will contact you immediately upon the freeze being lifted." It went on thanking me for my interest in the Highway Patrol.

Please, I thought as my hands shook. No, I didn't just read that. "Let me read it again," I said out loud. Out of state hiring freeze. What the #@#%??!!! All that waiting and bullshit, and that's it?

I just sat back down and read the letter about twenty more times to myself. I guess I was hoping the print would change. I put my chin in my hands with my elbows on the table and just sat there for about a half hour.

The phone rang about a half hour later and it was Bob with the same news. I'm glad he called because we vented on one another and by the time we hung up our moods had settled, and I felt better. Hey, I thought, it's still going to happen. The letter says the freeze gets lifted from time to time. I'll just have to wait, that's all, I pondered, I'll just wait. At least I know I got accepted. That's a good thing-right? "Damn," I mumbled.

I called my Dad to tell him what was going on. He just said to hang in there and it would work itself out. I felt better after getting his approval of the situation. There's nothing here I can control so I'm not going to worry, and I'll keep a good attitude.

I went back to work the next day somewhat of a different man. Now I didn't have to worry about getting hired, because I got hired. I was good enough to get hired. They offered me the position. It's just a little bump in the road that will iron itself out. I might as well concentrate on my job here.

I was trying to enjoy my job. The kids that worked for me were great. Most of them were 16-19 years old. Was I that goofy at that age? Yea, probably worse. Some of them are real head cases! But their all good kids. They were fun to be around for the most part.

A couple months passed and still no word from Ohio. I talked to my Dad about writing them a letter to find out what if anything had changed. We decided to hold off because they did state in their letter, they would be in contact with me.

CHAPTER **6**

First Born

A FEW MORE months had gone by and still no word from Ohio.

It was now late July and Cindy and I were over at my parents' house. Mom had made spaghetti for supper. Nothing like Mom's spaghetti.

I felt so sorry for Cindy. She had gone from 105 lbs. to 180 lbs. during the pregnancy. It was really hot in my parents' house. No air conditioning. Not too many people I knew had central air in their homes back then.

I noticed Cindy was doing a pretty good number on that spaghetti, and her due date was here. "You better slow down on that spaghetti," I said. If your water breaks, I don't think it's good to have a full stomach, is it?" Cindy looked up from her plate as she was trying to get the spaghetti to cooperate coming off the fork. She looked at me with that "F%#* you," look, and I knew I must have touched a nerve. "Well you don't want to be sick is all I'm saying," I stated.

My wife was a beautiful, kind, loving person, but she was thinned skinned. She didn't take any type of criticism well at all, and she was never hesitant to go to battle. I think it was her Russian ancestry, not real affectionate outwardly. I learned over the years that if she asked how something looked on her, it was a much safer play just to fib a little if something wasn't looking quite right. But that was rare anyway because physically she was a doll.

We went home and around 3am, yes, her water broke. Off to the hospital we went. She dilated very slowly and was in hard labor for

24

hours. Men in those days were allowed in the labor room, but not in the delivery room, and that was a good thing as far as I was concerned. My Dad told me that seeing a birth involving your spouse might have some negative psychological effect when trying to get aroused down the road with that memory in your mind. Ha-ha. Dad, what a character. Tell it like it is Dad.

Anyway, as predicted Cindy had thrown up the spaghetti early in the process. It was stuck everywhere. My heart broke for her as she moaned and cried, and occasionally spit out a cuss word or two. Finally, at around 4pm, after 13 hrs. of labor, the doctor said, "Time to go to the delivery room." Thank you, God. Get me out of this room please. I walked the halls for about 45 minutes and eventually the doctor came out and said, "Congratulations Mr. Munch, you have a fine-looking little girl. Mom and daughter are doing well."

I was tickled. A little girl, I thought. How cool is that!

A nurse came out a few minutes later and led me back to post op so I could see Cindy and little Angela.

Back then there was no knowing the sex of the baby until delivery. So, it was always a surprise. A very pleasant surprise. I got to hold Angela and kiss her little forehead. It was a great day! A really great day!! July 24th, 1978.

A couple weeks went by and all was fine. Mother and baby were home, and we were very happy. But, I finally decided to write OSP and ask what my status was. It was coming up on a year since I initially had applied. Time is a wasting, I thought.

About a week passed after sending the letter. I was at work and got a call. "Mr. Munch this is Tpr. Pasker from OSP in Warren, Ohio. How are you doing?" he asked.

"Good, I think sir. I haven't heard a word since January. Is the freeze still on?" I asked.

"It's been lifted for a while," he explained. I'll fill you in on everything when we meet. Can you come to the Ashtabula Post tomorrow for an interview?" he asked.

"Yes sir, what time?"

"Be there by 0900 hrs.," he said.

"I'll be there sir," I shot back.

I went home that night happy but guarded. I wasn't going to get my hopes up as high as last time. Cindy was happy again for me. The Tpr. didn't give me a chance to ask any questions, so I'm guessing the freeze is off or he wouldn't be calling. Or maybe they just are updating my application for future reference? I guess I'll find out tomorrow, I pondered.

I left the apartment that morning and made the 45-minute drive to Ashtabula. I had called work around 7am and told my assistant manager that had opened the store that I would be late. That was good enough, I thought. I'll make something up to tell my boss whenever I get there.

Upon arrival I entered the front lobby of the barracks and was greeted by a man in a suit. "I'm Harry Pasker," he said as he extended his hand.

"Fred Munch, Tpr. Pasker. How are you? Thanks for getting in touch with me," I said as we shook hands.

We sat down in the office and Tpr. Pasker explained that he had received orders to drop everything he was doing and update my background investigation because it had been a while since it had been initially completed.

"Do you know the Governor?" Pasker asked as he laughed outload.

"No, I don't know anyone over here," I said.

"Well they want this done ASAP because there is a class starting September 20th, and if all checks out with this, you're going to be in it," he explained.

"Really!?" I said surprised.

"Yea it looks like they misplaced some applications in January and yours was one of them. You should have been in the Academy class after the first of the year," he said.

"You mean they lost my application for seven months?" I asked.

"Well, yeah, but I don't know if you're supposed to know that, if you can understand," he said with a smile. "Sure," I said. "I'm just elated we're sitting here and it's going forward," I stated.

"Right," Tpr. Pasker said. "Well let's get through these questions and get this thing submitted because there isn't but about three weeks and that class will be starting."

I was hearing what he was saying, and understanding him, but I was screaming inside with total jubilation as to what was happening. Wow, wow, wow, I kept thinking to myself as Tpr. Pasker asked stuff like, are you still living where you were, same phone, any health issues come up? Sill married to Cynthia? etc.

"Oh, we had a baby!" I said with excitement in my voice. "We had a little girl!"

"Congratulation," Pasker said. "How's that going?" he asked as he chuckled aloud.

"Good," I said. "Real good."

"One thing," Tpr. Pasker said. "You're going to have to take the agility test again."

"Oh," I answered. "OK."

Wow, go through that again I thought. Nothing is easy when you want it bad enough. Dammit, that friggin Plymouth- again! Adversity breeds strength of character, I reminded myself. God- it must be Him helping me through this. That's what my Mom would tell me if I were to ask her.

After about an hour I left for home. I don't remember much about the short drive home because like I always do, I was agonizing over what was next.

The next day at work I got a call from Tpr. Pasker. He said all went well with his discussion with authorities in Columbus, and could I be in Columbus next Monday for the agility test? I told Pasker I could, and it was set. Next Monday at 1000 hrs., OSP Academy-physical agility test.

I thought I'd better call Bob, but did I want to get his hopes up. It's been seven months. Why don't I wait to see for sure? I don't know what else could happen, but maybe it's best to wait before letting him know.

A few days went by. I was a nervous wreck, and I had prayed and thanked God for what was happening-just in case there was a God. That's as far as I could advance in my faith and belief. I really wanted to believe, especially when good things happened to me. When something really good happened I always would think of the Almighty and say a few prayers thanking Him. But hey, I just wasn't a total believer? I couldn't get past that no matter how much I wanted to. God for me was this almighty power, older man type figure that you didn't want to bother unless you really needed something. If He was real, I'm sure He was way too busy with more important things and people than lowly me. I'd been told many times by my mother and religious people that God loved me and watched over me with His angels. That's pretty cool, if it's true. Again though, what about all the bad things in the world? Tragic things that happen? What about that? Would stuff like that happen if there was a God? Why would God let bad things happen?

Do I dwell too much on religion and God? I'd ask myself. After all, it wasn't long ago I seriously thought about becoming a Priest. I was raised by two loving God-fearing parents. I never felt embarrassed to talk openly about my beliefs if I was asked. And some people take offense when they hear people openly refer to God or a higher power, so I always tried to keep my opinions and beliefs to myself. I just continually felt guilt for being a "Doubting Thomas."

A car? I need a car, I thought. My Chevelle wasn't going to get me back and forth to Columbus on Monday. And if I attend the Academy I'm going to have to drive back and forth every weekend. I needed a good car. Cindy was driving an old Buick Apollo, ha! Yea, I needed a car I decided.

Monday came and I borrowed my Dads car to make the five-hour trip. I left early and got down there by around 9:15 am. I sat in the Academy lobby studying the displays. They had pictures from 1933 and through the history of Troopers and "Posts." In Pennsylvania they were called Barracks. Here in Ohio they are called Posts. They had a cool 1933 motorcycle roped off in the display. Man, I am really motivated. This dream is coming true, I thought as I walked around the displays. I thought of the Sergeants speech about integrity when we took the written test in Warren. I guess I can start to think of myself as being "special" like Sarge had said. "Not yet," I said aloud to myself. Big mission coming up. Got to get through this Academy.

"Munch," called a voice behind me. I turned quickly and there was Lt. Vassar standing at the lobby door in his PT clothes. "Ready to get on with this?" he asked.

"Yes sir," I answered.

We walked over to the gym and I changed in the locker room. I was the only person being tested. Then I had an idea. "Lt., do you care if I run first, and then do the agility?" I asked politely.

"No, that's fine," he said. "Why?" he asked.

"I tweaked my back last time pushing the car. It hurt to run afterwards. So, I'd like to run first, then push the car," I said.

"Fine," he replied.

I warmed up a bit and stretched out. And it all began again!

The run went well. Not as fast as last time. The agility seemed easier than last time for some reason, maybe it was because I wasn't as nervous this time. The car push went OK. I tried to stay more erect which took a bit of stress off the lower back and more to the legs. I finished the run a couple seconds slower but hey, it was over.

Lt. Vassar instructed me to go home and I would be receiving an acceptance/invitation letter this week. The Academy would start two weeks from this upcoming Wednesday. With that I left and started my drive home.

I had a lot of time to think driving home. I actually teared up a couple times thinking of how happy I was and how supportive my family has been. Then I made a "deal" with myself. The deal was, the only way I was coming home from the Academy without that title of "Trooper," was, "in a box." In other words, there was no failure going to happen. This was going to be accomplished, or I was coming home "dead." I don't think I'd ever been so serious in a conversation with myself. Ha, kind of crazy I thought, but that was it. That was the deal, period.

I got home late afternoon and I called Bob right away. I told him what was going on. I told him to write a letter a soon as he could. There was no way he'd get processed in time for my class, I didn't think, but hopefully he'd be in the next one. Bob was pretty excited.

By the end of the week the letter arrived. It was short and sweet. Basically, it stated that I was invited to attend the 104th Class of the Ohio State Highway Patrol beginning September 20th, 1978 at 8am., at the Academy on 17th St. in Columbus, Ohio.

I was so freaking happy. I had the evidence in hand. I was to present this letter of admittance upon arrival. I called Dad to let him know.

I couldn't tell for sure, but I think he choked up on the phone a bit. So, he was proud and excited.

After hanging up from Dad's conversation I turned to Cindy who was sitting at the kitchen table reading the letter again. "Well," I told Cindy, "we've set the table, to get ready for the party."

"What do you mean?" she asked.

"Everything I've done in my life was to get ready for this moment, like setting the table for a big dinner or party. Preparation I guess is what I'm trying to say. The table is set. Now I have to succeed in having a good party. The party of life," I said.

"You think too deep for a young guy," she said with a bit of a frown. "All your doing is going to a police academy. Just shut up and get it done."

I responded, "There you go! Hard, cold Russian popping up! You need to relax and laugh more. Share in this moment. Be happy!" I said.

"I am happy," she shot back. "I am proud of you. Just get it done now, that's all." Cindy was no dummy. She knew how to push my buttons and motivate me. Sometimes I needed to be "grounded."

The next day at work I notified my boss that I'd be leaving in less than a week. I decided that my last day would be the Friday before I left. My supervisor was disappointed, but I think he was happy that I was fulfilling a goal he knew I had set. The people at McDonalds were great people. The owners were classy people and had treated me well. I was leaving on good terms.

CHAPTER 7

"The Academy"

SEPTEMBER 19TH, 1978 was the day before the Academy began. I had driven to Columbus that afternoon and got a motel room. I wanted to get a good night's sleep rather than drive down on the morning of the 20th.

I went to bed and got up early, around 5am., showered got ready and drove over to a nearby McDonalds. Where else would I eat? I wasn't hungry because of all the butterfly's in my stomach but I ate anyway. I couldn't be sure when the next meal would be. I finished quickly and drove over to the Academy off 17th St. I pulled into the parking lot and drove to the rear of the Academy. I parked the car facing the rear doors so I could see where everyone was going to enter. I took a couple of deep breaths trying to settle myself.

Here I am I thought. This is it. This is what I've been waiting for. There is no way I'm blowing this, I pondered.

I saw a couple of other cars come in and I looked at my watch. It was 7:40. Twenty minutes, I thought. I felt nauseated, and I could feel a slight tingling on the back of my neck. I was really nervous.

I then noticed a uniformed Trooper come out of the rear door closest to me. He started walking around the parking lot. I saw him walk up to a couple other vehicles and shag the occupants out and point towards the rear door.

This is it, it's time to go. I opened the car door as the Trooper made his way towards my car.

"Are you a Cadet?" he asked.

"Yes sir," I responded.

"OK then, let's go," he said as he pointed towards the rear door.

"Yes sir," I said as I hurried to grab my suitcase out of the back seat.

I walked to the door and entered. Inside were two Troopers standing about ten feet from the doorway. Neither of them looked friendly.

"Good morning," I said as I looked them in the eyes.

"Name, Cadet?" one of them asked.

"Munch, sir," I stated. He checked my ID and took possession of my invitation letter.

"Get down to room 118. You'll find gear on the bed that's yours. Put on the uniform. When your complete stand outside your room door," he said authoritatively.

"Yes sir," I responded.

A million things were going through my mind. 118, 118, 118, I kept saying over and over to myself as I walked down the hall. I was also thinking, hey, they're not yelling at least. That's a good thing. As I walked by some of the open doors in other rooms, I couldn't help but look in as I passed by. There were other Cadets inside most rooms. Their as nervous as me, I reasoned to myself. I'll be ok.

I found 118 and went inside. There were two beds, two lockers, two desks, two lamps and one sink that separated the two areas of the room. Not real big, I thought, but nice and clean.

I looked at the bed closest to the door and it had a tag lying on it with my name on it. I set my suitcase down and started looking over the articles on the bed. Notebook, pens, a couple of manuals and a blue Cadet uniform. I guess I better get dressed, I thought as I picked up the shirt to examine it. It was a medium blue dress shirt with Ohio Highway Patrol Cadet insignias on each shoulder. There was a bag of chrome buttons with button clasps that I picked up to look at. I picked up the pants and held them up to my lower torso. Looks like they'll fit I said to myself. They might be a bit long though.

I put the pants on and took off my shirt. I had an undershirt under my dress shirt, so I put the uniform shirt on over it and tried to tuck in the shirt. Hey, wait a minute, there's no buttons on this shirt. It looks like you have to attach the buttons somehow.

Just then a man walked into the room. He walked over to the far bed and put his suitcase on the floor. He looked at me and got a big smile on his face and said, "You have to put the buttons on the shirt you know."

"Yeah," I said, "I'm just realizing that."

"I was a Cadet dispatcher at Lima," he said. "I'll help you with those buttons," he chuckled aloud.

"McCarthy, Jim McCarthy," he said as he stuck out his hand and walked towards me.

"Fred Munch," I said as we shook hands.

McCarthy went on to explain he had been hired as a Cadet dispatcher months before which qualified him for a Cadets position. He had gone through all the testing and was waiting for a class to start and worked at the Patrol Post dispatching. So, McCarthy was a great roommate to have because he knew a lot of things about the Patrol that he would relay to me over the next few weeks that helped me in various ways. Number one he showed me how to put those buttons on. I had never seen buttons like that. The button back goes into the hole on the shirt and the back is secured with a pin backing. Nothing too hard to figure out but considering being nervous and all the new stuff being thrown at me it was great to have a friend already.

I got the shirt to work and got it on and tucked in. Everything fit pretty well. There was also a hat to be worn. It looked like one of those old "milkman" hats worn in the 50's and 60's that milkmen wore delivering milk to your house. It was also blue with a chrome "Flying Wheel" insignia badge on the front.

"Cool hats," I said to McCarthy as I put it on and looked in the mirror.

"Looking good their Munch," McCarthy said as he put his hat on and we made our way to the doorway to stand in the hall as instructed.

As we got into the hall we stood on either side of the doorway. There were about twenty of us ready and dressed waiting. I could hear some commotion and loud yelling coming from down the hall. Some of the Cadets were coming in just before eight o' clock. The Troopers were yelling at them to move because apparently, they wanted us dressed and ready standing outside our rooms by eight o clock. So, these guys that are coming in thought they were on time, which they were, but now they weren't according to the Troopers. McCarthy and I stood outside the doorway for about fifteen minutes while the other Cadets got dressed and ready to go.

Our room was about fifteen feet from a joining hallway. There were about six of us standing in the middle of the hallway talking and waiting for instructions. Just then two uniformed officers came around the corner towards us.

"Get at attention and get up against the wall," yelled one of the officers. We scrambled quickly as they walked by at a fast pace. I could see the one officer that yelled was a Lieutenant. The other was a Sergeant as they continued down the hall.

It was not long and one of the Sergeants had us fall out and go outside where we had come in. He along with three other Troopers sized us up by height and assigned us where in the platoon we were to stand. They formed us up in two ranks with the tallest cadets at the front. The formation went from tallest to shortest to the rear.

"Memorize who's in front of you and behind you. This is where you will be when in formation," the Sergeant explained.

As we were in formation all the instructors left except for one Trooper. This guy looked like a model from a police magazine. He was about 6'2, 210 lbs. Obviously very fit with a small waist and big chest. He wore his Stetson kind of cocked at a downward angle towards his face. His movements even when he moved his arms to talk were ridged and controlled. Not robotic but "just cool," I thought. This dude was squared away.

"Alright, I am Tpr. Millner of the Academy staff. I'd like to welcome you, and I'll be requiring a lot from you," he said looking very serious. "Today, or should I say right now, I'm going to teach you how to march. Remember this, as he paused to make sure we knew what he was about to say was important. If you're going to be right, you first have to look right," he spouted. "And I promise you, we are going to look right," he said as his voice got louder.

For about the next three hours we marched, and marched, and

marched. Actually, it was kind of fun because we were starting to look pretty good. I felt a sense of pride that we were fitting so well together. Even Trooper Millner at one of the breaks said we were "starting to look sharp." And that's all he had to say to motivate us because in short order we all realized that we all really wanted to be there. Our group started to bond quickly, and the best way to describe it for me was "fun." I mean it was hard, and would get much, much, harder, but it would be rewarding.

At around lunch time we marched over to the cafeteria that is located near the front of the Academy. All the General Headquarters Staff usually drove to the Academy for lunch. GHQ is located in downtown Columbus. So needless to say, we were under watchful eyes throughout our training. The GHQ staff consisted of the Colonel who is the Superintendent. The Lt. Colonel, four Majors, and a lot of Captains and Lieutenants. In other words what was referred to be a lot of "Brass."

We ate lunch and were marched over to one of the large classrooms. The classrooms are located on the first floor down the hall from the cafeteria. The entire Academy is a big square in design. It has two floors, a pool, large gymnasium, indoor gun range, courtyard, and recreation room.

We took our assigned seats in the classroom. As we were sitting there, I took the opportunity to look around a bit. We were seated at tables that ran from left to right as you walked into the classroom. There were two tables abreast and four Cadets at each table, being eight Cadets across the width of the room. I counted 43 of us. Of the 43 we had five blacks and two females, one of which was black, and the rest white. I thought it was a good mix of people.

"Attention!" yelled the uniform instructor as he entered the room. The instructor walked to a podium desk combination located in the center of the front of the classroom. He looked at us standing at attention for several seconds as if he were looking at each of us individually one at a time. "Be seated," he barked.

"Good afternoon," he said loudly, as we squirmed in our seats trying to relax.

"Good afternoon, sir," we shouted back in unison.

"I am Lieutenant Sheafer of the Academy Staff and I would like to welcome you to the Patrol Academy," he said. "I am responsible for you and your welfare while you are Cadets here."

The Lt. was somewhat intimidating physically. He had a large protruding lower jaw, like an underbite that stuck out forward. And when he stood his posture was so upright that it looked like he kind of leaned back when he stood or walked. I don't want to piss this guy off, I thought as I cleared my throat quietly.

Lt. Sheafer went on to explain what is expected of us as far as our behavior goes. He let us know he was the man that was going to deal us doom and gloom if we messed up. He said the less we see of him the better it is for us. The first rule he had for us was when we are not in formation going somewhere as a class, there was no walking in the Academy by Cadets. All Cadets will run to wherever it is they need to go. He explained that during the first couple of weeks our ranks will get smaller due to guys leaving. He asked before we leave that he be given the courtesy of us telling him beforehand. He explained that Cadets sometimes leave during the night without notifying staff, and he would rather us tell him first. That way he and his staff don't have to look for us in the morning when someone comes up missing. When he said that he actually cracked a smile.

Wow, leaving during the night? I thought to myself. Sneaking out. Like trying to escape. Yeah, this place is going to get challenging.

The Lt. further explained procedures and schedules we would be expected to follow. Most importantly was the daily schedule. He explained unless otherwise changed in advance we would follow the same routine daily. Wake time was 0530 and fallout for PT (physical training). PT would end at approximately 0615. Back to the dorms for showers and cleaning assignments. Formation march to morning chow at 0700. Morning inspection 0730. At 0750 form up for Colors (flag raising). 0800 classroom until 1130. March to chow at 1135. After chow, commence work duties. Back to the dorm for cleanup and march to the classroom at 1300. Classes until 1500. Afternoon PT from 1515 to 1645. Back to the dorm for showers and march to evening chow at 1715. Evening class would begin at 1800. Evening cleaning duties would begin after evening class ended. If there were no assigned evening duties this would be designated as free time. Lights out at 2200.

Lt Sheafer explained the procedure when being "gigged."

Gigged I thought, what is that?

When violating procedure or any rules, a Cadet can receive a "Gig." What that entails is after a Staff member witnesses an infraction, he would then fill out a "Gig Slip" and hand it to the Cadet, or in some cases leave the gig slip on the Cadets bed. "For example," Lt. Sheafer explained, "let's say during morning inspection you fail to make your bed properly. The Staff member will tell you what the infraction is and immediately fill out a gig slip putting in the number of penalty hours to be worked, and then hand it to the Cadet, or," Sheafer continued, "if a room inspection is conducted during a time when you people aren't in the rooms, the Staff member will leave the gig slip on your bed. All gig hours will be worked off at a time that Staff decides. Most of the time will be worked off in the evenings after classroom work when you are allotted free time."

Did he say free time? I thought. Doesn't sound like there will be much of that.

Then Lt. Sheafer introduced Capt. Ricos the Academy Commandant. Upon introduction Capt. Ricos walked into the classroom. The class was called to attention and Capt. Ricos greeted us and began his talk. He basically explained that we were "special people" to be here. He was very positive in his demeanor. He told us what he expected and repeated what Lt. Sheafer had requested about anyone wanting to leave, would they not leave during the night, but wait until morning. Capt. Ricos gave us percentages on Cadet resignations as to how many usually leave per class. By calculating his numbers, I figured that we could expect to lose maybe 9 or 10 Cadets.

I looked around the room when he said that, and I couldn't figure that there were nine guys here that I thought would leave. I know it was the first day, but everyone seemed pretty tight. I didn't foresee that happening.

Captain Ricos then finished his talk and re- introduced Tpr. Millner who entered the classroom. Tpr. Millner stood at the front of the classroom and exhibited a large grin. "Now," he said, "until 1500 we're going to go over your Geography assignment due on Monday."

Geography? I pondered as I adjusted my sitting position. What kind of geography I thought? We all know where Ohio is, don't we?

Tpr. Millner passed out sheets of paper with a map of Ohio on it. On the map were drawn the 88 counties and listed were the County Seats. For example, looking at the top right corner of the map, Ashtabula county is drawn out. Ashtabula is in large letters on the county drawing. In smaller print is the County Seat which is Jefferson. That's where the county courthouse and county services are. Each county has a County Seat.

Tpr. Millner explained that on Monday we would be having our first test on geography. We will be required to fill in a blank map with all 88 counties and their County Seats.

I think I heard a slight gasp in the room along with some muffled moans. The room went dead quiet as Tpr. Millner smiled from ear to ear looking around the room.

Monday? I thought. Shit that's only five days from today. How can I memorize 88 counties and where they go on the map along with their county seats? He's got to be just screwing with us, I joked to myself as I scanned the room. It was like Tpr. Millner had heard my thoughts.

"Yes, you will be able to memorize all 88 counties and county seats by Monday, and you all will pass the test," he said, as he looked a bit more serious. "It's not that hard once you get started and remember, you have to keep your grade average at eighty percent to continue training."

OK, I thought. We're only in the middle of the first day. Let's not panic yet. All these other guys have to memorize this stuff too. I can do as good as any of them. Can't I?

The rest of the class time, until 3pm., Tpr. Miller spent on going over the map and Districts within the Highway Patrol. I learned there are 10 Districts that divide up the state and Post's which also had to be memorized.

CHAPTER 8

Leapfrog

AT 1500(3PM.) WE marched back to the dorms and got dressed for PT class. Once we got back to the room McCarthy was chuckling about the memorization assignment. "I already got them memorized," McCarthy said as he laughed.

"Yeah," I said, "you've been sitting around your Post at work for the past six months studying, right?" I asked.

"Yeah wouldn't you?" he continued to laugh. "It really isn't that hard once you get a few of them down pat."

We formed up in the hall and marched over to the gym. The weather was great for late September. The temperature was in the low 80's, and after count was taken, we marched outside to the front of the Academy. There is a large grassy area about two football fields long and about half that size width out in the front area off 17th St.

Lt. Vassar and Tpr. Bellinger were our Physical Training instructors. They would be working with us daily whenever PT was called.

We started out in formed lines and stretched out for a while. Then Lt. Vassar had us run starting single file around the circumference of the yard a couple times which was measured out to that mile and a half distance. We were all in decent shape and we were timed for the mile and a half. It was hot, and it took a lot of seconds off of our entrance test score. I was surprised how slow we ran it. My time didn't qualify me for a pass if this were the final PT test. I was a bit worried, but everyone was slowed because of the heat.

After the run and without not much rest time he had us form up in single file with about ten feet between us circling some of the field.

"Today we are going to play leapfrog," the Lt. announced in a loud voice so all could hear. He went on to explain the way he wanted us to do the exercise. We were to wait in line bent over with our hands together and our elbows resting on our thighs. The last guy in line would start forward jumping each man in front of him and continuing until you jumped the 42 Cadets. As you got past the last man that was bent over in line, you then assumed the bent over position. The next guy who was now the first man would start forward in the same manner on the Lt.'s command. Also, when you jumped a Cadet you were to put both hands in the center of the back of the Cadet, and leap over trying not to have much contact other than the hands in the back.

"This ain't gonna be hard," said a voice from behind me. Yeah, I thought, it doesn't look to hard until we get tired.

The exercise started smoothly but as it went on, and the line got more constricted, and guys started to get tired, it became a fiasco.

After about two laps around the yard guys were not leaping. Guys were "rolling" up on top of each other because the bent over guy would eventually collapse. Collapsing because every few seconds you had some Cadet crashing into you, falling over you, sweating all over you, etc. Tempers got short because if the guy that was trying to get over you wasn't giving it his best; all his body weight would be on your back. Needless to say, words started being exchanged like, "Get up you lazy #@#%, get your weight off me." Ha, it was a comedy because the Lt. wouldn't let us slow down, so it was a continuous flow of bodies trying to pile over you. Then when the last guy would jump over you, it was your turn to start running forward and attempting to leap over people. They would then collapse when you put your hands on their back, and here comes the next guy behind you.

We leap frogged for about 20 minutes in that heat. It sounds like a sissy exercise, but it was tough. This exercise wasn't so much to build you up physically, it was to promote teamwork. We were supposed to be helping one another.

We were all pretty shot when Lt. Vassar called an end to it. A few torn gym clothes and grass stains. We formed up and marched back to the dorms to get ready for chow.

Once back to the dorms we showered and got to rest for a few minutes before forming up.

"That was @#%#ked up," Cadet Mallac said from across the hall. I looked over towards his room and he was standing in his doorway.

"Yeah, it was a lot harder than I thought it was going to be," I said as I was brushing my hair.

I spoke with Cadet Mallac for a while. He was a good guy. He was slightly overweight, but a big built kid. He was from southern Ohio where most people in the south are pretty laid back. Not a lot gets them nervous.

Mallac would turn out to be one of my best buddies in the Academy. He always could make me laugh with his demeanor and ability to tell a joke. That comes in handy when your stressed continually to have someone like that around.

Cadet Rennie had been chosen by the Staff to be the Class Lt. for the week. Every week Staff would select a Cadet to basically lead for the week. Any problems you had, or any problems that would come up the Class Lt. would deal with them. He was basically the conduit between the Staff and the Class. The Class Lt.'s main responsibility was to get the Class to wherever we were supposed to be on time and follow the schedule. Cadet Rennie had prior military, so they selected him to lead this first week. It was a big job to keep everyone together and on time, especially being week one.

Rennie got us formed up and we marched to evening chow. After we ate, we went back to the dorms and got ready for the six o'clock class. We had about fifteen minutes to do nothing. The bathrooms were located on each end of the halls, so there were two. Each had about six showers and four toilets along with urinals, a couple sinks and mirrors. There was a medium sized sitting area that divided the hallways. There were about a dozen chairs and a TV. Although we were told we could not watch TV at the present time in our training.

At 1750 hrs. we marched down to the classroom and took our seats. Tpr. Bellinger entered the classroom as attention was called.

We've got that down pretty good, I thought, as I looked around the room a bit. Everyone looked a little tired. I knew I was.

I looked over at Cadet Mead who was one of our female Cadets. She was seated off to my left in the same row I was in about four Cadets over. She was a decent looking girl. She was just a bit on the heavy side. Not fat but "thick" as one of my old buddies use to say. She didn't look very happy. It appeared she might be in some pain. She hadn't done to well in the PT class because it looked like her knee was bothering her.

Tpr. Bellinger instructed us in how to build notebooks. We would be required to maintain three notebooks that would contain type written notes from each class session. As it worked out you would take handwritten notes in class and keep them sorted by class name. Then on the weekends you would type the pages out as required, and add the pages each week to the notebooks. The notebooks were to be kept with us always and eventually be turned in prior to graduation for grading.

It was around eight pm. and Tpr. Bellinger told us the class was over. He instructed us to go back to the dorms and then we were to assemble in the gym at eight-thirty. (2030 hrs.)

We marched from the dorms to the gym and stood in formation. Tpr. Bellinger addressed us there and explained he had some evening work duties for us to perform. He gave the list of duties to Lt. Cadet Rennie and advised he would return later.

There was some quiet murmuring amongst us and maybe even a couple of complaints wondering when the day might end. Cadet Rennie divided us up into several groups. We were provided with cleaning supplies in a storeroom located off the gym. We grabbed the necessary cleaning supplies we thought that our group would need and commenced cleaning.

My group had to clean one of the lower boiler rooms located in the basement. It was kind of cramped down there because there were about eight of us in the one boiler room and we divided up cleaning rags, brooms, and a couple mops. Everyone was quiet. Not really any complaining because I think we were too tired. I took a moment to thank God for getting me through the day as I closed my eyes for a second, and kept sweeping, as to concentrate on getting my message to

Him. Thanks Lord, for getting me this far today. Please stay with us all, I prayed to myself.

"They're just doing this to us on purpose to see how much we can put up with, and to see if anyone will quit," said a voice from behind me as I was sweeping the one corner of the room. I turned around to see who was talking. It was Cadet Chris Borne whom I had met earlier in the day during PT class. Cadet Borne's brother was a Trooper who had several years on the job. So, Chris always had a lot of inside information for us. "It's going to be like this until they get guys to quit and thin our ranks. They'll let up on us after four or five weeks," Borne said, as he too was sweeping.

It was around ten-thirty pm when Rennie summoned us upstairs. We secured our equipment and marched back to the dorms. Cadet Rennie went over some procedural things and we then went to our rooms.

Cadet McCarthy and I cleaned up our room and went to bed. I laid there for a while trying to put the day in perspective. It was a good day, I thought, assuring myself that I was going to get through this. Day number one was over.

CHAPTER **9**

Gigged

0500 CAME EARLY. It was Thursday, day two of the Highway Patrol Academy, I thought as I threw the covers back and slid to the edge of the bed. I looked around and saw McCarthy already dressed in his PT gear standing there with a smile on his face. One thing about McCarthy I would learn, he was always smiling. He always had a good attitude.

"You up already?" I asked.

"Yep," said McCarthy. "Time for PT," he said, as he walked towards the door to see if anyone was up and in the hallway.

I got dressed quickly and ran to the bathroom. The guys were starting to form up in the hallway when I returned. I got in my assigned position and we were off, marching over to the gym.

Upon arriving at the gym, we were met by Lt. Vassar. He led us outside and we ran out front and did a couple laps around the front yard after we had stretched out. We did some calisthenics and more stretching, and after 20 minutes that ended the morning PT session.

We got back to the dorms and showered up before chow. McCarthy and I cleaned the room again. McCarthy said the morning inspections he heard were thorough, so we made sure to move the beds to get every inch of the room clean.

We formed up and marched to chow and got back from breakfast at around 0715. McCarthy and I agreed not ever to use the sink in the room because it was too hard to clean. We would use the sinks in the bathrooms. It was a little inconvenient carrying toiletries over to the

44

main bathrooms, but it was easier than getting in trouble for a water spot on the sink.

At 0730 some of the instructors entered the dorm area for inspection. We were required to be in full uniform and standing at attention at the foot of our beds. It was Sgt. Cotrell who entered our room. Sgt. Cotrell would earn the nickname from our class of "Rotten Cotrell" by the time of graduation. It was well deserved. He genuinely took great pleasure in making your life as difficult as possible.

"Good morning," he said sharply as he entered the room. He walked over to McCarthy's side of the room and began looking everywhere. Window ledges, tops of dressers and baseboards, and then stood in front of McCarthy face to face and looked over his uniform. He then stepped over in front of me and did the same. He then stepped around me and got down on one knee and reached under my bed. He stood up and walked back in front of both of us. He started to chuckle and extended his right-hand palm up towards my face. He opened his hand, and there was a dust ball the size of a golf ball. "What's this Cadet Munch? I got this from under your bed," he said in a forceful tone.

"That's a dust ball sir," I replied.

"Did you clean today Munch?" he asked.

"Yes sir, we did sir," I answered.

"Well, apparently not good enough," he chuckled. "That's two gig hours. One for each of you," Cotrell stated as he walked out of the room.

I looked over at McCarthy while I was still frozen in the position of attention. "He had to bring that in with him!" I exclaimed to McCarthy.

"Damn right, these floors are spotless," responded McCarthy. "And he took the dust ball out with him when he left," McCarthy said.

"Yea," I said. "He's going to use it again on somebody else!"

"He sure as shit is. He's gonna burn somebody else with the same dust ball," exclaimed McCarthy.

"Yea, He probably puts it in a small plastic case and takes it home at night," I said. "He has a pet dust ball!"

I had been gigged for the first time! It was like a baptism of sorts. There would be many more gigs to endure in the upcoming weeks.

McCarthy and I straightened the room and got ready for morning class. We formed up and marched out to colors. As we were marching, I was thinking of what just happened. I had to fight back a smile on my face because if you really think about it, the whole thing was pretty funny. Although I also felt a bit angry, I realized their trying to get you mad here. They want to sort out people with short fuses or anyone that can't handle an insult or harassing situation. It's all part of the training I thought, as we marched along. You have to learn in here how to control your temper.

The rest of the day was a repeat of the first day. Classes, lunch, work hour, classes, PT, evening chow, classes, and then we were allowed to work off any gig hours. Everyone in the class had been gigged that day for one reason or another. So, the whole class was again working late into the evening.

Friday, day three started the same as the previous day. Morning PT, Showers, chow, inspection, colors, class, lunch, work duties, class, afternoon PT, and showers. But on Fridays, we did not stay for evening chow. After showers was room cleaning and inspection at 1700 hrs. After inspection we would be released for the weekend. That's not quite how it went.

During the 1700 hrs. inspection some guys were getting gigged. After the instructors would find a violation, they would leave the dorms while it was to be corrected. This cut into us leaving on time. We were supposed to get out of there around five- thirty. The instructors would wait about fifteen minutes before coming back. Then the entire class again would be inspected, which took time.

We went through three inspections and didn't get out of the Academy until around seven o' clock. Guys were really pissed at one another for not being responsible to the "team." We're working together. We're supposed to be a single unit.

CHAPTER 10

Weekends

AFTER WE GOT permission to leave, I quickly packed everything I thought I would need to bring home for the weekend. Dirty underwear, socks, and t- shirts had to be brought home to wash. I got my notes, as I reminded myself to take home to be typed. That was it, as I grabbed all my stuff and exited the rear of the Academy. I loaded the car and pulled out of there and hit IS-71 northbound. I had about four and a half hours to think about the last three days. I should hit Erie at about midnight, I thought to myself.

As I drove north, I remembered the words of warning from staff about speeding tickets. Basically, they told us not to get one. I didn't know what type of punishment that may bring, but I wasn't going to find out. The speed limit of 55mph would be strictly observed. Staff also told us to identify ourselves as Cadets if we are stopped. It wasn't to try and get out of a ticket, but it was to make sure the staff would find out about the violation because Troop's in the field were advised to make notification if they stopped Cadets.

As I started to relax a bit and got north of Columbus, I started thinking about the last three days. I was very satisfied that I got through basically unscaved. I had made quite a few friends. I enjoyed the structure and discipline, and the set scheduling it required. I chuckled about a few funny things that had happened. I felt a general air of confidence about the whole situation, although the pessimistic side of me kept saying don't get too comfortable, there's a long way to go.

I thought about the upcoming physical demands. I was in decent shape for 185 lbs. I had just put on about 25 lbs. in the last two years. I guess I was a late bloomer, I thought as I concentrated on the road. I only weighed about 145 lbs. in high school, and I put on 30 lbs. during my college years, but the last year and a half seemed to be good muscular weight that I put on due to some weight training.

I also thought of God. I spent a few minutes praying and thanking Him for helping me and watching over me. It always seemed the only time I would feel like praying was when something extraordinarily good happened, because loyalty required thanks. Sometimes I'd think of God if something bad happened, and I'd ask Him why, or ask Him for help. And the underlying question for me was, does God exist? And then the overwhelming guilt it made me feel because I was a doubter. That was the most frustrating part for me because I wanted to be a true believer, but had always fallen short of that goal. I had never read a Bible before. It's amazing that attending six years of Catholic schooling that we never opened a Bible. I just thought the Bible was a feel-good story book.

I was thinking about how I had basically quit going to church regularly several years ago. I'm not sure why. I wasn't getting anything out of Mass anymore. I had been raised pretty strict in my religion, and I had just kind of forgot about it. That bothered me and I always wrestled with the fact that I had been so blessed in my life, and I couldn't spend one hour a week to go to church and give thanks? Every Saturday night I would tell myself that I was going to go to church tomorrow, and then end up not going. On Sunday nights I'd suffer through a little self-imposed guilt trip.

About 12:15 am I pulled into my driveway in Erie. Seems like I've been gone a lot longer than three days. I got out of the car and grabbed my suitcase and opened the apartment door. Cindy was asleep on the couch and the baby was in her crib. Cindy woke up and was happy to see me. We talked for about a half hour before I told her I had to turn in. She was genuinely interested in what I had to say about the Academy. We would "talk more tomorrow," I told her, and I knew I'd get in touch with my Dad. I told her I had about four hours of typing homework to do, and also having to memorize the state map and counties.

"Homework?" she asked.

The next morning, I got up and drove to my Dad's house. He was in the garage working on some project he had going. We talked for a couple hours as I explained just about everyday hour by hour. I could see he was happy and proud, but knowing him he was cautiously optimistic.

The remainder of the weekend I spent typing and studying for the geography test. I had a decent handle on the task. By Sunday afternoon I could fill in the map satisfactorily with the counties. The county seats I was learning but I just needed more time.

We had been told we were allowed to spend Sunday nights at the Academy. That was great because I didn't have to rent a room or get up and leave early on Monday morning. So, it was convenient to leave Erie on Sunday afternoon at around 4 pm.

On Sunday at four o' clock I said goodbye to Cindy and the baby, loaded the car and headed south. Cindy even packed me a lunch to eat on the way!

We were told we had to sign in at the Academy before 10 pm. because that's when they locked the gates.

I arrived at the Academy Sunday night at around 9pm. There were about ten or so Cadets already there. I walked down to my room and turned on the light. Ah! I thought, no gig slips on the bed! I entered the room and started to unpack. While I was putting my clean underwear away in one of the drawers Chris Borne walked into the doorway. "Chris," I said, "what's up? You came down early too?"

"Yeah Freddie. Me, Haltz, and Heft drive together. We all live near Youngstown so we're going to take turns driving," Chris explained.

"That's cool," I answered. "Who? Haltz and Heft?" I asked.

"Yea, it's about three hours for us so we figured its less stress just coming down the night before than get up so early on Monday morning," he replied.

Cadet Haltz then walked up behind Chris. "Hey Munchie, you came down early. How long does it take you?" he asked.

"It's about four and a half to five hours," I replied. "It's an easy drive though."

"You Pennsylvanian's are used to driving up and down mountains, aren't you?" Chris said jokingly.

"Yea," I replied, "We're all a bunch of backward hill rods," I answered.

It was kind of ironic because the only other Cadet in our class from out of state was Frank Mercer. Frank was from Kentucky, and the first thought I had when I heard that was of a hillbilly, barefooted, sitting in front of a log cabin, with fifteen kid's running around. It's amazing the preconceptions we can have, and I would learn year's later how perceptions can be so, so, wrong, and so unfair.

CHAPTER **11**

Week Two

THE STAFF HAD posted on the bulletin board in the dorm that Cadet Rennie would be the Class Lt. again for week two. That made sense, I thought. That gave us a chance to study Rennie for the week and get an idea of what we had to do if we got picked for Class Lieutenant. Cadet Rennie had a good handle on what was going on. Rennie had said the staff told him they pick people that show good leadership potential for Class Lt. I didn't want anything to do with that right now. I had my hands full just figuring out what I had to do, and not be responsible for the whole class.

Monday morning came fast and 0500 came way too early! McCarthy had just arrived from home driving in, and I got up and got dressed. I did my trip to the bathroom and we formed up in the hall. Rennie took attendance and announced all Cadets had returned.

Good, I thought. This unit is tight. Everybody came back.

The day progressed like the previous three. During morning class Capt. Ricos came in and introduced Major Hammel. He was an older guy. He walked slow and had a definite hunch back. I knew the mandatory retirement age is 55 years old, so he couldn't be older than that. Although I thought anyone over forty was near death anyway, ha-ha. I guess all 24-year old's think that way.

The Major talked about the legacy and traditions of the Ohio Highway Patrol. He was impressive in his speech and demeanor. He stressed family and good values of being most important to the "Division." He also mentioned that there were about 1800 officers statewide. That kind of surprised me. I guess I hadn't thought about that before. With only 1800 officers the Highway Patrol could really pick the best people for their ranks. I was proud to hear that, I thought, as the Major finished his talk and left the room.

All went well after class. We had lunch, then work duties washing staff patrol cars before afternoon class. There was no mention of the Geography test? I'm not saying a word about it, I thought. I don't think they forgot about it. Well, I pondered, it gives me another night tonight to study.

After afternoon class we all fell out for PT in the gym. Tpr. Bellinger organized the exercises and conducted them along with us. That's pretty cool, I thought. They (the instructors) participate right along with us. That earns respect from us. Tpr. Bellinger then ran us outside in the front yard for-yup, Leap Frog.

"Shit," I mumbled to myself. I'd rather do anything than this again. I know most everybody else was thinking the same thing.

Then it began. Same as last week. Everybody eventually got tired and guys were falling over each other. Guys were shoving and pushing one another, and a couple wrestling matches broke out. Tempers got hot. Tpr. Bellinger ran around yelling at us, "What are you going to do when you got some truck driver sitting on your chest trying to pound your face, and take your gun? Get up, don't quit!! No grey shirt ever quits, stay tough, you cannot lose. You wear that grey shirt. You will not lose. You will survive," he kept yelling, and yelling.

Wow, I thought. Really intense. It kind of all makes sense as to why we're doing this. This job is no joke, I pondered. Survival at all costs, but you must be in shape. This is great training, and really motivates you to want to stay fit.

The reality and seriousness of this job came to light for me that day. And I was so happy to be getting some of the best training in the world. Tpr. Bellinger was a bad ass dude.

The rest of the day went as usual. We got a chance to work off our gig hours again that night. Class ended at 2000 hrs. and my assignment was to rake leaves in the courtyard. I was out there with about eight other guys raking and bagging. When it got dark, we used our flash-lights. Adapt, adapt. You can rake leaves in the dark- just adapt.

We all got turned in by 2330 hrs. I laid in bed again like the previous days analyzing the day and what might be to come. The bottom line though was, I was happy. I even made the conscious decision to pray every night at this time. I prayed a lot when I was younger, I thought. Why did I get away from that? So, I found myself with the need to thank the Almighty every night, and to ask St. Michael to watch over me. I knew St. Michael was the Policeman of Heaven. He had been the one to kick Satan out when the dark angels revolted, as the story goes in Genesis. He was the Patron Saint of policeman. Yea, I said to myself, St. Michael can watch over me, but what I didn't realize at the time was, I would keep St. Michael very busy over the upcoming years.

CHAPTER 12

Lost One

THE NEXT MORNING 0500 I got up, teased McCarthy about his snoring, went to the bathroom, got dressed and fell out in PT gear in the hall.

Cadet Rennie took roll call. "Hartness. Where is Hartness," Rennie asked yelling out to us in formation. "I got up and he wasn't in his bed," said Cadet Brill who was Hartness's roommate. "I think he left during the night."

Oh shit, I thought. We lost one. During the night too. Just what staff asked us not to do- leave during the night.

We went to PT, breakfast, room inspections, colors, and to the classroom at 0800.

As we broke formation in front of the classroom, I could see Lt. Sheafer inside standing at the podium. Oh, I thought, Sheafer must have bad news.

After we were seated Lt. Sheafer confirmed we had lost Hartness and that he had contacted him at his home this morning to verify his resignation.

We were kind of bummed about it, but hey, that's his decision, I thought. Maybe yesterday's dose of reality during PT class made him decide this wasn't for him?

After that Lt. Sheafer left the room Tpr. Millner entered. "Attention," we shouted out as he entered.

"As you were," Tpr. Millner responded, as a big smile broke across his face. "Did you think I forgot about the geography test yesterday," he laughingly said.

"No sir," we all chanted in response.

"OK," he said, "Here is the test. You have 30 minutes. I'll be back then."

Tpr. Millner left the classroom as we started the test. It was deadly silent in there. I saw a couple wandering eyes on a few guys seated in front of me to my left. But that was about it. No one got any answers from anyone else. It was tempting though. Hey, they probably have a camera in here and they can see us all anyway, I thought. You get caught cheating that's an automatic trip home. "Not going to happen to me," I mumbled to myself.

Tpr. Millner came back and collected the tests. Then he passed them back out to be graded. We were going to grade each other's test.

Tpr. Millner said no one has any excuse to fail because he gave us the extra day for us to take advantage of. If we were stupid enough not to use the extra day that was our fault. He wanted us to learn the importance of making the best out of any situation and relating it to life's challenges. He also said this was a confidence building exercise because the task five days ago seemed unrealistic, but we accomplished it.

It took us about fifteen minutes to grade the test as Tpr. Millner read off each county and county seat. When I got my test back, I had missed three, and I think that worked out to like a 94%. Eighty percent was passing. No, I won't be class valedictorian, I chuckled to myself. But I'm glad that's over with for sure. I didn't hear of anyone failing the test, but I guess there were a couple of close ones.

Tpr. Millner said to review that map from time to time because week nine would be a mid-point exam that would be comprehensive from week one thru nine covering all subjects. He said reviewing occasionally helps you to retain what you have learned.

There were only two of us in the class with degrees which really surprised me. It was me, and Cadet Mossy. Ironically, we sat right beside one another. Mossy was quite a character. He was from deep southern Ohio and had a strong drawl. I often wondered if it was real, but it fit him well. He was quite a comedian when prompted.

The reason I even wondered about the lack of degrees was because something my Dad had always drummed into me. And that was when you get out of high school there are only two options he would accept for me and my brother. It was Military service or College. He felt those years from 17-21 were prime character development times. He thought coming out of high school and just going to work somewhere was a true waste because "you can work the rest of your life," he used to say. "Coming out of high school is the time to set yourself up to become a man, both educationally and morally." He felt just going to work every day at that age didn't create enough adversity in one's life. And adversity builds character he always said. "What's the worst thing going to happen to you during those years going to work in a shop every day?" my Dad asked me once. "The most stressful thing might be your toilet at home might plug," he said jokingly. "You're going to go to college or military to experience stress and adversity," he said. "It builds the ability to become responsible. It's good for you at that age."

And today, I couldn't agree with him more. Dad was a pretty sharp guy. He realized that the military tragedies he had witnessed and the adversity he experienced at such a young age made him a stronger person.

The morning ended after a class in Accident Investigation. Accident Inv. would be the number one priority in our studies and training. Two of our notebooks would eventually be filled with information and studies on accident investigation and prevention, and traffic law enforcement. The primary mission of the Highway Patrol is highway safety, traffic enforcement, and turning out the most professional, thorough accident investigators in the country. They certainly excel in these area's nationwide.

After lunch it was the usual car washing, and some of us were assigned cleaning details, along with some outdoor cleanup of the courtyard.

Back to the classroom at 1300hrs. And at 1500 it was back to the dorms for PT.

We formed up and marched to the gym. Tpr. Bellinger and Lt. Vassar were waiting for us. We started our stretching and after that did our calisthenics. To pass the final PT test for graduation involved a minimum number of pushups in two minutes, sit-ups in two minutes and the one and a half mile run within time limits. So, each PT session was tailored to include the pushups, sit-ups and usually ended with the run. Circuit training was starting to get popular around the country at the time, so they mixed running and resistance training a lot together during our hour and forty-five-minute workouts in the afternoons.

It was also explained to us that we would spend two weeks studying self-defense techniques which would involve Troopers from the field coming in and teaching.

Also, two weeks would be dedicated to boxing. The first week would focus on defense and technique. The second week we would actually box every day. On the Thursday of the second week we would box in front of Academy staff for critique purposes. On Friday, the next day, we would all box matches in front of the GHQ staff.

Wow, we're going to be boxing in front of all the Majors and the Colonel, I thought. That ought to be a bit stressful.

Tpr. Bellinger explained it has been a Highway Patrol tradition and is called "Boxing Week." Usually the two weeks of boxing week is scheduled around the ninth and tenth week of training. Its purpose primarily, he explained, is first of all to teach us defensive techniques. Secondly, it's to prepare you for "getting hit" out on the job. "Some of you in here may have never taken a punch in your life," Tpr. Bellinger stated. "We're going to make sure you do in here, so it doesn't come as a big shock to you when it happens to you on the road."

Ha, my problem throughout my teenage years was trying not to lose too many skirmishes. It was unavoidable in the neighborhood I grew up in, and the kids I hung around with, not to get into something now and then. Somebody was always challenging you. I never backed away from a fight, but the problem had been I wasn't really big, and sometimes caught the worst of it. I had been hit in the face more than I'd like to admit, including a few chipped teeth.

We would hear a lot of stories about past boxing weeks in the upcoming weeks of our training. Everybody would be talking about it. Well, I thought, it was about eight weeks away.

We stayed in the gym that afternoon running circuit for the remainder of the PT session. What? No leapfrog? When we ran inside the gym floor would get wet and slippery from sweat. It really was usually over and hour or more of running, pushups, sit-ups, nonstop. According to Chris Borne, he said they'd be pushing us hard to get into shape, and to get rid of the people that really might have doubts about being here. It was a good way to test one's fortitude about really wanting this job.

I guess in this business I don't want to be working and depending on someone with my life that really doesn't want to be there. So, it was good that we were going to have a lot of pressure to deal with throughout this training. When I get to the Post and I'm working the road, I want the people I work with to be "all in."

The gym class ended, and we were off to showers and chow.

Evening classroom ended and we worked off gig hours that evening until the standard time of around ten-thirty. We got to bed around midnight after McCarthy and I talked about the day's activity. McCarthy and I thought a lot alike. I guess I could figure that everyone in the class had similar personalities. Maybe that's what the entrance test promoted was a certain character we all share. I don't know, I know I hadn't met any Cadet there that I didn't like. But that would soon change.

CHAPTER **13**

Bad Asses

THE NEXT THREE weeks went relatively smooth. PT got harder. We were running longer distances, but everyone was handling it pretty well. We hadn't lost anyone, and no one had "slipped out" during the night. The females struggled with PT but didn't quit which is the most important thing. Cadet Meads' knee seem to get worse, but she continued to try.

We had a couple Cadets that were older. They were at the max age limit of 30 when they were hired. It's funny how when your 24 or 25, you consider someone that's 30 as being old. We all felt that way. One of the "old" Cadets (I'll keep him nameless) passed all his PT requirements but usually fell behind now and then. He was quiet and didn't make too many friends, but everyone accepted him as being a quiet guy. He also had somewhat of a slender build, and in other words not real physically intimidating.

On the other end of the spectrum were a few of the 21-year old's. They were a just PT freaks. They aced just about every PT test. Two of these guys became close friends, but both were a bit immature. They were your standard jocks like in high school, and these two acted sometimes like they were still there. They didn't bother me, and I didn't bother them. They seemed to have their own little three or four man click.

One day a rumor circulated that these two Cadets weren't happy with this older Cadet because he wasn't their picture of the perfect Trooper, and that he wasn't a stud when it came to PT. Apparently, they were going to ask him to quit, or the inference was they would make him quit.

I personally got really pissed when I heard the rumor. We were starting the fourth week and these two seemed like they were going to "take over." What they didn't understand, and most of us did, was that we're all in this together as teammates. That's the main quality the staff wanted to see in us.

Most of us decided to keep quiet and not confront the two younger Cadets until they actually did something. I had talked to the older Cadet about the rumor. He said he had heard about it and was somewhat concerned. I and a couple other Cadets told him that was not the wish of the majority, and we would wait to see what happened.

A day or so later prior to one of our classes beginning these two cadets stood up and addressed the class. They were vague in their accusations, but it was clear they weren't happy with one or two cadets because of their "look" and their "PT standard."

Several of us Cadets in the room told them basically to shut up and sit down. We let them know that they weren't in any position to say who meets standards and who doesn't, and that is up to Staff to decide.

They were a bit embarrassed and angry when they sat down. Just immature, I thought. They think their studs and everyone else has got to be as good as them. As long as these older guys are giving it their all, and passing required standards, that's all that matters. I didn't like those two at all. And neither did anybody else.

The rest of that day was a bit tense to say the least.

The next morning as we broke formation for class, I saw Lt. Sheafer standing in the hall near the door. "Shit'" I mumbled. Here we go.

We sat down, Lt. Sheafer entered, the class was called to attention, and Lt. Sheafer took the podium. He was leaning back on his heels. His head was straight and somewhat pointed skyward. His lower jaw was sticking out, as he began to speak.

"It has come to my attention that there has been some disrespect shown to Cadet members by other Cadets," he said very forcefully. " I cannot stress enough the importance of teamwork. What you have to learn here is that one Greyshirt can handle just about anything, but two

Greyshirt's together *can* handle anything, and that is because of team-work. Now I don't care how you take care of this problem you seem to have developed, but it's going to stop. And if it doesn't stop, I'll stop it. There will be people here going home. Does everyone understand," he spouted as he scanned every face in the room. "Yes sir," we all shouted in unison, as Lt. Sheafer walked out of the room.

"I hope everybody gets the message," said Cadet Riler from the back of the room where he was seated. "We don't want to hear any more bullshit. Worry about getting you own ass through this before judging someone else," he said, as most of us nodded.

Cadet Riler had been an unspoken class leader basically from about the second week. He had prior military service and called cadence every time we marched somewhere. He was about one of the coolest guys I'd ever met. He was very confident but not boastful. Actually, a pretty humble guy that got along with everyone. I, as most of the class, had a lot of respect for him. He wasn't any kind of PT stud and wasn't going to score the highest on academic tests, but this is the type guy I would want to back me up on the street when the shit started flying.

CHAPTER 14

"Spiderman"

BY THE BEGINNING of the sixth week all was going well. Just about everyone that was going to quit had, or so we thought. The only Cadet we had lost was Hartness.

On that Monday at the start of class Capt. Ricos came to the classroom to advise us that Cadet Mead had resigned. Her knee had continually given her pain and she and Staff decided it would be best for her to leave and recycle into the beginning of another class after her knee healed.

We were not surprised, and it had become obvious she was not going to pass any running standard for graduation. Most of us felt sorry for her although there were those who had the opinion that there was no place in front line police work for females. I personally was on the fence about it. There is certainly a need for females in law enforcement. I just wasn't sure how I felt about having a female working beside me on the front line. What a lot of people don't understand is that when in a confrontation, gun security has to be the foremost thought in the officer's mind. Any fight or altercation that an officer is involved in, he or she brings a gun to the fight, the officer sidearm. That gun is controlled by the first person to get their hands on it.

If I'm in a wrestling match with a suspect along with my partner, I am depending on my partner to be able to retain their weapon, so it's not used by the perpetrator on me or my fellow officer. With females, they don't usually have the same strength as the average male officer, so the likelihood of her having her gun wrestled away from her is higher than if it were a male officer. It's always a little more to worry about when working with a female unit.

One day during lunch duties I was in the courtyard raking leaves. Unfortunately, being late fall the leaves just seemed to be a continual onslaught in the courtyard. Windows surround the courtyard, and from the inside of the Academy it's a nice view into the courtyard. I was raking with Cadet Riler and several other Cadets.

At one point I looked up and saw Cadet Riler watching a large spider that was on the outside of one of the widows and was ascending the window. I was standing about ten feet from Riler when I observed him pull a lighter out of his pocket and "torch" the spider. Those of us that saw it got a bit of a chuckle out of it, although if I'm outside I always leave nature alone. I hate spiders so I wasn't upset. The only time I can remember killing a spider was if I saw one inside my home. Nothing much was said as we continued our duties and then secured to get ready for class.

After cleaning up in the dorm we marched to the classroom in formation. As we broke formation, I could see Lt. Sheafer inside standing at the podium.

"Here we go, what now?" said Cadet Stanley as we rounded the corner of the doorway.

As we all sat down Lt. Sheafer began. Again, with his head back as if he was going to fall over backwards and his lower jaw sticking out, he began a quiet ass chewing.

"It has come to my attention that there was a disrespect for the value of life committed during lunch in the courtyard. We are here to save life, not destroy it," he said as he leaned a bit forward to make his point.

The Lt. went on to lecture us further and explained that by the end of the day he wanted the "actor or actors" involved to come forward for the "benefit of the Class" he said. He then left the classroom and the scheduled class was given.

At the 2pm. break while we all stood outside the classroom, everyone wanted to know what had happened. Cadet Riler admitted to the group that it was him, and he was going to go to the office to report that it was he who burned up Mr. Spider. Riler then walked towards the office as we all went back to the classroom.

"Do you think they'll kick him out?" a question came from the back of the room. "No, they're not going to kick him out for that, do you think?" asked Cadet Rennie. Needless to say, we were all pretty nervous for Riler as class started without him.

At 3pm. we broke from class and formed up. We marched to the dorm for PT., and we saw that Riler had just gotten back from the office. He was dressed for PT. and we were all relieved.

"What happened," asked one of the Cadets. "I have to do a 3000-word essay due tomorrow," explained Riler. Staff had punished him for his conduct and required him to write an essay on the "importance of the sanctity of life." We all got a big laugh out of the whole fiasco, but it was them teaching us self-control. Riler was up most of that night writing the essay.

As week six winded down and Friday came it was announced by Tpr. Millner in class, that next week would be "Driving Week." It was explained that the entire week would be off the normal schedule, and every day would entail instruction by staff and Troopers from the field in the art of safe driving. The focus would be on pursuit driving, high speed skid recovery, officer violator contact scenario's, etc. There would only be morning PT because the afternoon and evenings would be also driving instruction, and night driving. "Man, that sounds really cool," whispered Cadet Mossy to me who was sitting beside me.

"And the Class Lt. for next week will be Cadet Munch," stated Tpr. Millner, as he looked directly at me.

I felt a rush of blood to my face and scalp. Did he just say my name? I thought as I looked at Tpr. Millner who continued to look at me.

"It's going to take a lot of organization Munch because you'll all be off the normal schedule, and you'll be required to be together at certain times in certain places on the back Fairgrounds where we set up the driving events," Tpr. Millner explained. "It's going to be a fast-paced week with a lot of unexpected changes in scheduling because we don't want to waste any time with the Troopers in the field being here as instructors. So, it's all valuable time."

"Yes sir," came out of my mouth as it still hadn't registered totally as to what Tpr. Millner was saying.

"Munch we will give you daily written schedules to follow and your assistants for next week will be Cadet Brill and Cadet Slayton. They will be your Sergeants."

"Yes sir," again I spoke.

After Tpr. Millner finished, class ended, and we formed up in the hall to march back to the dorm to get ready for PT. "Hey Munchie, you da man for next week," came a voice from behind me in the back of the platoon.

"Looks that way," I said as calmly as possible trying to not show the shock I was in. As we commenced marching thoughts started running through my head. Me? I thought. Why? Man, not that week. It's going to be crazy trying to keep everyone together and on time. Not to mention having to concentrate on my own training and getting through the course. Shit, I thought. It'll be something to worry about all weekend.

Friday 1700 hrs. came, and I began the drive home. Here we go I thought, as I started northbound on IS-71. I turned on my radio and fidgeted in my seat to get comfortable. Driving has always made me relax and gather my thoughts. In the past if I was agonizing over a problem, or if Cindy and I had a tiff, it was always easy for me to get in my car and just drive. I started thinking and putting the last week in perspective. I was happy with myself and how I was doing in the Academy. For the first time I really started to think what things might be like beyond the Academy? Where I might get stationed? How would Cindy feel if we were hours away from home? We had certainly already discussed that, but it looked like it was going to become a reality. Wow, exciting, I thought. Then my thoughts turned again to; Me, Class Lt. for next week? Quite an honor I pondered. Going to be very stressful though. It would have been a lot more fun for me next week if I didn't have the added responsibility, but what the heck, the staff is putting their confidence in me so I'm going to give it my best. That's all I can do is give it my best. "Right God?" I mumbled. Everything will work out, I thought.

The drive home was uneventful although being late November there was always the worry about snow and storms. I had been very fortunate to this point not to run into any bad weather since the Academy began. I arrived home that night around 9:45. Cindy was up sitting on the couch and the baby was asleep in her crib. It was always great to be home, but I was beginning to get this eerie feeling that I didn't belong in Pa. anymore. Psychologically my allegiance and my heart were shifting to Ohio. I guess the training and brainwashing was working.

The next day I typed up my notes for the week and then visited my parents. It was a pretty uneventful weekend, and Sunday at 4pm. rolled around fast. Part of me wanted to stay home for a couple days, but the biggest part of me couldn't wait to get back and get this part of my training over with.

CHAPTER **15**

Driving Week

I ARRIVED AT the Academy that evening on time and said hello to the usual bunch of guys that drove in. I really felt a part of something big and important for the first time in my life. "Hey LT.," came a voice out in the hall. It was Chris Borne. Chris stepped into my doorway. "Hey Lieutenant, are you ready for the big week of command and control? he chuckled.

"Yea Chris I guess I have to be, right?"

"Yep. said Chris. "We're all behind you. You're not going to have any problems."

"Thanks Chris. Yea maybe next week it will be you and I'll be supporting you," I said with a smile.

Morning came quick and I had put my silver bars on my uniform which Tpr. Millner had brought down at reveille. I got together with Brill and Slayton my two Sergeants and filled them in on what Tpr. Millner had told me, and I went over the times for the morning events. We had to be out on the Fairgrounds at 0800 in formation. That was the first thing to get accomplished.

The Ohio State Fairgrounds is measured in square miles. How many I had no idea but its huge and you can run for miles without seeing a vehicle or pedestrian. It is an ideal area for what we were going to be doing concerning our patrol car operation and obstacle events.

When we got out to the fairgrounds, we met our instructors. We were broken up into groups of three and assigned a patrol car which was driven in by the instructor we were assigned to for the entire week. Tpr. Francis was my instructor. Two other Cadets and I shook hands with him as he explained what Post he was from and how long he had been with the Highway Patrol. Cool guy, I thought as he talked about what was going to transpire during the week.

"There are nine events," he stated as he looked over the three of us. "You'll be required to pass all nine events by the end of the week. Also, you will have to pass a high-speed skid pad test and recover your vehicle properly, and we'll expose you to some high-speed pursuit driving."

The four of us got into the car and drove to an area where we set up a reverse backing on a curve event with cones. "This is our event," said Tpr. Francis, as he paced off the width and length of the cones we had set up. "It's called reverse serpentine on a curve. We'll practice this event for a couple hours and then move on to another one. This event location is where we will meet every morning," he said.

I think the first three or four attempts at backing that patrol car through that curve the three of us knocked down a hundred cones. Ha, after a couple hours of taking turns we improved to where we still hadn't completed it successfully but had improved greatly.

"This is my Patrol car," spouted Tpr. Francis. Every time you hit a cone your putting little marks on my car. That's why you're going to wash and wax it on Friday afternoon before I leave," he said with a grin. Tpr. Francis jumped in the car and drove backwards through the curve on a hill at about 15 mph and never nicked a cone, and on his first try. I couldn't believe it.

"That's how you gentlemen will be able to operate that vehicle by the end of the week," he said as he swung his legs out of the car. "When you begin an event, you tap the horn. The instructor will start his stopwatch. When you complete the event, you tap your horn. The instructor stops the time. Each event is timed and must be done within parameters," he said.

Wow, I thought. And there's eight other events to learn too. With that we drove over to the next event. The first day flew by and we all had plenty of opportunity to practice each event.

Day two was like day one. Drive, drive, drive, from 0800 until 2200

(10pm.) We also had night driving events and violator stops which were simulated by a carload of instructors. They allowed three cadets in a police car and put three instructors in a car designated a violators car. We took turns practicing stopping these violator cars at night, and simulated officer violator verbal contacts stopping the violators. It got tense a few times when the violators didn't want to cooperate with the Cadets. A few scuffles ensued in an attempt to arrest the violator/s. Ha, it was a riot.

"These guys are really intense," I said to one of my Cadet partners. "They really are testing our courage."

"You know we're not going to get through the week without getting our asses kicked by one of these guys," said Cadet Mossy with that southern drawl.

"Yeah someday maybe we'll be the instructors and we can kick some Cadet ass," said Cadet Haltz.

The rest of the week flew by. I had delegated a lot of my worries to my Sergeants. Something I had learned to do when I was in management at McDonald's. Fortunately, we were not late for any event throughout the week. On the last day I was stopped by one of the Academy staff and thanked for keeping the class on time and focused, and for my leadership. I did that? I asked myself. I guess things did go very well.

On Friday afternoon all Cadets passed the required testing. There was an air of confidence that you could feel amongst us all. We were truly changing for the better. Becoming confident people with a focus towards completing the mission. It felt great. We thanked Tpr. Francis as we handed him his keys to his newly washed and waxed patrol car that we had finished cleaning by 5 p.m. "Great job guys," Francis said to the three of us. "I hope you guys get stationed at my Post or maybe my District."

Ahh. That was a huge compliment I thought as I watched him get in his car and drive off. Now we were done for the week and we all left for the weekend.

CHAPTER 16

Boxing Week

THE NEXT TWO weeks concentrated on handgun qualification and academics pertaining to the Vehicle and Crimes Code. A lot of classroom note taking, and a lot of time spent on the indoor gun range. Each of us had to show proficiency in handling our issued sidearm.

We had a couple Cadets have trouble qualifying but eventually did. I was no crack shot, but I had hunted before and was somewhat familiar with guns. We learned position shooting, weak hand shooting etc. Sgt. Wilson was our firearms instructor and was very committed to what he did, although he was quick to crack a joke often to break the tension. I really enjoyed being around all the instructors except for one, yep, Rotten Cotrell. He just had this demeanor that screamed out that he enjoyed harassing us and giving us extra work duties at night which could really screw up your day. Time was a precious commodity at the Academy with all that had to be done. He seemed to go out of his way to take that time away from you.

Parts of week nine were spent developing self-defense moves. Tpr. Stillman came in from the field and taught us come a longs and some useful defense techniques, along with handgun retention. He had a black belt in high degrees in some type of close in fighting art. What I learned that week would help to save me a lot of injury in the years to come.

Tpr. Bellinger ran the PT training that week because he was a skilled boxer. He taught us proper stances and how to punch correctly, and how to fend off a punch. We practiced every day during PT in preparation for the upcoming "boxing week."

Then came the week that had been talked about by staff and Cadets since arrival. Admittedly we were all scared. Not of being beat up, but of losing in front of our peer's. It seemed so important to maintain the respect each of us had earned with one another.

There were people here who had never been punched in the head or face and had never hit anyone. Not the case with me. With my last name and having thin skin in sixth, seventh, and eighth grade, I think I was always tearing up my clothes. I know my Mom got so angry with me tearing out the knee's in my pants that she eventually refused to sow or patch them anymore. I sure loved my Mom....

Monday morning came and we were told to report to the gym at 0800. The staff wasted no time as we entered the gym in formation. "Fall out," chirped Tpr. Bellinger. "Form up around the mats and listen for your name to be called for your bout's."

We all got around several mats that they had set side by side to form two square areas resembling a boxing ring. Tpr. Bellinger began by calling two names and instructing them to put on the gloves and headgear provided. Within a couple minutes two Cadets were squared off in the first ring and Tpr. Bellinger was giving instruction on what was next. "On the whistle," he shouted. "You will commence boxing and maintain form that we taught you last week."

We were to fight three one-minute rounds in our first fight. The whistle blew and the first two Cadet's began their combat. Within five seconds the form went out the window and these guys were round housing and winging and trying to take each other out. It was some of the most entertaining fighting I have ever witnessed. One match pitted Cadet Fulton who was a medium built unintimidating kid. But no one knew except the Academy staff that he was a Junior Golden Gloves boxer in his teen years. Against Fulton was Cadet Baxter, who was a stalky well-built, kind of intimidating guy. I think Baxter thought he was going to dismantle Fulton on the whistle. We all thought that until the whistle blew. I don't think Fulton gave Baxter a chance to even throw a punch and hit him ten or fifteen times in the first 30 seconds. I was in shock.

Baxter took a real beating. To his credit he never quit or ran backwards. Ha, what a pummeling. I was convinced that if I drew Fulton during the week, I was just going to have to go ballistic on the guy till he knocked me out. I wasn't going to take a beating like that for sure.

My first fight I drew Frank Mercer the Kentucky'n. I think that was by design. We were the only two guys in the class from out of state. Admittedly Frank was good with his hands, but as even as the fight went, I think I came out a little less lumpy than Frank did. We all got in our first match prior to lunch.

After lunch we assembled again in the gym. Then it was announced. "You will keep the same fighting partner you had this morning," spouted Tpr. Bellinger. Ohhh!!, I said to myself as I looked over at Cadet Baxter, at the same time everyone else did.

"Oh man," I said to Cadet Cavinwood who was standing beside me. "Baxter is going to get another ass kickin'."

"Yes, he is," chuckled Cavinwood.

Again, to Baxter's credit, he got in the ring and put his hands up. I think Fulton actually felt sorry for him because Baxter after the first match at lunch time had to have a q-tip up each nostril to stop the bleeding so he could eat. I would guess Fulton only hit him a dozen times during the second match, but you could hear Baxter wince and grunt with each blow. Baxter earned a lot of respect from most of us that day. Oh- and so did Fulton. No one was going to mess with him.

My afternoon match with Frank went more in Frank's favor. I walked right into a straight right Frank threw and it dazed me to where I wasn't sure what day it was, ha! At the end of the day I had to take a couple Advil to stem the headache Frank had given me. None of us left that ring untouched. The staff made sure of that. If you weren't giving it 100% the staff member would step in and box a few minutes with you. That was to be avoided at all costs as far as I was concerned. Like I said it wasn't a beating anybody was afraid to take, it was the fear of not giving it 100% and losing the respect of your fellow Cadets. I have to say that even a couple of the older guys that we didn't expect much from did their best. We had become a very tight knit bunch.

Day two was a repeat of day one. A fight in the morning and a fight in the afternoon, keeping the same partner for both fights. I drew Cadet Askins who was taller and lankier built than I was. He had good reach over me, but I was able to get inside on him and hold my own. I bumped up the aspirin dose at the end of day two, because the head-ache was a little worse than the day before.

Day three was again a repeat of the two previous days. Fulton had beaten up the biggest kid in the class in the morning fight. So, by the af-ternoon they had mercy on people, and I don't remember Fulton having a match that afternoon. I survived my two fights on Wednesday and did pretty well. I hadn't embarrassed myself and was satisfied with how I did. By the end of the day on Wednesday we were all pretty lumped up and sore. The staff announce at the end of the class before going to the showers that because we had given it our all and were pretty damaged, that they would give us Thursday off from boxing and have just regular PT. We were pleased with that decision, but we knew they wanted us ready for the big show on Friday morning when we were to box in front of the GHQ staff and the Colonel himself.

As promised on Thursday we had no boxing. Just a lot of PT in the morning and afternoon. But it was nice to take a break from the boxing. Thursday ended and we were all very anxious about what was to come on Friday.

Friday morning came and we assembled in the gym all standing around wondering who we would draw for our final fight. It was tense. Tpr. Bellinger came out of the locker room and announced that the Colonel would be unable to make the trip to the Academy, and that there would only be a couple of Major's witnessing the bouts.

"Well that takes some of the pressure off, right John," I said as I turned to Cadet Simms who was standing beside me.

"Yeah Freddie. But I think this Guinea pig thing sucks anyway for their entertainment," he said with some distain.

The Majors arrived and as they walked across the gym floor, we all were kind of in awe. "That's the big brass from downtown," said Lou Reese from behind me. Intimidating, I thought as they took their seats and all that gold and silver hardware on their shoulders shined in the brightly lit gym. They were smiling and talking amongst themselves as

73

the first names were being called out by Tpr. Bellinger.

The matches began and after about seven or eight of them I heard my name called along with Cadet Askins. Him again? I thought. Stay inside on him. He hits hard if you don't get in close. I'll have to take a shot or two to get inside of him but stay in tight, I kept telling myself.

"Box," yelled Tpr. Bellinger, as me and Askins squared off. Again, I got hit pretty good getting inside, but I had learned how to absorb punches with my gloves. I retaliated in close and held my own throughout the match. It was a good showing from the two of us. I liked Askins, and it's hard because you don't want to hurt somebody you like. So, we couldn't like each other in this setting. Ha…

"Good job," yelled one of the staff as our match ended. Oh, that's cool, I thought. Somebody liked the performance.

Boxing week was finally over. I got to watch the remaining matches and say a prayer of thanks. I was running my tongue under my upper lip because I could taste blood and could feel the fat lip starting to swell, along with the ringing in my ears from a good straight right from Askins. I've got to learn how to duck faster I guess. Ha, it's just part of the game I thought as I watched the rest of the days matches and thought about what was to come in the final weeks.

CHAPTER 17

Getting Closer

WE WERE DISMISSED for the weekend and again the drive to Erie began. It was getting old driving back and forth, I thought as I set my cruise control on 60mph. At 9:45pm. I got home. Cindy was asleep in bed. I made myself something to eat and crashed on the couch to watch TV. I was watching TV but thinking about what we had gone through so far. I was so grateful. Thanks God, I wish I had the faith my mother has. There's no doubt in her mind that God is real and there for her. What a great way to go through life I thought. Being certain you have divine intervention in your day to day life. What would you be afraid of? Nothing, right? Life could be pretty stress free if you were convinced that everything that happened to you was God's wish. I really think too deep sometimes, I reminded myself as I laid there on the couch. I guess we will all know someday for sure what the answer is.

The weekend went fast. I didn't have any notes to type because we hadn't had any classroom last week with the boxing. I was able to spend much more time with Cindy and little Angela that Saturday. My Dad always wanted to know how it was going, so Sunday during the afternoon I set aside time to visit him and Mom. They told me they had been going to church every Monday night together and offering their prayers up for me to help me get through the Academy. I got choked up when they told me. I thanked them and assured them that their prayers were working. I was certainly blessed with great loving parents, and I had thanked God many times in my life for them; but was He really listening, or am I just getting lucky in life lately? See, I just am such a doubting Thomas. Why am I? I don't want to be. How can I improve my faith was the mystery for me?

The next couple weeks were spent concentrating on academics. Ethics and code of conduct set forth in our Policies and Procedures were learned and emphasized. We had taken a comprehensive midterm exam that was especially important in calculating our grade percentage for graduation. A score of 80% had to be maintained throughout the program, and that was the minimum for graduation. I had scored a 93 on the midterm and was well above the 80th percentile to this point. As far as we knew everyone was maintaining at least the minimum standards.

Accident Investigation (AI) was the Highway Patrol's bread and butter. Many, many, classroom hours were spent on accident reconstruction, learning formulas for speed evaluations, skid mark comparisons and statement taking techniques. Photography was also taught because of the necessity of Patrol units in taking on scene accident photos.

I had gotten a new roommate. I was crushed to see McCarthy go, but was happy to get Larry Heft as the new roomie. I don't know why they decided to change us up, but they changed the whole class. Larry was from Boardman Ohio near Youngstown. He and I hit it off and became close friends quickly. He was much quieter than McCarthy, so we meshed well together.

All 41 of us had made it to this point. We didn't have a quitter in the bunch. Staff had mentioned that our class was breaking all records as far as not losing Cadets. We were all proud of that.

It was nearing Christmas and we had less than a month before graduation. In a couple of weeks, we would individually be called in and given our duty assignments, so the stress levels were starting to spike. We had been given what were called "dream sheets." We were to list three Posts that we wanted to be considered for assignment. I had picked Ashtabula, Chardon, and Warren in that order. They were the three closest Post's to Erie. I figured the closer I could get would be best for Cindy because I knew homesickness had the potential to become a real issue.

There had been nothing earthshattering happen at home. Christmas came and went. We had been given Christmas off and the day after. We were down to a couple of weeks to go and the mood of the staff lightened considerably. We all began to believe these instructors could be warm blooded and human. Hey, they're just doing their job, I always told myself when I'd get mad at one of them for something they did to me or someone else. They were paid to put pressure on us. They had to see what we could take. The staff had done their job's well, and with graduation approaching they were accepting us as equals. As one of them. It was a great feeling.

CHAPTER 18

Duty Assignments

WEEK 15 BEGAN knowing that sometime early in the week we would be called in to the Personnel Majors Office for an interview regarding our duty assignments. Then on Friday find out where we were stationed via announcement in class by Capt. Ricos the Academy Commandant. On Monday each of us made the trip to the Majors office. During my interview I was told I'd probably be going to Steubenville. Steubenville? I thought, as I heard the words come out of the Major's mouth. Shit! I had heard nothing but bad things about Steubenville. It was supposedly a depressed steel town, dirty, and the economy in shambles. I heard it called "the ass hole of Ohio." Oh well, I thought as I got up from my seat after being dismissed by the Major, nothing I can do about it. Looks like Steubenville it is then. I'll have to break it to Cindy very gently when I get home Friday night.

During the rest of the week a lot of guys were upset because most of us were being assigned to places we didn't care to go to, mainly for geographical reasons not being close enough to home. "We don't know for sure until Friday," chirped Cadet Riler as we were eating lunch on Wednesday afternoon. "Everybody should just relax," he said. I hope he's right I thought as I dumped my tray in the trash and left the cafeteria to go wash cars.

Friday morning 0800 Capt. Ricos entered the classroom with the assignments in hand. He had a huge grin on his face as he stood at the podium. "I have your duty assignments here," he said as he held up a couple sheets of paper. "I'll read them off by District. He mentioned a couple other issues and then began.

"District One, Post VanWert. Cadet Heft," Capt. Ricos said as he looked at Larry.

Oh no I thought, Heft to Van Wert? Oh man he is going to freak out! Larry just sat there. Van Wert is on the far west side of the state at the Indiana border. All the way across the state from his hometown. That's what you get for being unmarried and free, I thought. I was wondering if Larry heard the Captain. He stared straight ahead and never even blinked. Capt. Ricos continued to read off names and District's.

After a few minutes of reading through District's two and three, "District four, Warren Post 78 DHQ, Munch and Kraft," I heard the Captain say. Warren? Warren? I repeated to myself. Not Steubenville? Hey, not bad, I think? Warren-Youngstown area. Very fast paced area. A lot of accidents and drunks. A District Headquarters. A lot of brass there at DHQ. Only about an hour and a half from Erie, I was thinking to myself. Cindy will be satisfied and relieved with that. Yea, Warren, OK!

We got back to the dorms after being dismissed. I walked in the room and saw Larry sitting on the end of his bed. He had tears in his eyes as he looked up at me. I knew this was going to be a tense moment.

"What did I do wrong Munch?" he asked as I sat down on the end of my bed.

"Nothing buddy," I replied. "Your single and unattached. They're going to launch unmarried guy's and put them where no one else wants to go. You know that," I said in a soft tone.

"Yea I figured I'd end up somewhere crazy, but you can't get any farther away from Youngstown than that," he said as he even chuckled a bit.

"It's all going to work out fine," I said, as we both started packing for our drive home for the week.

We were dismissed at noon on Friday because we were to make arrangements to visit our assigned Posts that weekend. We didn't graduate until next Friday, but they wanted us to make an appearance at our Post's this weekend. I made the drive home and got home around 5:30 p.m. I told Cindy where we were going, and she seemed somewhat relieved. I told her we would take a ride there tomorrow.

The next day I pulled out of the driveway with Cindy and we drove to Warren, Ohio. It ended up being exactly one hour and thirty-five minutes from Erie. I arrived at the Post around noon. While there I met the Post Commander Lt. Shatzer. He was happy to meet me and said that they were looking forward to getting a couple of "New Troop's" out of this class because they were quite understaffed. I spoke to the Lt. for about a half hour and he showed me on a map where he preferred me to live in the County.

That afternoon I found a two-bedroom apartment in the vicinity the Lt. told me and placed a deposit to hold the rental. I knew the following weekend I would have to be moved in for work on Monday. Yep, it was all happening very fast.

CHAPTER **19**

Graduation

I GOT TO the Academy that Sunday evening at the regular time. The same old guys were there. The mood was festive to say the least. "Last week," yelled Jimmy Haltz as I walked past his room with my suitcase on the way to my room.

"Got that right," a voice came from across the hall. We were all very pumped up and it felt good to be doing it with people I now considered my brothers.

Graduation would be on Friday at noon. The ceremonies are held traditionally in the gym. We were allowed to have guests attend. The number was left up to us, but it had to be reasonable because the guests would have lunch with us in the cafeteria after the graduation. My parents were going to attend as well as Cindy's Dad. My sister also was coming along with one of my aunts. My brother couldn't make it because he had just taken a job with a firm in Philadelphia and couldn't get away.

The beginning of the week seemed to really drag. We had been bussed to GHQ in downtown Columbus for final uniform fittings. There was also paperwork to be filled out concerning insurances, pensions, survivor beneficiary forms. It all seemed an endless train of paperwork.

The Academy staff now was treating us like we were brothers. It's a weird feeling being so scared of somebody and then all of a sudden, the guy is your buddy? Huh, it was hard to relax around these instructors no matter how nice they were to us. It's like getting bit by a crazy dog, and now the dog comes up to you wagging his tail wanting to be petted. I don't think I'd be too quick to extend my hand to pet him.

Thursday night came and I don't think any of us slept much at all. I know I didn't. Larry had gotten over his duty assignment shock and was back to his normal self. He had driven to VanWert on Saturday like I did to Warren. He had found a place to stay temporarily and was reluctantly happy with the area.

Friday morning, we assembled for PT at the usual time. Showers and breakfast afterwards. Nothing was going to change even on the last day. After we ate, we stayed in the cafeteria and Capt. Ricos along with the entire Academy staff joined us. Capt. Ricos addressed us and gave words of encouragement and advice. Then each staff member spoke and conveyed a story or two about an incident or incident's they found funny or interesting during our training. Like the time Cadet Baxter almost shot the underside of the bill of his hat attempting to get in a prone position during qualifications. Like the time Riler torched the spider. Like when Cadet Richards got caught speeding and had to scrub the kitchen grille every night before he went to bed for several weeks. We had nick named him "Range Rider." We all laughed and joked. The mood was festive.

Then a couple of the Cadets asked if they could speak. A couple thanked the staff and spoke for all of us regarding our appreciation for their commitment to making us as ready as possible for what lies ahead. Then Chris Borne stood up. He had borrowed a pair of glasses and set them on the end of his nose. He stood erect and leaned back as far as he could without falling over. He stuck his lower jaw out and began a drop-dead impersonation of our disciplinary officer Lt. Sheafer. It was an amazing rendition. "You people are tipping the canoe," Chris said as he rocked back and forth from his heals then forward to his toes. "Some of you people may not be here tomorrow," Chris went on. We were all roaring, including the staff and surprisingly Lt. Sheafer. It was a great moment for all of us.

At 1000 hrs. we were dismissed to our dorms to get dressed and ready for the ceremony. We had practiced several times during the week so we were all confident that all would go well. We all got dressed in our Class "A" uniforms. We spent the remaining time straightening up the dorm and checking each other's uniforms for lint and corrected any uniform problems. Then it was time.

At 1159 hrs. we marched in platoon formation through the gym doors. I could see my parents seated in the first row behind the last row of where we would be sitting. It was hard not to choke up. We all looked straight ahead as we marched around the gym and into our seats. The stage was very large and accommodated a lot of dignitaries that were in attendance. The Governor, the Director of Highway Safety, the Colonel, GHQ Majors, and a few guest speakers. "Quite a production," I mumbled out loud to myself. The day had finally come I thought as Capt. Ricos was the first to speak and introduce all the dignitaries on stage.

There were several speeches to listen to, and after about an hour the time came. We were called individually up and walked across the stage. We shook hands with each dignitary and were handed our Commissions by the Colonel. Then when we all had made the walk across the stage we sat back in our seats. We were then ordered to stand, to recite the oath of office. Needless to say, I felt I wasn't really there. It was like an out of body experience. I was reciting the words and understood their meaning and what was going on, I knew my right hand was in the air, but it didn't seem real. Was this really happening after so many years of goal setting and worry? And then, it was finished. We were Troopers, as we shook hands and congratulated each other.

We were dismissed. I turned to exit my row of seats and the first person I saw was my Dad. His eyes were welled up with tears, and that kind of made me lose it. Not totally, I didn't create any scene, but my Dad and I hugged and we both fought back tears as he told me how proud he was. And as usual as I had said to him many times before, "Thanks for being my Dad."

Cindy came up and gave me a nice hug along with my Mom and Aunt and my sister. It was a great day, but I knew now that all the hard work would begin in the upcoming months.

CHAPTER 20

"Post -78 Warren – DHQ"

IT WAS THE Sunday after graduation. It was cold and snowy, and Cindy and I had driven back to our new apartment that afternoon from Erie because we had to pick up the baby. Cindy's Mom had been watching Angela all weekend.

It was a fairly nice duplex in Bloomfield Township off of SR. 45. The rent was $275 a month. It was a two-bedroom ranch style duplex with a kitchen, living room and bath. Pretty simple I thought, as I was carrying some of the last boxes from the trunk of the car through the back door.

Several of my friends from Erie, my Dad, and Cindy's Father had moved us in the day before all day Saturday. Cindy and I were tired and wanted to go to bed early. Cindy drew bath water to give the baby a bath and the water had a brownish tint to it. "Well water I think," I said to Cindy as I watched her look at me with those eyes and look of disgust? Was that the right word, disgust? Pissed, I guess would be a better word. It was clear to me that Cindy wasn't as excited as I was to be there starting a new life and a new job.

"I'll call the landlord in the morning and ask what's up with the watercolor. I 'd wait to bathe her," I said with a sheepish grin. I was really trying to make the best of it all and trying to keep her happy. I knew things might get pretty tense in the months to come waiting for her to get overwhelmed with being homesick.

Morning came quickly and I had to be at the Post at 0800 hrs. I said goodbye to the wife and daughter and left the apartment at seven o' clock dressed in my uniform. I was extremely nervous with all the standard worries that face a person on the first day of a new job. Would I be accepted? Would I live up to self-expectations?

Hey, I thought, to heck with it. I made it this far and did well throughout the Academy. Why wouldn't I continue to maintain a good standard? Just relax a bit, enjoy what's happening. Easier said than done I thought as I pulled into the parking lot.

As I walked towards the building, I could see the District Captain getting out of his car. Oh Boy, there's the top dog. I know to salute him if we get within speaking distance. As I approached the rear door of the Post, I saw him enter at the side door of the attached building which physically is the DHQ part of the complex. Well I guess I dodged meeting the Captain for now.

Upon entering the back door and walking into the office area there were several Troops standing around doing paperwork and kibitzing. "Good morning," I said as I walked over and stood near one of the tables.

"Hey men," one of the Troops said, "We got a new face in the mix here." The Troop walked towards me with his arm stretched out. "I'm Ben Carter," he said with a broad smile.

"Hi Ben, I'm Fred Munch and I'm new here," I said as I chuckled out loud nervously.

"Great to see new faces here," he said as he turned to the rest of the Troops. "Guys this is Fred, Fred Munch."

"Welcome," one voice said.

"Have a seat," another stated.

I sat down on one of the chairs as the group shot questions as to where I was from, was I married, how many kids did I have. One of the guys brought me over a coffee and said, "We only drink it black here," with a smile on his face.

"That's fine," I said as I lifted the cup to my mouth. Don't spill it, don't spill it on your pants I thought.

"The Lieutenant will be in shortly Fred. He'll want to go over some things with you first thing," Ben said.

"OK"' I said as I carefully set the coffee on the table in front of me.

From across the squad room there was another office door labeled Sgt's Office. The roughest toughest battle-hardened looking man walked through the doorway from that room. His uniform was a bit wrinkled and didn't appear to fit him very well. He was wearing Sergeants stripes on his shirt and had a few ribbons above his badge.

The Highway Patrol has several awards programs that recognize Unit's in the Division for various above and beyond the call of duty awards.

As I scanned him up and down, I thought, this guy has got to be the saltiest human being I've ever seen. "Salty" is a military adjective for someone that's been through the ringer and around the block a few times. A veteran of many campaigns.

I swallowed kind of hard as he stepped towards me. He looked at me as our eyes met, and with a gruff snarly kind of voice asked," Your Munch?"

"Yes sir'" I shot back as I extended my hand to shake his.

"Don't ever call me sir again," he said as he reached out and grabbed my hand. He got his hand way deep into my palm where I couldn't respond with a decent grip. He squeezed my hand so hard I felt one of my knuckles pop.

"Yes sir- I mean yes Sergeant," I said with what probably was a look of terror on my face. "My names Bob Spader," he barked.

"Hi Sarge, Fred Munch. Nice to meet you," I said in a forced deep voice.

"Where are you living?" Sgt. Spader asked.

"Bloomfield," I said.

"Bloomfield?" a voice came from one of the Troop's behind me.

"How the hell did you end up in Bloomfield?" asked Spader.

"I'm not sure," I said. "The Lieutenant told me on that Saturday I visited the Post before graduation that he wanted me living north of Rt.5. So that was the first place I found that was pretty decent and affordable."

"That's a half hour from the Post," Spader chuckled. "You'll eventually want to move closer to town. You're out in the sticks up there."

Just then the back door opened, and the Lieutenant walked in. "Hey

Lieutenant, how come you told Munch to live in Bloomfield?" Spader said jokingly.

"Bloomfield? I never told him to live in Bloomfield, although that's north of Rt. 5, but by about 10 plus miles," he laughed. "He'll be ok there for a while," the Lt. said.

The Lieutenant then set his briefcase down and shook my hand welcoming me to the Post.

"I hear you did pretty well down there at the Academy. You must have, to have been stationed here at this Post. We're one of the busiest in the state and you have to be pretty sharp to make it here. It's a fast Post. Lots of action," the Lieutenant stated.

"Yes sir," I responded. "The Academy was challenging for sure."

The rear door opened and in walked my Coach. We had met at the Academy during driving week. The Patrol sends all the Coaches that will be training the new Troopers to the Academy during driving week. They set time aside that week so you can meet your Coach and start to build some rapport. My Coaches name was Trooper D. Gemco.

"Hey Fred, you made it huh?" he said.

"Yes, it looks that way," I said as I couldn't help but crack a big smile.

"Good Fred. Now the fun begins. Swinging shifts, midnights, drunks throwing up on you. Crashes, injuries, hospitals, statements, photographs, people resisting arrest, drunk drivers. You're going to learn it all my boy."

"Sounds good Coach," I said.

Then walked in Cadet Kraft. He was the other Unit stationed with me from our class. Now, he was Trooper Kraft. Fortunately, then all attention was diverted to him as I followed Trooper Gemco up the staircase to the Troopers locker and report room on the second floor.

"I'm really nervous Dennis, meeting everyone," I said as we walked up the stairs.

"Don't worry about anything until I tell you to worry," he said, which made me feel a whole lot better.

The rest of the day went fast. A lot of personnel paperwork to get through. Dennis, I would learn, was such a nice guy and had a laid-back approach in how he trained a new Troop. Dennis had "Broken-in," a couple guys before me, so this wasn't new to him. His theory was a relaxed atmosphere for learning, although all that would soon change.

My first shift in a patrol car would take place that evening. They sent me home at 4pm. that day and I was instructed to be back at 11:30 pm. for work. Wow, I thought, this is called a double back. I had learned that term in the Academy and it was not uncommon the way the Patrol had their scheduling laid out. There was also what's called a triple back where a Unit works 8 on, 8 off, 8 on, 8 off 8 on. Kind of confusing at first but triple backs weren't very common. Double backs happened at least once a month going from day shift to night shift.

The Highway Patrol schedule was of a fixed nature. It started out on a Tuesday at 4p-12a and work seven days in a row. Then two days off. Then out for day shift on a Thursday at 8a-4p and work seven days in a row. Then two days off, and then that Friday night out at midnight and work till 8am and work six in a row finishing up on a Thursday morning at 8am. Then have the next four days off and come back out on the next Tuesday at 4pm. That gave you from Thursday morning until Tuesday afternoon off. It was nice to get what was called the "long weekend" every month, but believe me, you paid for it. Those seven-day runs were long days. And those six midnight shifts every month tore up the body, because you were rotating your sleep patterns every week, and never getting used to any type of routine.

After grabbing about three hours sleep, I arrived on station that evening at 11:30 pm. I reported to the Post for my first day of Patrol. Of course, I'd be with Dennis every minute for the next three months glued to everything he did and said.

The Warren Post 78 was responsible for Trumbull County. The county is a mix of urban and industrial areas in the southern areas, and rural farm in the north. Warren is located in the southern end of the county. Just south of Warren is Girard, and Youngstown in Mahoning county. The area is blue-collar working-class people. The job market was stressed and unemployment at all-time highs. The home mortgage rate was 13%. Homes weren't very affordable to say the least. Generally, the area was depressed due to the closing of area steel mills and related industry in recent years. After graduation, my pay rate jumped to around $7 an hour. Just under $15,000 per year. Most of the people in the area worked at GM Lordstown, and Packard Electric, where they were making twice that.

Dennis met me in the squad room and went over some procedural things I needed to know for my first day. We had a short roll call lasting about ten minutes and then we were on our way to the parking lot. I threw my briefcase in the back seat and got into the front passenger seat. I looked over at Dennis. He was seated leaning with his chest on the steering wheel looking at me with a big smile on his face. "What?" I asked as I smiled back at him.

"Here we are," he said.

"Yeah, what?" I replied.

"You'll never forget this moment," he said.

"No, I don't think I ever will," I said. "It took a long time and a lot of worry and hoping to be here. And the only way I'm quitting or going back to Erie is in a box," I said as I laughed out loud.

"Don't say that!" said Dennis, as he put the car in drive and pulled out of the parking lot.

We were assigned the east zone Interstate 80, SR. 193 area. It was a Monday night and not much going on. Dennis showed me all the boundary lines and city limit areas. I had to memorize each township we drove through and he would ask me periodically during the shift to repeat the townships and court jurisdiction boundaries. There were three different court jurisdictions in that area, and it was mandatory to know whose court jurisdiction you were in at any given time in the event you had to write a summons or ticket, or made an arrest. IS-80 is a big commercial route for truckers traveling from New York City west towards Chicago. We started checking speeds with the radar and stopped several tractor trailers over the next couple hours. Dennis did all the talking, and it didn't take long for the truckers to figure out that I was a boot Troop. Haaa.

Dennis was always polite and professional, and I was impressed with the respect he commanded without having to act like a tuff guy. That's the way I want to be, I thought as Dennis handed the driver his

SEARCHING FOR MY FAITH

ticket and the driver thanked him. Wow, I thought, the guy thanked him even after getting a ticket. It was because Dennis treated the man like a man, and never spoke down to him. Yep, I'm paying attention to Dennis. He's pretty cool.

"Ok Freddie let's get a coffee and then come back out and you can do all the talking with the next guy we stop."

"Really?" I asked. "Do you think I'm able to pull it off?"

"Sure," he said with a grin. "Now's a good time to start don't you think"?

"OK," I said slowly and with a lump in my throat.

We had a ten-minute coffee break at Denny's and back in the car and off to the Interstate. The whole time I was having that coffee I don't remember even being waited on. I was thinking about this first traffic stop.

"You'll be driving right around the ten-day mark," Dennis said. "So, pay attention to how I stop these vehicles and positioning of the patrol car for safety purposes because you'll be doing it soon."

"OK," I said as I saw the radar go off reading and flashing 67,67,68,68,67.

"That's a good one coming in the passing lane," Dennis said. "I'll stop him on the other side of the next exit so we can get him to pull off on to the entrance ramp to get away from traffic."

"Ok," I said. I was really nervous. I could feel my heart beating. Dennis called in the trailer plate registration as we pulled in behind the trailer and activated the overhead emergency lights. All the patrol cars have CB radios in them because we monitor emergency Channel 9, but it also scans and picks up the trucker's channel 19.

"Hey Smokey's got somebody," chirped a voice from the CB.

"Ahhh, feed the bear, feed the bear, did Smokey get mad at somebody again?" said another voice.

"Dumb ass cop, that's all they got to do is mess with us," said yet another voice.

Dennis got the truck stopped and positioned the car behind the trailer. The driver had pulled off on the entrance ramp and on to the right berm, so we had lots of room to walk up the left side of the truck.

"Be careful your hat doesn't blow off when the semi's go by," he said. "They try and get close sometimes hoping to blow your hat off. They've got mine a couple times," he said with a smile as we opened our doors and started walking up the side of the truck. "Just ask him for his license registration and paperwork. He'll know what to give you," Dennis said.

We took about ten more steps towards the cab. I could see looking up at the driver's side mirror that the driver had turned on his interior dome light and was looking through his paperwork. I saw the window coming down and the drivers head turn towards me.

"Afternoon," I mean good morning," I said as I tried to clear my throat. "I need to see your license, registration, and paperwork."

"What paperwork do you need?" asked the driver.

I looked off to my right where Dennis was standing with a blank look on my face.

"What paperwork do you need?" again asked the driver.

Dennis spoke up, "Medical card and bills of lading," stated Dennis.

Fortunately, the driver had a lot of patience because I was stammering and stumbling through the whole contact. For his reward he got a warning and we had him on his way. As we got back in the car, I was shaking my head in disgust.

"Hey, you're just learning my man," Dennis said. "It takes five years to get a good handle on this job. Five years, and don't forget that."

"OK, Thanks for your patience," I replied.

"Now since we're on the subject, I want you to understand the correct way to inform a violator that you're giving them a ticket," Dennis said intensely. "You never stop anyone to just give them a warning. If the violation isn't serious enough to warrant a ticket, then you shouldn't stop them because here's what happens. You see a minor infraction so you're going to stop the guy and be a hero and give him just a warning. But you get up to the vehicle and the guys an ass hole and starts popping off. So, you get pissed and write him a ticket because of his attitude. That's writing a bad pinch. Rule number one. Don't stop anybody to write a warning. If the violation isn't good enough to write a ticket, then don't stop the car. You can decide after speaking to them to issue a warning- that's ok. But don't write a bad pinch because of someone's attitude. You will develop a reputation in the courts concerning the quality of your work, and you want it to be a good. Understand?"

"Yeah that makes sense. I never thought of it that way. So, they can talk you out of a ticket, but don't let them talk you into one, because if you stopped them for something minor, then you look bad in court writing chicken-shit pinches, right?"

"You got it," Dennis replied.

"There's a lot more to this job than meets the eye, huh coach," I said half-jokingly.

"Yep," Dennis replied. "And another thing," Dennis went on. "You look them in the eye on your first approach and tell them, I'm issuing you a citation for whatever. Then go back and write it. Some guys don't tell the people and go back to their car and write it. Then they come up and give it to them, and quickly try and avoid a confrontation. You don't keep people in suspense. Be a man. Tell them to their face. Sir, Ma'am, I'm issuing you a citation for the offense, and I'll be right with you. Go back and write it and then come back up with it. If they want to vent sometimes that's ok, as long as they don't disrespect the badge. They may chirp at you a bit, that's ok. We're paid to take it a little bit. But if it gets personal towards disrespecting the badge and becomes more than a bit of venting, then other actions may be warranted. I'll never tell you to be a whimp and take a lot of abuse from somebody. But they do pay us to listen to someone having a bad day and venting a little. You will learn the difference quickly out here. Especially in this Post area. There's a lot of struggling people living in this depressed steel area."

"OK," I responded. "But when it gets to swearing and threatening, that's when you change gears and take action necessary to protect yourself?" I asked.

"Sounds about right to me," Dennis replied.

It was getting near 6am and we had pulled into a crossover on IS-80 just west of the Pennsylvania state line. I could feel my eyelids getting heavy, and as hard as I tried, I could not keep them open. I could feel my head bobbing.

"Hey!" spouted Dennis. "Stay awake. Don't be putzing out on me," he continued. "We can't afford to sleep on midnights. That is not what they pay us for. If you get tired pull over. Don't ever wreck a car or get hurt falling asleep at the wheel. There is no excuse for that."

"Sorry Dennis," I replied. "I've never been up this late without sleep that I can remember. I'm seriously trying to stay awake."

"I know," he said. "But get used to it. The trick is to get enough sleep during the day and take a nap just before you come in. That's what helps me. Just think, you only have a little less than 25 years to go!"

"Ha, that all?" I responded. "Maybe I'll end up being the Colonel and I won't have to swing shifts."

"Maybe Fred," Dennis said with a grin. "Somebody's got to be the Colonel, and why not you?"

The next two hours seemed like days. We pulled into the back lot of the Post and up to the gas pumps. I felt terrible. My eyes burned, my clothes had a funky smell, my face was shiny and greasy. I was hungry, and I had a dry awful taste in my mouth.

"Is this the way you feel at the end of every shift on Midnights?" I asked Dennis.

He chuckled out loud, "Yep, and you never get used to them. I don't care how long you work them their just impossible to feel good on. The problem is every month you have to work seven straight. It is a bitch, and guys hate 'em."

"OK, well I'll try and go to sleep right after I get home and hopefully sleep until four or five o' clock," I said.

"Good luck with that," Dennis said. I go to bed right away also, but maybe four hours is all I can get. Then lay down around 7 o'clock for an hour and a half or two before coming in."

At the end of the shift I got in my personal vehicle and made the drive home to Bloomfield. The Highway Patrol assigns each Trooper a patrol car. The Troop is responsible for maintaining the car, keeping it clean, etc. The vehicles are allowed to be taken home and kept at the Troopers residence. New Troopers are not assigned cars until they get through the coach/pupil period. It's a twenty-minute drive home up north in the sticks. About halfway home I kept nodding and had to pull off and get out for air. I'm definitely going to have to move further south closer to the Post I thought, as I got back in my car to finish the ride home.

Upon arrival Cindy and the baby were up and of course full of energy.

"I've got to go right to bed," I said to Cindy as I took my coat off and hung it in the closet.

"OK" she said, "How did it go?"

"Oh, yea, work. It went good. Dennis is a real patient laid back guy and is really focused on the task of training me. I'm lucky to have gotten such a good guy."

"That's great," she said, "What time do you want me to get you up?" she asked.

"If I'm still sleeping past four o'clock come in and get me up."

I laid down and within a couple minutes I was out. I looked at the clock once I remember and it was 11:30am. Have to get more sleep, I thought to myself. Back to sleep. Woke up at 1:30 pm. and I sat up on the edge of the bed. I feel like I've been up all night, I thought to myself. I *was* up all night. That's why I feel like shit.

I got up and walked into the living room. Cindy and Angela were sitting on the floor watching TV.

"Did I wake you up?" Cindy asked.

"No, I just can't sleep any longer," I replied.

At the end of that work week of night shifts, I was beginning to realize that I was not a night person. As the week ended, I reflected on what had transpired. I handled three accidents. One of which was an injury accident, and I learned how to report to the hospital after clearing the scene and take written statements from the drivers. And something I wasn't really comfortable with, was issuing a citation to an injured party while their being treated. If their injured to where their near incapacitation, then the statements and citations are taken care of later. But the last thing someone injured, or their family want to deal with, is receiving a ticket in the hospital, but that is the procedure. It is hard to issue grandma a ticket for running a stop sign, while Grandpa and grandmas' kids are standing in the room. Even after years of learning how to be tactful about it, it was always difficult for me.

We wrote several tickets that week for various violations. It was a lot to absorb and very challenging both mentally and emotionally, but I loved every minute of it. God was good to me in allowing me to chase after my life's dream. It had all happened so fast, and I hadn't focused on giving thanks. All the good that had happened to me and I was still a doubter. It was a part of me I wanted to change.

CHAPTER 21

"Salty Dog"

IT WAS THE middle of the third week of Coach/Pupil training, and all seemed to be going well. I was making my share of little mistakes, like not remembering a court jurisdiction, or forgetting to enter some minor information on a report or citation etc. All mistakes to be expected at this stage of training.

Dennis and I got along really well. He was about ten years older than me and I was starting to consider him like an older brother that I never had. His style was calm and laid back. Aggressive with people only out of necessity. Dennis preached to treat everyone the same no matter who they were, or skin color, or how they looked, or how they dressed. It was always sir or ma'am until they pushed your nasty button. In other words, treat everyone with respect until they make you treat them otherwise. If they become disrespectful, then it may be necessary to change into someone different, and maintain composure seasoned with whatever force necessary to effect an arrest if warranted. In other words, be nice until they are not. Then deal with them in terms they wish they had not pushed you to. We ran into a couple people during that period that got Dennis to change from nice guy to not so nice. I learned a lot about how to breathe and oxygenate on the way to a hot call or accident. Deep breathing slowly and calmly. There was a lot to learn in a wide spectrum of techniques. Dennis was just the epitome of a smooth operator.

We were working the four to twelve shift for a couple days. Usually that is the busiest time for call volume. So, it's a fast running shift and the time usually flies by. As I walked in the back door of the Post just prior to the start of roll call, Sgt. Carnival walked out of the Sergeants office and saw me. "Hey Junior, follow me," he said.

"Hi Sarge. What's up?" I asked, as I followed him into the Sergeants office. Sarge sat down at the desk and then slid a teletype across the top to me. As I was picking it up to read it Sarge said, "Your Coach got promoted this morning. Sgt. D. Gemco will be transferring to District 9."

As I heard his words, I was reading the promotional announcement on the teletype. "Wow that's great!" I exclaimed. I didn't want to show it, but I was in a bit of shock. I was just getting comfortable with Dennis and now he's leaving, damn it.

"Your new coach is Jack Martin, the "Salty Dog," Sarge said.

"Tpr. Martin?" I asked.

"Yep," said Sarge. "He'll be here shortly to meet up with you. He was on day shift but we're changing his schedule to get into rotation with your squad."

"Oh. OK," I said as I could feel my stomach tighten.

I hadn't met Jack because of conflicting schedules, and he was on a different squad. I knew he was younger than Dennis, maybe in his upper 20's, about five years older than me. He had a reputation around the Post and District as being a "Hard Charger," which means highly productive, and fairly aggressive in his demeanor, which is putting it nicely. In other words, Jack had the rep of being a big-ticket writer, and didn't take any shit from anybody. He's a bit different in style than Dennis. Plus, Jack only had about six years on the job, and that would be an early selection time wise for being a coach. There was an occasional 5-6-year promotion, but most Troopers were in that 8-12-year window when promoted.

"I broke the Dog in ya know Bud," said Sgt. Carnival.

"You were his Coach Sarge?" I asked.

"Yep sir," said Sarge. "He was the quietest meekest little lamb you ever met when he came here from the Academy. He was easy to break in, never mouthed even a peep about anything. He got out on his own and got comfortable, and the rest was history Junior. He turned into a high speed hard charging never slow down type Troop and hasn't looked back. He's got into a few scrapes because he stops a lot of drunks, and within a couple years, he got nicknamed the "Salty Dog." Not like a mean junkyard dog, but in a good professional way. So that's who's going to be your "Daddy" is the Dog."

"Wow," I said. "sounds a little different than Gemco, Huh?" I asked.

"That can be a good thing for you Bud," Sarge proclaimed.

"You get to see two different styles of policing. One is laid back a bit, and the other is faster paced. Maybe you'll pick somewhere in between. I think it's a good learning experience for you Bud."

Sarge was a big old farm boy from Columbiana County. Mid 40's, hair cut high and tight, no one to mess with, and with Sarge it was straight and true, red white and blue, hardcore American, and I heard if he liked you, he called you "Bud."

"Yeah that sounds pretty good Sarge," I said. "Gives me a perspective maybe other guys would never get to see."

"Yeah Bud. The Dog's probably going to put a little heat on you, and I want you to hang in there. If anything comes up you have a question on, I want you to come see me," he said with a grin.

"Sure Sarge, thanks a lot," I said.

"Yep, I broke the Dog in, and a good Coach put's you under pressure to get you used to it. That's because the day you go out there by yourself, you want to have the confidence you can do the job without someone sitting beside you helping you."

"OK. I see what you're saying," I said.

The desk phone rang and as Sarge answered it. I went outside to smoke. All this news got me a little jacked up and I needed a smoke to relax me a bit. I was standing on the back walk when a brand new 78 Plymouth patrol car pulled into the lot. I could see the driver get out. It was Tpr. Martin. He parked and got out and started walking towards the rear walk. He looked up to greet me and adjusted the tilt on his Stetson.

"Tpr. Munch," said Jack as he held his hand out.

"Hi Jack," I said as I forced a smile.

"We haven't formally met," he said as we shook hands. "Being on different squads we've kept missing one another. I see your Coach got promoted," he said.

"Yea isn't that something. Sgt. Gemco transferring out," I said.

"'They told you I'm taking his place coaching you?" Jack asked.

"Yeah Sgt. Carnival just told me a few minutes ago," I replied.

"Pop told you?" he asked.

"Pop?" I asked.

"Yeah, Pop, Sgt. Carnival," Jack Stated. "I call him Pop. He broke me in so he's my State Patrol Daddy. I call him Pop for short," he said with a wide grin.

"Oh," I said. "I get it."

"So, if you make it and I sign the paperwork for you to go on your own I'll be your Daddy," Jack said.

"If I make it?" I asked with another forced grin.

"This is a tough business we're in and not everyone can cut it," Jack continued. "The Academy is a breeze compared to the three months of Coach/Pupil."

Awwggg- I could feel my stomach tighten as we both turned and walked up the sidewalk towards the back door of the Post. This guy is going to be intense, I thought as my stomach continued to slightly burn. Nothing- not even the Salty Dog Jack Martin is going to keep me from getting through this, and I asked God for some acknowledgement. Right God? I thought and asked the Almighty. Hmm, no answer from the big guy upstairs. I guess it's because I have that continual 10% doubt wondering if He's really there.

We walked inside and were greeted by Dennis who had been upstairs in the report room when I was inside the first time.

"Hey Dennis," I said as I extended my hand to shake his, "Congratulations."

"Thanks Fred. Sorry I'm leaving you. But you'll be OK with Tpr. Martin here," he said as he looked at Jack with a half-smile.

Jack didn't say a thing. "So, don't ruin this kid," Dennis said as he looked at Jack and then back at me. "You'll do fine, just keep doing what you're doing."

"Thanks Dennis," I said in kind of a lamented tone.

Jack looked at me and said, "Let's go Junior. Get upstairs and clear your file. Make sure there's no notes or Hp-22's from anyone," (Inter office communications) he said in a forceful tone.

As I was taking the stairs two at a time to get upstairs and clear my file, and get ready for the start of the shift, I was recalling some of the stories I had heard about Jack over the past three weeks. I'd say he was liked by most of the Troops at the Post. I know of a couple older guys that thought he was arrogant and too cocky for a guy that only had five years on the job. The Staff must really like him to assign him a coaching responsibility. This I'm sure is a big deal for Jack and wants to do his best no matter how it turns out with me getting through it. I guess I should be thankful that I got a Coach as highly motivated as Jack? Right God? I asked. Again, I didn't hear any response from the big guy?

I was back downstairs ready to go within about five minutes. "Check the zone assignments and tell me where we're going," Jack stated, as I walked into the Sgt's office and checked the roll call slip.

"We're assigned East, SR. 11 and 193," I said as we were walking out the back door with me following.

"You're sure?" Jack asked.

" Yes, I'm sure," I said as we walked down the sidewalk.

"Zone assignment are a guide as to where your responsibility lies," he said. "But if something big goes down outside your zone, you have to clear it with the Squad Sgt. to leave a zone. Did Dennis go over that with you?" he asked.

"Yes, he did," I said as he opened the driver's door to get in.

"I saw that you started driving with Dennis the other day, but for a few days I'm going to drive," he said with a smirk as he sat down and adjusted his seat. "This is a brand-new car and we're going to keep it looking nice."

"OK," I said as I pulled my seat belt across my lap and fastened it.

"What Township are you in right now?" Jack asked as he started the car.

"What?" I asked.

"I said what Township are we in right now? I'm going to be asking you geography and court jurisdiction questions throughout the training, so you'll memorize all this stuff," he said forcefully.

"Oh, OK," I said. "The Township were in is Southington," I answered.

"OK," he said. Get used to me asking questions when there isn't much going on. It's so important to be right on these affidavits that you'll file at the courts. We have three different courts here in Trumbull County. Did you know that?" he asked as he turned his head and looked directly at me.

"Yes, I know that," I responded.

"Then name them."

"Uhh," I hesitated.

"What are they?" Jack somewhat shouted.

"Uhh. Warren City, Brookfield East County, and," I paused. A couple seconds went by. "Newton Falls West County," I quickly blurted.

"Don't hesitate," Jack strongly emphasized. "Don't hesitate on this job it can get you killed."

"Remember if you're going to be right, you have to look right. And to look right, you have to want to be right," he said. "It's all about desire. This job every cop loves for the first few years. It's fun, and it's a novelty. Then you start to see bad things happen to people, like assaults, bad accidents, and you start dealing with bad people every day. Then after some more time goes by you start thinking everybody's a jerk. But you have to keep that in perspective. It's easy to treat everyone like a jerk, but it's all about desire to do good for people. Treat everyone with respect until they show you- yeah, this guy is a jerk. Then deal with him differently because he doesn't respect you or the rights of law-abiding folks."

I could feel the sweat running down the middle of my back between my vest and t-shirt. Wow this guy really makes me nervous. I agree with everything he's saying, so I guess that's a good sign. This conversation is similar to one Dennis had with me. These guys here in the field are pretty sharp characters. I think I should start to feel a bit more confident in myself. I've made it this far. Is being this nervous good for a leaning environment I asked myself? I guess I'm going to find out what pressure is like. I felt I had just gotten comfortable with Dennis. Well, I guess I'd rather have it challenging and learn more, than have it too easy and not learn much.

"Does that sink in and make any sense Junior?" Jack asked.

"Yes sir," I responded.

"Don't call me sir," he shot back.

"I do have one question though," I said.

"What's that Junior?"

"Why do you and Pop call me Junior?"

Jack laughed. "You're the Junior unit here at the Post. Actually, it's kind of an affectionate title because everyone here looks out for the newer guys," he stated.

"Oh, OK," I responded. "I thought it was something maybe negative."

"No, you're the boot Troop at the Post right now. You'll have the title of Junior until some new guy comes and then it's on him," Jack stated with a chuckle.

We drove over to the east side and checked our main responsibility by driving the entire length of IS-80 in Trumbull County. Primarily, unless taken away from the Interstate by other calls, the Interstate is a priority patrol helping disabled motorists and enforcing traffic laws. At the County line, which is Mahoning County, Post-50 Canfield covers IS-80 west. Post- 50 is a busy and fast pace Post area also and encompasses all of the greater Youngstown area. Youngstown has a reputation of being inhabited by a bunch of tough people. Steel people, laid off steel and auto manufacturing people who like to drink.

The shift flew by. When we weren't investigating accidents, we were running radar on the Interstate, and patrolling SR 193 on the north side of Youngstown looking for drunk drivers. And during the entire night, Jack shot questions at me related to geography and Division policy and procedures that have to be memorized. Jack treated me fairly good. He asked about my family and what I had done with my life prior to taking this job. We had quite a bit in common I felt, as I started to relax around him just a little bit by the end of the shift.

As we pulled into the back lot and up to the gas pumps Jack threw the car in park and jumped out. "Gas her up Junior and make sure the windows get cleaned on the inside," he spouted.

"OK Jack," I answered.

As I stood holding the gas nozzle in the tank, I looked up into the night sky. Very dark and cold I thought. Is this it? Is this what I've been waiting all my life to do? Am I man enough to pull all this off, taking my family out of state and attempting to master this job? Is this going to be a happy time for my wife and family? Is this why God put me here on earth, to do this? I cracked a smile and continued to scan the stars. I guess Gods there, right? I had to keep my confidence levels high.

Cindy was asleep with the baby when I got home around 12:30am. I made a sandwich and sat back in my chair. "Forget about everything for an hour and then go to bed," I mumbled to myself. Clear my mind and rest. I felt good but I had to admit I was apprehensive. But of what? Failure, I guess? Worried I'd fail? I'm sure I'm not the first guy that ever thought this way.

CHAPTER **22**

First Drunk

IT WAS THE fourth day with Jack and he had me drive that evening. It was about mid shift around 8:30 pm. and we were driving eastbound on the By-pass SR 5 which is busy, and the main four lane highway that circles Warren. We were in the passing lane driving above the speed limit passing cars as not to back up traffic by driving the speed limit. When a cop drives the speed limit on four lane roads, traffic tends to back up because no one wants to pass.

"I feel like a bear with a sore ass tonight," stated Jack as he looked at me with a smirk.

"Why is that?" I asked.

"I don't know. Kid's got on my nerves today."

"Oh," I responded. "I guess I better not mess up then," I stated with a forced chuckle

"Slow down a little," Jack spouted.

"What?" I asked.

"The fourth car up is 19," he said. (19 is the subsection in the Ohio Revised Code for DUI.)

"He is?" I asked.

"Yea watch his left rear tire. He's hitting the white lane markers weaving in his lane," he said.

"OK," I said, as I slowed and changed into the right lane.

We followed the car for about a half mile when Jack said, "Yea he's 19. Go ahead and stop him near the upcoming exit ramp."

I waited for a few seconds and activated my overhead lights and called in the stop to the Post.

"199 Warren Signal 3," (traffic stop) I said, as I was trying to see the plate.

"Go ahead 199," the Post answered.

"Ohio, Adam, Tom 4 5 0, be on the Bypass eastbound west of Larchmont," I said into the microphone, "A white Ford Pickup."

"OK," the Post acknowledged.

"Let me talk to this guy," Jack said as we started towards the driver's side. As Jack approached first, I was directly behind him and I could see the drivers face as he turned to look our way. Holy shit, I thought as I looked at the guys face. He's waxed! (drunk) How did Jack spot this guy so easily? I pondered. I would have never known to stop this guy!

"How are you doing sir," Jack greeted the driver.

"I'm doing good," the driver responded in a mushed mouth slurred voice.

"I stopped you for weaving," Jack explained to the driver.

"No, I don't think I was we-we-weaving," he stammered.

"How much have you had to drink tonight?" Jack asked.

"Oh, only a couple beers after work," he said.

"What time did you get out of work?" asked Jack.

"3:30," he answered.

"So, you've been at the bar since 3:30?"

"Yea that's all," the driver responded.

"Do you know what time it is right now?" Jack inquired.

"I'm not sure- 5, 5:30 maybe," the driver answered.

"It's 8:45," Jack informed him. "Looks like you've been drinking for the last 5 hours," Jack stated.

"That's not that long," the driver replied.

"OK, step on out here I want to give you some coordination tests," Jack said.

The man complied and stepped out of the car. He was obviously having trouble maintaining his balance as he stumbled while walking back in between our cars.

"If you will watch me first, I want you to do this. Walk heel to toe touching your heel to the toe of your other foot in a straight line," Jack said as he demonstrated how he wanted the man to perform. "Then count nine steps out loud and turn around pivoting and walk back where you started," Jack explained.

While Jack was demonstrating, the guy took a cigarette out of his pocket and started to light it.

. "No smoking prior to the test sir," I said as Jack realized the man was attempting to light the cigarette.

"The Officer said no smoking," Jack said as the guy ignored both requests.

"This is America, and if I want to smoke you can't stop me," he barked in a slurred gasp. With that statement Jack reached over and took the cigarette out of the gentleman's mouth and stepped it out on the berm.

"You can't do that you son of a bitch," the man spouted as it was obvious that Jack's actions had angered him. The man reached into his coat again and pulled out another cigarette and put it between his lips.

"No, I said you can't smoke before any breath testing," Jack said and reached up and again took the cigarette snatching it from his mouth stomping it on the ground.

"You young punks," the man screamed as he lunged toward Jack. I reached out and grabbed the man's left arm and pulled him towards me, as Jack grabbed his right arm and pulled it behind the man's back. The berm had spots of ice here and there and someone slipped. We all went down with the both of us landing on top of the driver. There was granulated salt on the berm from the salt trucks, and this poor guy's face went straight down on the ice chips and salt brine.

Oh shit, I thought as I stood up and pulled the man up off the ground. He looked like somebody shot him with a load of bird shot directly in the face. He had small tiny little abrasions and cuts all over the right side of his cheek and nose from the rock salt and had started to bleed.

"Settle down," Jack shouted as the man continued to resist. "Cuff him," Jack ordered as I leaned the driver over the hood of the patrol car and put the handcuffs on.

"Put him in the back seat," Jack said, as he was attempting to brush the salt and dirt off the side of his uniform.

"Great, just great. The old man had to have a cigarette," Jack said out loud as I helped the guy into the back seat. "Call a wrecker Junior," were towing the car. He can pay for a tow bill too," Jack stated.

I shut the back door and walked around the back of the Patrol car to get in the driver's seat and took a deep breath to compose myself. I sat down and grabbed the microphone, "199 to Warren we'll need a wrecker here."

"OK 199 wrecker in route," the Post responded.

"You guys are bad seeds," the now prisoner said yelling from the back seat. "You guys are rotten bastards treating me like this," he went on.

"Be quiet," yelled Jack. "All you had to do was put the cigarette out and you might not be sitting where you are," Jack chimed. "Now we have to do a resisting case! These drunks don't listen to simple requests."

"Did you get hurt Junior?" Jack asked me.

"No, I'm fine. You?"

"Yeah, I'm fine," Jack said. Damn that berm is slippery there isn't it?"

"Yeah I can't believe how fast and hard we went down-Boom!" I exclaimed.

"Look at my face. Look what you ass holes did to me," the guy bantered.

"Shut up your fine. It's just a little blood that's all," Jack said.

As I pulled out into traffic after the wrecker had taken his car, I couldn't help wondering what just happened. Here is an average guy that drank too much and he gets pissed off because we can't let him smoke, and now he's looking at two counts of Agg. Assault, resisting arrest, DWI. Wow going to cost him his license and a lot of money. But I can't feel sorry for him, I thought. All he had to do was follow simple instructions and a simple request.

We will call our drunk driver Mr. Smith. He whined and complained all the way during the 10-minute drive to the Post. We pulled in the back lot and I walked around and opened the door for Mr. Smith.

"Bastard," Mr. Smith said to me as I leaned in to unbuckle his seat belt.

"Com'on Mr. Smith, I replied, "All you had to do was listen to Tpr. Martin and you might have been on your way home right now. But you had to overreact and charge at him."

"Who are you anyway? Some know it all rookie I'm guessing?" he stated.

"Well your right, I'm a rookie, but know it all? Not yet," I answered.

Mr. Smith got out and I walked with him holding on to his arm as we negotiated the snow and ice on the walk. Don't let this guy fall down handcuffed I thought as we got to the back door. Jack was holding the door as we entered.

"And you're a real smart ass, aren't you?" Mr. Smith said to Jack.

"You got that right buddy," Jack replied. "Smart enough to be standing here while you're standing there with handcuffs on," Jack laughed.

Just then Sgt. Spader stepped out of the Sgt.'s office and looked at Mr. Smith and then looked at me.

"What happened to him?" Sgt. Spader asked.

"He fell Sarge," I said as I swallowed a little harder than normal.

"Fell where?" Sarge asked.

"He lunged at Tpr. Martin and when we grabbed him and turned him around, we slipped on the berm and we all fell," I explained.

"These guys kicked my ass for no reason Sarge," Mr. Smith bellowed, and then started to whimper.

"They did, huh?" replied Sarge.

"Yeah I was just driving home and wasn't doing nothin wrong," he continued. "Then the stalky guy smashed my cigarettes and laughed at me. Then the rookie pushed me down and jumped on top of my face!! Look at my face," he yelled.

"Well when you're feeling better tomorrow you might have a better recollection as to what happened. For right now the best thing you can do is quiet down and do what they ask. Ok partner?" Sarge said.

"Yeah," Mr. Smith replied. "I'll do what they want only because you asked me to. Your older and smarter than these young punks."

"You got that right," replied Sarge. "I know I'm older, and I think I'm a little wiser than them," Sarge said with a big grin as he looked at me and started walking back into the Sergeants office.

Mr. Smith did cooperate and took the breathalyzer test for which he tested a .17 BAC. The legal limit is .09 and below. We drove Mr. Smith to the Trumbull County jail for lockup. In Ohio there is a set bond for every offense.

Upon arriving at the jail, the intake officer looked at Mr. Smith and said, "Guys I can't accept him in that condition. You will have to get him cleared at the hospital. Then we can take him."

"There just superficial cuts," explained Jack.

"Whatever, but I'll need a clearance from the hospital, sorry," said the officer.

Off we went to Trumbull hospital which was just down the street. We walked into the emergency room and up to the registration desk.

The blood from the scrapes had run down his face and soaked the white fur on his coat. We had used the first aid kit at the Post and cleaned his face with towelettes, so there wasn't much dried blood on his face. The small cuts had swollen a bit, and Mr. Smith looked worse than he actually was.

"May I help you?" asked the registration clerk.

"Yes, Ma'am he needs to be treated for these abrasions," said Jack as he pointed to Mr. Smith's face.

"Ok, have him sit in the chair and I'll be asking him some questions," she stated.

For some reason I felt like we had done something wrong. Everybody in the waiting room and even some hospital staff were giving me and Jack the evil eye. I wanted to just stand up and yell, he fell! But I knew I couldn't. Shit they wouldn't believe me anyway, I thought. Fortunately, Mr. Smith was in full cooperation mode and very quiet. I think he's really tired, as I noticed his head drop and his chin touch his chest a couple times. After a lot of clerical information taken, we were eventually escorted back to one of the exam rooms. About 20 minutes passed and a nurse and doctor entered the room. The exam was quick, and they put an anti-biotic cream on Mr. Smith's face, and we were on our way back to the county lock up.

We arrived back at the jail within an hour of leaving to go to the hospital. Pretty fast I thought, as I was taking the handcuffs off of Mr.

Smith, and then one of the jailers took custody of him.

Jack and I got back in the car and it was near shifts end. I was re-hashing the whole thing in my head when Jack said, "Ok Junior, you banged your first drunk. Did that make you feel good?"

"Yeah, I guess," I responded. "Maybe he would have killed somebody if we hadn't come along."

"You never know about what could have happened, right?" he said.

The next couple weeks went pretty well. Jack and I were getting to know one another. He was a stickler for neatness in report writing. His printing looked like it was block typewritten. I tried my best to print in perfect block style and be neat as possible, but it was nothing near the quality of his work. Content, I thought to myself. As long as the content is thorough and concise who cares if the printing is pretty.

The onslaught of constant questions persisted. It got to be where I wasn't that nervous expecting his next question.

We had finished the seven days of afternoon shift and were on days. It was a Saturday morning at around 9am. "Let's go up on 11 and see how you handle some high-speed driving," he said.

SR. 11 is a four-lane highway which runs north and south right down the middle of the County extending from the northern end of Ashtabula County, down all the way through Trumbull and south through Mahoning and Columbiana County. It's kind of desolate in the northern part of our county, and especially on a Saturday morning. We got up to the northern county line and turned around through the cross-over and headed south.

"What's the fastest you ever drove a car?" Jack asked.

"I don't know," I answered. "Maybe 100 or 105 at the Academy fairgrounds."

"Ok, well keep the car right in the center of both lanes and hit it," he spouted.

I punched in that 440 and when the four-barrel kicked in that Plymouth snapped my head back a little. The sound of the four barrel is something you have to hear for yourself. We got up to 100 in no time and I had tons of pedal left. I could feel my heart pounding and I took a couple of slow silent deep breaths as not to let Jack think I was scared.

But I was. Haaa.

"How fast do you want me to go?" I asked as I raised my voice over the road noise.

"Stay in the middle," Jack said loudly. "Go as fast as you feel comfortable."

I glanced at the speedometer and it read 105. Oh shit I thought. I hope a deer doesn't run out in front of us now. I couldn't help but to crack a little smirk as I glanced over at Jack. "Keep your eyes on the damn road Junior," he barked.

I glanced down, 110, 120, and slowly climbing. That's it I thought.

"Keep going," is all I heard from Jack.

"Shit," I mumbled under my breath. Now 125, this is crazy, 125, that's it for me I thought, as I backed off the accelerator.

"No balls Junior?" Jack barked with a big smile on his face.

"That's enough adrenaline for me boss," I yelled. "That's enough for me Coach," I said again. I backed the speed down to around 90 and it seemed like we were standing still after the 125 plus-mph blood rush.

"Pretty good, pretty good," Jack spouted. "I haven't had her much faster."

Wow I thought. I think he just paid me a compliment. He said pretty good!

Day shifts were filled with running from accident to accident, especially in the winter. Radar enforcement was a priority as was writing a consistent amount of tickets every month. It was expected for the average Troop to produce around 70 plus tickets a month. Some Units wrote more. Much more, like 100 plus. There were no quotas to speak of, but you were expected to do more than drive around just burning gas. So, if you wrote a minimum of three tickets a day and worked twenty days a month, you were well within satisfactory numbers. Commercial pinches were a priority. Yes, semi-trucks. Poor truck drivers, they're just trying to make a living. Yeah, but there are some drivers out there that shouldn't be. So, the more truck drivers you stopped the better. And of course, DWI enforcement was looked at closely. Definitely the Highway Patrol's number one priority. On a typical seven-day string of night shifts every month it wasn't difficult to get five DWI pinches. That would average out to around 50+ a year. I'd say that was a minimum number. The numbers had to add up to maintain productivity.

By the end of the first month I had worked every shift. I don't know that I had a favorite because each one offered different challenges. Day shift was busy with accidents and radar enforcement. Afternoon turn as they called it was always the busiest with a variety of just about everything. Night shift was focused on DWI enforcement.

I felt at this point I was getting a grip on some of the procedures. I guess I was feeling more comfortable with Jack. He was certainly intimidating. I hadn't made any major mistakes, like wreck a car, or call in sick. Using sick leave was only if your half dead. I was still being grilled on just about anything Jack could think of to ask me. I had just accepted that part was going to be never ending.

I drew a diagram backwards on an accident report. It took me about twenty minutes to draw it because it was a complicated multi vehicle wreck. Jack apparently saw that I was drawing it wrong but let me finish it, then he told me to do it over. The diagram is on page two of the accident report. He wouldn't let me tear the first page off and attach it to a new second page. So, I had to re-do the entire first page also. It was things like that got me mad. But I would think back to Sgt. Carnival's words of wisdom, and remind myself that its Jack's job is to put pressure on me to see how much I can take, number one. And number two, when I get out on my own its more of a relief to not have him sitting beside me, and I'll be more relaxed and confident.

The second month had gone well. I was getting comfortable with officer violator contacts and how to reason with most people. I had stopped a few difficult people, but I handled those stops Ok. Jack taught me to let people vent if they need to as long as they didn't insult the badge or be threatening in their tone. It surprised me how many people actually thanked me after writing them a ticket. One thing you didn't want in your personnel jacket were multiple citizen complaints. They were almost unavoidable if you came in contact with enough people. Eventually you're going to run into that one contact that no matter how nice you are their going to file a complaint knowing it makes your life more difficult.

With just about a month to go before I got "cut loose," which is the terminology for making it out on your own, we were working afternoon turn. We were stopped at a red light on State Rt. 5 at the intersection in Heartscrabble, which is the nickname of an area east of Newton Falls. It's a busy area known for a lot of bars and party folks. It was about 2100 hrs. (9 pm), and a car abruptly tried to stop when the driver saw us and slid partially into the intersection.

"Turn right and get in behind this guy," Jack barked at me. I turned right and within a few seconds the light turned green for the targeted driver and I began to follow him. "He'll do alright driving for a while because he knows we're behind him, and he's pumped full of adrenaline," Jack stated. "Give him a minute to relax and he'll start weaving."

Sure enough after about a mile of being behind him he started drifting off the right side of the road and then back into his lane several times. "He's 19," stated Jack.

"Yeah, he is," I responded. "Look at this guy," I exclaimed. "He can't keep it together at all and he knows we're behind him. Unbelievable!"

"Let's stop him before he takes somebody out," stated Jack.

I turned on the overheads and got him stopped off the roadway and on the right berm. We approached the vehicle and spoke with the driver advising him why we had stopped him. He was a white male in his late 20's. Let's call him Mr. Jones.

Mr. Jones failed all coordination test and was placed under arrest. I handcuffed him and searched him. He was placed in the Patrol car and transported to the Post for processing. Upon arrival he was escorted to the Intoxilyzer room to be given the breath test.

"You go ahead out and start the paperwork Junior and I'll stay in here with him and give him the test," Jack stated.

"OK," I responded, and I then walked out of the room and into the Sergeants office to use the desk to start my paperwork.

After about 10 minutes passed Jack stepped into the Sergeants office. I looked up from doing my paperwork and looked at him. He had this crazy looking angry expression on his face. He slammed his hand down on the desk in front of me.

"What's this?" he shouted. He lifted his hand and there laid a small pocketknife, about three inches long.

"What?" I asked in total surprise. "What's that? Where did you get that? Is that his?" I asked, meaning our arrestee.

"Damn right it's his," he spouted as he looked at me with fire in his eyes. "You missed it Junior. You patted him down and missed this knife," he continued. "You're going to apologize to my wife the next time you see her for putting me at risk, along with everyone else here in the building, because you missed this knife on your drunk driver."

"I'm really sorry Jack," I blurted out. "I can't believe I missed that. I patted him down and went through his pockets before I put him in the car," I exclaimed.

"Apparently not good enough Fred," he responded. "What would you say to my wife if he slit my throat when I was processing him?"

"God, I'm sorry man," I lamented. "That will never happen again," I said as I wiped the sweat off my forehead with the back of my hand. "I feel really bad," I said as I stood up to follow Jack out into the hallway as he was walking back to attend to Mr. Jones.

"I could have you written up for that but let's keep it between us," he answered. "I don't want to see you get jammed up. I just want you to realize what can happen when you're not thorough," Jack said.

As I turned and walked away headed back to the Sergeants office, I had a sick feeling in my stomach. This friggin job is going to give me an ulcer I thought as I sat back down in the chair. I can't believe I missed that knife. I know I put my hands and fingers inside each of his pockets.

I went over and over that pat down in my mind and had a clear visual recollection of it. No way, I thought. Then it dawned on me, could Jack have brought that knife in with him from home?

Then I remembered the dust ball that Sgt. Cotrell brought into my room at the Academy so he could teach me a lesson in floor cleaning. OK I thought, Jack brought that knife to work with him because I know I went through the drunk's pockets. I don't know, maybe I did miss it? Regardless, it's something I'll never forget, I anguished to myself, as I tried to focus on completing my paperwork.

For the next 29 years, every time I put handcuffs on somebody, Jack's face, and the look on it, would flash in my mind. Looking back, it was a great training experience. Weather I missed it or not on the pat down, only the "Salty Dog" knows the truth.

Millcreek PD

Trooper Pic

Sister

"My Mom" 1989

Wedding Day Aug 76

Wedding Day 3.16.19

Me and Dad

Me and Kids

CHAPTER 23

"Judge Reed"

I WAS ENTERING the last month of the Coach/Pupil period. My confidence was good. I admit that it was the hardest couple months of my life. I guess Jack had something to do with that! I had a long weekend coming up. That's the five-day break between night shift and afternoon shift. Cindy and I hadn't been home to Erie in a while. My heart ached for her because she was so close to her mother and missed her so much. The weather had been bad which hindered visits from her folks. She was excited that I had only one more night shift to go and would finish up on Thursday morning at 8am. I wasn't going to sleep when I got home, and just leave that morning for Erie. That would put us in Erie by mid-morning on Thursday, and Cindy could enjoy the next four or five days with her family. There wasn't a lot of room at her parent's house, so we decided she'd stay at her parents and I'd stay at mine. Almost like being single again!

It was Wednesday night and I arrived on Post at 11:30pm. to start the last shift before break. Jack and I loaded our gear in the Plymouth and we were Signal 2 (In service).

I swung the car out on to Rt. 422 and headed east towards the Bypass and Warren city limits. We had arrested four drunk drivers that week which was adequate, but it would be nice to grab at least one more tonight I thought, as I drove onto the entrance ramp.

"You and the wife going back to Erie this weekend Junior?" Jack asked as he leaned his head back on the headrest and let out a big yawn.

"Yep, yes we are!" I said enthusiastically with a smile on my face. "Cindy is really climbing the walls and is looking forward to being around her folks."

"That's nice," Jack said. "What day are you driving to Erie?"

"Probably right when I get home this morning," I replied.

"Warren to 199," the radio cracked. "Go ahead Warren," I responded. "Signal 31A, SR.82 and Howland-Wilson Rd." (Signal 31A is an accident with injuries) "Ok Warren, in route," I replied.

I activated the overhead lights and hit the siren and we were off. Traffic on the Bypass was light, and we were there in about a 4-minute response time.

It was a two-car crash in the middle of the intersection. Somebody must have blown the stop sign I thought as we were walking up on both cars. The ambulance had already arrived and was treating the driver of one of the vehicles.

"Go ahead and get your pictures Junior and I'll watch traffic," Jack barked as he waived on an approaching car.

I grabbed the camera and took a series of a dozen pictures of the resting points of the vehicles, and the damage. I was having trouble with the flash. "I have to change the batteries in the camera," I shouted to Jack so he could hear me.

After changing the batteries and finishing the photos I began a field sketch. The Patrols policy is to take photos and written statements on all injury accidents. Accidents involving injuries always takes time because you have to be meticulous with measurements.

"You about done Fred?" Jack asked as he walked towards me.

"Yea Jack," I said. "Just about ready to clear."

After being on scene for about 30 minutes we were finished with what had to be done immediately. We determined it was a failure to yield from a stop sign and the person at fault was the driver that was transported to Trumbull hospital.

"Ok let's clear and get to the hospital and see if the driver's drunk or not," Jack stated.

"Right, I responded, she's an older lady maybe around fifty. I doubt she's drunk because I didn't smell anything on her when I spoke to her in the back of the ambulance. But she popped that stop sign, so I'm going to have to write her up for that."

We cleared the accident scene and arrived at TMH. The driver was being seen in the ER and the nurse told us we could go back to talk to her.

The Highway Patrol's policy is to issue traffic citations if a violation is determined at accident scenes or hospitals, in person. For me, it had been the hardest thing I had done in my illustrious two-and-a-half-month career. Several times I had stammered through issuing a citation to someone lying in a hospital bed. I mean their day is obviously not going to good to begin with, and here comes Mr. State Trooper to make it much worse. Usually their suffering some injury, and it was extremely difficult to advise them I'm writing them a citation in their time of distress.

We entered the room, and somehow a couple of the lady's family members had already arrived. At first glance it appeared to be two of her children. Her son, probably about 20 years old, and her daughter, about my age. She was drop dead gorgeous and emitted a smile that made me lightheaded. I tried not to look obviously smitten by the young lady, but it was more than difficult not to stare at her.

I took the lady's written statement as to what happened as I wrote it out while she dictated. She then read what I had written, and she signed it.

This was the time to start my rendition that the violation which caused the accident is failure to yield the right of way from a stop sign, and I'm issuing you a citation for the violation.

I paused. I cleared my throat. I paused a second time. The people in the room were looking at me. The daughter smiled again. I felt like I was going to panic. I turned to Jack who was standing behind me near the door. "Can I talk to you for a second," I mumbled as I walked past him and out into the hallway.

Jack followed me out into the hall as we stepped out of hearing range of the room.

"What the hell's wrong with you?" Jack asked. "Huh?" he said. "What's up? What are you doing?"

"I, I, I'm having trouble telling this lady I'm going to pinch her," I again mumbled and stammered. "I've never wrote up anyone this old with their family in the room. I don't know if I can do this one? Can you do this one?" I whispered.

"No. Is that plain enough for you?" he whispered loudly. "Now get in there and get this over with. We've spent too much time on this crash to begin with, and now your dragging it out even longer. We have to get back on the road!"

I took a deep breath. I walked back into the room and explained the violation, and that I was issuing her a ticket. The daughter quit smiling at me. The son asked if we could have sent her the ticket via mail rather than upset her more. I wanted to answer him by saying I couldn't agree with him more, but I had to explain it was a matter of policy and procedure.

When we got back to the car, Jack had nothing much to say. It's hard enough stopping someone and penalizing them monetarily for a mistake. It's something more to show no empathy for someone's misfortune and writing them a ticket and embarrassing them in front of their family. That's pretty cold I thought. For the first time I wondered if maybe I was too empathetic towards people to be a policeman. Although that's why I wanted to be a policeman was to help people.

"Having trouble writing people in the hospital Junior?" Jack asked.

"I guess I am. Pretty hard. Seems kind of cold," I answered.

"What if she committed the same violation, only killed somebody? Would you still feel bad about writing her a ticket then?" he asked.

I had to think about that for a couple seconds before I answered. "No, I guess I wouldn't feel bad at all," I said.

"OK then," Jack responded. "You're not the judge. You don't have anything to do with punishment. Your job is to enforce the law. Let the judge decide on how serious the violation is. Don't get caught up in the emotions this job throws at you. If you do, you won't be able to sleep at night. Just enforce the law. Let the judge decide as to degree of guilt and maybe feel sorry for her. What the judge does we have no control over. We did our job. Get ready because you're going to lose cases that were good arrests. Don't get caught up in the politics of the judicial system."

The rest of the night went by and I pulled up to the pumps behind the Post. "Your pretty excited about leaving this morning for Erie?" Jack asked.

"Yes we are. Cindy's home right now I would guess all packed up. We're leaving around nine," I answered.

"OK Junior, have a good weekend," Jack responded.

I drove home and arrived about 8:30am. Cindy was pretty excited. I took a shower and grabbed a bowl of cereal. I started to load the car and the phone rang. It was around 8:50am. "Who could that be?" asked Cindy.

"I don't know," I responded.

"Hello," I said.

"Junior," the voice chirped.

"Yeah, Jack? What's up?'" I asked surprisingly.

"Get dressed in uniform. Get in your car and meet me at Warren Municipal Court in a half hour. Judge Reed wants to speak to you," he bantered.

"What? Why?" I asked.

"That citation you wrote that lady last night, you put the wrong Township on the citation. We were in Howland Township and you wrote in Warren Township. The judge is pissed, and he wants to see you, now!" said Jack.

"OK," I responded.

I hung up the phone and looked at Cindy. She had that "oh no" look because she figured something was going ruin us from getting to Erie.

"I have to go down to the courthouse. I don't think I should be there too long," I said as I walked towards the bedroom to get dressed.

"Are you in some trouble?" Cindy asked.

"I'm not sure," I responded. "One of the judges wants to talk to me about something."

I arrived at the courthouse shortly after 9:30am. As I entered the front lobby Jack was standing near the elevator. "The judge wants to see you Junior," Jack said. "He's going to chew you a new ass hole I would guess," Jack said as we stepped on to the elevator.

"I don't remember putting Warren township on the ticket. I knew it was Howland township," I said.

Jack piped up, "You just say yes sir no sir. Don't offer any excuses. Just take it, thank him, and we'll leave."

As the elevator doors opened to the third floor, I could feel a bead of sweat running down the middle of my back. We walked into the judge's outer office and we were greeted by his receptionist. "Hi fellas. The judge is in his office. I'll tell him you're here," she said.

I had met Judge Reed a couple months before when Tpr. Gemco took me around to meet all the county judges the first week of my coach/pupil period.

As we walked into his office Jack was in the lead. I could see the judge look up at Jack as he began to greet us. "Good morning Troopers, and what do I owe the pleasure of this visit?" he asked.

"Uhh-Uh what we talked about on the phone judge? About the ticket that Trooper Munch wrote?" Jack said as he glanced at me and then back at the judge.

"Yes, yes, the mistake on the ticket," the judge went on. "Please be careful in the future Trooper because if it's something like listing the wrong township, it has to be amended."

"I understand your honor," I replied. "I won't do that again," I said as I looked over at Jack.

I turned slightly to look at Jack's face and saw the judge smile at him. "Thanks, your honor," Jack said as he turned towards me and pointed towards the door.

I thanked the judge as I walked towards the door and out into the waiting room.

Huh? I thought to myself. That was far from an ass chewing. Took about 30 seconds. I think I've been spoofed. I think Jack went home knowing I was going to Erie early and to keep the pressure on high, called the judge and arranged for us to come in on the premise that I was to be scolded for making a mistake on the ticket. Another "Salty Dog" learning experience, I thought.

We made our way outside and I apologized again for the mistake. Jack wished me well and I was on my way home. Yeah, I thought, just a couple more weeks and I'm a free man on my own away from the wrath of Tpr. Jack Martin.

CHAPTER 24

Finally Snapped

THE TRIP TO Erie and five days off flew by, and by Monday afternoon we were headed back to our apartment in Bloomfield.

Tuesday rolled around and I reported for the 4-12 shift. With two weeks to go I was feeling anxious and couldn't wait to get away from Jack. He had certainly accomplished his mission of getting me wanting to go out on my own and having the confidence to do it, rather than be hesitant and still depending on someone to be with me. But the last couple episodes with Jack had taken its toll on my psyche. I guess I couldn't decide if I loved him or hated him?

The first few days of 4-12 afternoons were very busy. The weather was bad, and we had several accidents to investigate per shift. It was very hectic and stressful, and Jack was still asking me questions and keeping as much pressure on me as he could.

On the fifth day which was a Saturday evening, again it was extremely busy. We had just cleared an accident and were traveling east across the Rt. 5 By-pass when the Post called.

"Warren to 199," cracked the radio. I picked up the mike and continued to look over the dash to see where I was driving because of the heavy traffic.

"Go ahead Warren," I responded.

"Go to the intersection of Elm Rd. and (Garbled) for a reported drunk in (garbled)," the dispatcher said.

"What did he say," I asked as I looked over to Jack who was slouched in the seat leaning up against the passenger window.

"Don't know Junior. Ask him to repeat," Jack answered.

"199 Warren you broke up repeat your last," I said into the microphone.

"199 go to-"(Garbled not understandable).

"What did he say Jack?' I asked. "Go to Elm and Rt.5 and where for what?" I asked Jack again.

Jack wouldn't answer. He just looked at me. "What did he say Jack?" I asked again. Jack had no response.

"Did you copy 199?" the Post asked.

"Negative," I responded. "repeat," I said. Again, the transmission broke up, but I knew Jack knew what the Post was trying to dispatch me to.

"Are you going to tell me what dispatch said," I asked as I raised my voice because of my frustration, as I glared at Jack.

"What are you going to do when you're on your own and you don't understand the dispatcher?" he asked in a forceful cocky tone.

"I don't know, I guess I'd have to pull over somewhere and call him if it got that bad," I responded. "Is that what you want me to do is pull over and call him?" I asked as my voice got louder. Jack just shrugged his shoulders and mumbled something, and turned his head away looking out the right-side window.

I felt a hot flush run from my neck straight up through my face to the top of my head. I thought of grabbing the back of his neck and shoving his face into the side window.

"That's it, enough of this shit," I yelled as I clinched the mike and forgot I was driving.

Jack being somewhat surprised at my response looked at me kind of wide eyed as he shouted, "Watch the damn road!"

I pulled hard on the wheel and drove onto the right berm and started to brake hard. "I'm done," I said as the car came to an abrupt stop. "I don't know what you expect of me, but apparently anything I do isn't good enough. So, you can take this job and stick it somewhere, because I've given it my best shot, and I've had enough of your bullshit."

It was like an out of body experience. I could feel my lower lip quivering I was so pissed. I knew what I was saying, but it was like I was outside of my body watching it unfold. I knew I had really lost it, and this was probably my last ride like it or not. At the same time, I threw the microphone fairly hard up on the dashboard. I remember just seeing red and yellow haze around everything I was seeing including Jack's face. I thought about punching him. I pictured my fist driving into the bridge of his nose and his head bouncing off the right passenger window, but the thought left me quickly. It's bad enough to quit, I thought, I don't need to get arrested for assault. And I don't think the general motoring public would understand why two Troopers were rolling around on the berm trying to kill one another.

"Screw this," I said as I looked him squarely in the eyes. "You drive back. I'm too pissed to drive," as I started to open the driver's door.

"Whoa, whoa their Junior," Jack said. "Take a deep breath and calm down!"

I turned again to my right to look at him. He had that damn smirk on his face. What is this? The son of a bitch thinks this is funny.

"You're not going anywhere," he said. "I finally got you to crack. I have put more pressure on you than I thought I'd ever have to. You took it all. Day after day," Jack bantered, as he continued to smile and chuckled aloud.

I still wasn't sure if I was going to be able to control myself.

"Just relax. I just kept telling Pop; Pop I can't get the kid to crack. What should I do?" Jack explained. "And Pop said just keep up the pressure Dog. Keep up the pressure." Jack continued, "I finally got to you, and now that we know how much you can take, you've shown you can handle this job."

For a moment I felt like I was dreaming. I was looking straight ahead through the windshield over the hood of the patrol car. I wasn't sure how to respond to what I just heard. My hands were still trembling, and the sweat had run down the sides of my face.

"No, you're just saying that to keep me from quitting. You don't want to have to explain to the Lieutenant why I just quit and walked home," I said in response.

"Fred, it's all part of the training. You'll understand it all when you get on your own. You'll be breaking somebody in someday and you'll be doing the same thing to them," Jack explained.

"No, not like this. Not like this," is all I could think to say.

"Now let's go," Jack said. "There's a drunk in the road over on Rt. 5 south of Elm, near North Rd. That's what the Post has been trying to tell you."

I put the car in drive and pulled back out on the By-pass. I was still sweating and felt nauseous. My dislike for him had overwhelmed me. I had really lost it.

All the way driving to the call I seriously was thinking about quitting anyway. Did I want a job that put this kind of stress on me? I was starting to realize why the average age of policeman dying we learned in the Academy was 58. And only a national average of three years of retirement.

The rest of the shift was tense to say the least. There was very little spoken, and what had transpired between us wasn't discussed.

The following couple of days were noticeably different. No more questions shot at me. Every call we handled Jack stood off and out of the way. I handled everything myself like he wasn't there. His demeanor had changed, and he seemed more relaxed. I guess he felt he had accomplished his mission by getting me to snap, and he was satisfied with letting me do everything without his input. With only about a week to go until the big day when I got to go on my own, I was feeling relaxed and confident, but I wasn't feeling any love for the "Salty Dog."

CHAPTER 25

"Hey Man"

IT WAS THE last few days of afternoon shift when Jack explained we'd be doing two drivers Ed speeches. It was getting near spring and time for High School graduations. The Patrol was responsible for participating in the driver's education programs around the county at each High school.

I had never done any public speaking, except for getting up in front of class in some of my college courses for presentations. I wasn't very good at it to say the least, and I was fearful when it came down to it.

Instead of starting at 4pm that last Monday of 4-12 shift Jack had told me we'd be working 12p-8pm on Monday and the same on Tuesday. He had scheduled our talks at one o clock each day at each school.

On Monday we had given a short presentation to a group of about 50 kids at the first school. Jack had been kind enough to give the initial presentation and then followed by a short question and answer period. It went well, and I was impressed with Jack's demeanor and attitude towards the students. It was structured and informative and the students and faculty were very receptive and respectful.

"You did a nice job there Coach," I said as we were getting back in the car and leaving the school to resume patrol for the rest of our shift.

"Yeah Junior," he said. "It's part of the job. Tomorrow you'll be doing the speech and answering the questions."

"Me? Really? Do I have to?" I responded with a sense of fear in my voice.

"Yep," Jack replied with that grin on his face that I learned to dislike so much.

On Tuesday I got on Post before noon and was anxious thinking about the speech. I had prepared some notes from a couple brochures we had at the Post. Some statistics and info I jotted down on my notepad. I figured if I got up there and panicked, I could read from my notes. I think I'd rather be shot at than have to give this speech, I thought to myself as I saw Jack pulling up in the rear lot.

We drove over to the High school assigned to us and arrived promptly at 12:45pm. We were greeted by the school principal and escorted to a large double room that had the folding wall that slid open to make two classrooms into one large one.

The room began to fill after the 1:00 pm. bell, and I stood near the podium while Jack sat at a desk in the front of the classroom. As the room filled, I could feel my stomach tighten and I was having trouble breathing.

Relax, take deep breaths I told myself. This isn't important shit like working with nuclear bombs. It's just a bunch of goofy high school kids who could care less about being here. I looked over at Jack a couple times. He was sitting up straight and surveying the attendees.

The principal walked across the front of the classroom and asked everyone to be seated and direct their attention to the front.

"We have two State Troopers here today," he said. "Give them your attention because with Prom coming up, I'm sure they have some important advice for all of us."

With that he introduced us and nodded to me as he walked up the center isle to the rear of the classroom.

I cleared my throat and greeted the group. "Good afternoon. I'm Trooper Munch of the Ohio Highway Patrol. It's a pleasure to be here today and hopefully I can relay some information to you that may help you in your decision making during the Prom and graduation season."

I could feel my throat tightening up a bit, but I just kept telling myself that most of these kids don't care what I say, or how I say it. If I get through to a few of them then I've done a good thing.

I emphasized the importance of being responsible and not to include alcohol or drugs in their upcoming events. I read a few statistics and a few minutes elapsed. I was actually starting to relax, and for a moment or two I felt like they were learning something. It was a good feeling.

Then from the center of the room came a male voice interrupting me. "Hey man, who cuts your hair, man?"

I looked up and was able to pinpoint the young man who asked the question. He was your typical long hair, radical style moron with a big smirk on his face.

Wouldn't life be great if you could act on your impulses without consequences? Wouldn't justice be served if I could walk down the aisle in kind of a rhythmic, sauntering gangsta style gate, stop in front of his desk, reach out and grab him by the hair, wrap it once or twice around my wrist, and hair drag him up and down the aisle as he yelled for help from his cowardly teacher? That's what really needed to be done, because after that, he'd never disrespect anyone again. All those thoughts blew through my mind in less than two seconds.

But instead, I smiled back at him as the class erupted in laughter. I looked over at Jack who was obviously keyed in on the kid. Jack had this unmistakable eye piercing jaw tight look on his face.

The late seventies early eighties guys wore their hair long. The only men who had short hair, or military tapered cuts were either in the military, a cancer patient, or someone who might be crazy or mentally unstable.

I didn't say anything and kept on with my prepared speech. I thought to myself, if that would have happened at my high school, my principal would have sprinted over and got whomever it was in a headlock, and dragged him or her out of the classroom. Ha, these teachers are afraid now a days to even correct a student verbally, and forget about any physical discipline.

I continued with my talk ignoring the young scholar.

A few seconds went by. "I like to drink and drive," stated the same kid. Again, quickly my mind regressed to what I had just thought about after his last comment. No, I thought, don't do it. I ordered myself to ignore. I stopped, but I had to respond.

"Apparently you're not a very smart person then," I said as I glanced over at Jack who now was somewhat leaning forward partially out of his chair and visually locked on to the young man.

The teachers in the classroom again said nothing as a murmur filled the room. There were some kids who appeared annoyed at this jerk, and there were kids that were getting a kick out of the whole thing.

I didn't say anything else to him and continued with my rendition. A couple seconds later again from the same kid, "I drive better when I'm drunk," he blurted.

"Like I said," I responded. "you're a dummy then. You're going to end up hurting yourself or someone else."

All went quiet. The teachers did absolutely nothing and when I looked over at Jack he was out of his chair and had stood up and was obviously glaring at the kid.

"I'm going to drink and drive and there's nothing you're going to do about it, man," he chirped and laughed out loud. He tilted his head back and blew a large pink bubble with his chewing gum.

Ohhh-Ahh, I thought to myself. I'd pay a million dollars to be 16 yrs. old again just for today, just for an hour, so I could kick this kid's face in after school. My neck got tight. It wasn't funny anymore. It's one thing to bust someone's balls and interrupt them once, then shame on you- but if I let you do it to me a second and then third time, shame on me.

What I couldn't believe the most was that the teachers in the room did nothing. Not even a verbal reprimand.

A few seconds went by as I was looking at the principal who just kind of stared into space. He wouldn't look my way. I think he was acting like he hadn't heard any of these comments. Maybe the other teachers couldn't respond because it was the principals place to do so.

Suddenly, I saw fast movement from my left out of the corner of my eye. It had been only a few seconds since the kid's last comment. It was Jack flying by me headed up the isle towards this brain donor. The look on Jack's face I could only describe as a hungry lion about to pounce on a piece of raw meat.

My mind went blank for a split second. Is Jack going to "jack" this kid? Should I stop him, or should I help him? Huh, I thought? No crime committed other than the kid being a complete dick head. I better stop him, I thought, as I started up the isle behind him.

Suddenly Jack stopped about halfway up the aisle, about 10 feet from the young man's desk. His face was red, and he was pointing his finger.

"You know what's going to happen to you, you little punk," Jack chirped. "You're going to see me in your rear-view mirror. And then you're going to enter my world, and your mommy isn't going to be there to help you. And mommy won't be able to tuck you in at night because you're going to get locked up."

I wanted to say something to the little ass hole, but Jack had done a great job. Why ruin it by saying anything else? Haaa.

The kid surprisingly sat there and didn't say a word. He still had this shitty little smirk on his face, but I think he realized he had pushed the Troopers button, and wasn't willing to take it any further.

And just as Jack finished, finally, one of the male teachers had started to walk over to the isle. "OK sir, we can take it from here. Thank you for coming and sharing your insight," he said.

Jack just stood there for a couple seconds looking at the kid. The room was dead quiet. I had stopped directly behind Jack, and when he turned around to leave, I could see this smile come across his face.

"Ok. Thank you for your time," Jack stated, as we both walked towards the door and out into the hall.

"Well that went well, hey Dog?" I asked with a questionable tone.

"Yes, it did Junior, yes it did."

"Were you going to crack that kid Jack?"

"Only if he would have been dumb enough to stand up and walk towards me."

As we walked down the hall towards the exit, I could barely keep from busting out laughing. The Salty Dog, the Salty Dog, I kept saying to myself. I witnessed the "Dog" in action.

We got back in the car and finished the shift. The day was over, and I was happy.

CHAPTER 26

"Cut Loose"

WE FINISHED THE last two days of the 4-12 shift. I had taken my two days off and it now was Friday morning, day shift 8am-4pm. Today was going to be my first day by myself. "Cut Loose," to terrorize all the law-breakers roaming the streets of the state of Ohio.

As I walked up the sidewalk to enter the Post through the back-entrance Jack was standing inside on the other side of the door. As I opened it, he stepped back into the room away from the door and held out his right hand.

Here's the keys to the car you're going to be using today Junior. "Congratulations and don't wreck it," he said with a smile.

I stepped towards him and he reached out and shook my hand. "Thanks Coach," I said. "I'll take care of it."

I looked at the keys and realized it was car #938. It was the oldest car in the fleet at the Post. It was a 1976 Plymouth Grand Fury with a single bubble light on top. If you ever were going to be in an accident, this car would help you to survive it. It was a tank. It was the only car we had without the more modern Visabar that extended across the entire roof line.

"Car #938," I exclaimed. "she's an old war horse. I'll take good care of her," I said as I thought about the 1976 Plymouth we had to push at the Academy agility testing. "She's a beast. I'm proud to take her out on my first patrol."

I got all my paperwork together I needed for the shift. I picked up my briefcase and raincoat and headed out to the parking lot. I felt a tingling of excitement as I walked towards the car, and a sense of confidence I had hoped I would have.

I opened the driver's door of the car and hit the unlock button to open the rear doors. I set my coat and rain gear on the back seat and shut the door. I sat down in the driver's seat and looked over the equipment.

All the cars are set up identically but old #938 had an older radio console and siren setup which I hadn't used in the newer cars. I adjusted the mirrors, shut the door and started her up.

I took a couple of deep breaths and got ready to key the mike knowing the entire District 4 staff and units would be listening to me go in service.

I keyed the mike, "199 Warren Signal- 2, Car #938." I took my right thumb off the red transmit button on the mike and waited. A few seconds went by. No answer? Ten seconds, fifteen seconds. Should I repeat? She's probably busy I thought. Be patient. Did I say that right? Don't doubt yourself!

Then finally, after 20 seconds which seemed like two days, the Post answered, "OK 199."

"Ahh." A sigh of relief. I was putting too much pressure on myself. Why am I a self-doubter? Why am I doubting the existence of a higher power? Doubt, doubt, doubt. Why not relax and enjoy the minutes of each day? Why make things harder than they really are? Do I want the final days to come and ask myself why I worried so much? Or do I want to say I did my best and enjoyed every minute of it all?

All these thoughts floating around in my head. I need to concentrate on what I was doing. "Haa," I chuckled outload. Then I thought to myself and asked: Is it crazy to laugh outload when you're the only one listening? Yes! No? Who cares?

I pulled out on to Rt. 422 and headed towards the Bypass Rt.5. I had a million thoughts shuffling through my mind, mainly my wife, my kid, my parents, all these people that had helped me accomplish this goal, and lastly God. He had to be real. I couldn't have done this without some divine power helping me at every turn. Again, thoughts of my Mom and her unwavering faith. Why can't I be a believer like she is?

What must happen for me to truly believe?

But I was bustin'. I didn't know whether to laugh or cry. I was full of intense emotion. This dream had really happened. I was a cop. And I was a State cop, just like I told my Dad that morning years ago at breakfast. That was his dream. It had become my dream and reality.

It took about a half hour of driving to relax enough to get these thoughts under control and concentrate on what was going on around me. I was having a blast at just riding down the road basically doing nothing.

Doing nothing? I thought. Yeah, I better do something or their going to think I froze up someplace and I'm hiding under a bridge somewhere. "Haa," I laughed out loud, again!

Shortly thereafter I drove up on a vehicle parked on the berm eastbound on Rt.5. I got a little nervous. OK don't screw up your first stop and transmission. Don't sound like a dummy. Take it slow.

I slowly pulled off the roadway and in behind the vehicle. I activated my overhead bubble, put the car in park and keyed the mike. "199 Warren Signal-37, (Disabled vehicle) Rt. 5 eastbound, west of Elm Rd., Nora Sam William -233."

The Post quickly responded. "OK 199." I stepped out and walked up on the left side of the vehicle. All the times I had done this before in training for some reason this felt different doing it on my own.

I visually checked the back seat as I walked up to the driver's window and checked the front seat. Empty, I said to myself. Just an abandoned vehicle that probably broke down and the driver went for aid. It's well off the roadway and not a hazard, I'll put a 48-hr. tag on it.

I walked back to the Patrol car and sat down. Am I doing everything right here? I asked myself. Com'on man. It's a simple disabled vehicle. How could you screw anything up? Relax, you've done this a hundred times in coach/pupil.

Oh shit, I thought. It dawned on me; I'm missing Jack! That's why this all feels different. I sincerely miss him. He'd tell me if I was doing something wrong or forgetting something. This is all on me now. Nobody to ask for help. That's why I feel different.

Once I realized why I was feeling anxious everything fell into place for me. I was on my own now and they trusted me to be able to handle this job. And I've shown them to this point I'm more than capable. OK I thought, that's why that man put all the pressure on me. Most importantly that taught me to trust myself, so I must void myself of these thoughts of insecurity. It's normal because it's a new job. I'd never been insecure in most anything I'd ever done. Why would I start now, although this kind of responsibility is enormous and can be overwhelming.

I wrote the 48-hr. tag and attached it to the windshield wiper. I walked back to my car and got in. I checked my mirrors and pulled out into traffic and keyed the mike, "199 Warren vehicle abandoned and tagged, Signal 45." (resuming patrol)

I was in the passing lane traveling a couple miles over the speed limit so as not to back up traffic. I got about a half mile down the road and I noticed the vehicles in front of me in the right lane were braking and partially pulling off on the right berm.

"What's that guy doing?" I mumbled out loud. "Oh shit," I spoke aloud. I realized I had forgot to turn off my overhead bubble. Here Mr. Trooper is driving down the road with his bubble rotating, and traffic is scrambling out of his way.

Rather than shut off my overhead and look like a total idiot, I kicked old #938 in the ass and busted down the road for about a half mile to make it look like I was in a hurry to get somewhere. Now if I shut it off, it looks like I got called off the hot call and resumed normal speed. Maybe I am crazy?

The day flew by. I didn't write any tickets, but I did stop several vehicles for vehicle defects. I also was sent to a couple of fender benders in Howland township. No major crashes.

I also had not handled or been present at a fatal accident. It was one thing Jack was concerned about as to how I would deal with it.

That week of day shift passed, and my squad was coming out on a Thursday night shift 12-8am. I had gotten a little more acclimated to night shift since my first night with Tpr. Gemco. The trick to staying awake is to stay busy. Stop cars, stop cars, stop cars. Headlight out- stop it. Speeding - stop it. Weaving- stop it. Driving over the white lane marker- stop it. Driving to slow- stop it. License plate light out- stop it.

No front plate attached- stop it. On night shift any violation was prob-able cause to stop and look for a drunk driver.

I arrested my first drunk driver by myself the first night I went out. There were a couple nights I came up empty but being a new guy, I didn't feel a lot of pressure to land a drunk every night. One night I arrested two. One was out of an accident at the start of the shift, and the second was a few hours later when I stopped a guy for weaving. I worked with some Troops that consistently would come up with one per night, and a few guys would get two or three. The most I had heard of was a Trooper that made five DWI arrests in one shift.

CHAPTER 27

"Youngstown Hardhats"

ABOUT TWO MONTHS had gone by. I was enjoying the job as much as anyone could. I looked forward to coming to work regardless of what shift it was.

Cindy and I had moved! We found a house to rent in Champion Twp. It was only 10 minutes from the Post and much closer to shopping areas etc. Ironically, it was about two blocks from Champion High school where I had taken the written test for OSP, which seemed so long ago.

The house was a nice two-bedroom cape cod which sat back off the street with a long driveway which we wanted, considering traffic and Angela's safety. The next-door neighbors (the Marshall's) were in their late 60's early 70's, and immediately took a liking to Cindy and Angela. They visited every day, and sometimes most of the day, which was fine with me. Their attachment had grown quickly, and they seemed a good substitute for Cindy's parents. She was much happier, and that was a relief for me.

It was now late summer, and Cindy told me she had an announcement. She told me she was expecting! I was thrilled. I loved Angela so much and a second child was certainly in the plans.

I hadn't experienced a full-blown resisting arrest. Oh, I had my share of drunks giving me attitude. A few had gotten mouthy and mumbled threats, but that was expected in this line of work. Fortunately, I had developed thick skin over the years because of my last name.

In grade school "Munch a bunch of Fritos," was one of the first clichés that would set me off. There were many more that were worse and a bit more X-rated. My Dad had a talk with me about the draw backs to fighting and the need to control my temper. Plus, I lost more fights than I won, so eventually it dawned on me that it might not be worth it. All in all, it made me a bit fearless, which wasn't always a good attribute to have.

I considered myself an average to above average producer. Especially considering being a new Troop. I was pretty good in the ability to talk people out of doing stupid things. I wasn't crazy about fighting people, although if you disrespected the uniform and I had to protect myself, then you were going to see a different side of me without hesitation.

If they threatened my family or me, or someone I was working with, then I didn't put up with it. They would get charged appropriately and if they resisted that was on them. To sum it up I didn't look for trouble that wasn't there.

It was near Thanksgiving, and I was working night shift. I was dispatched to IS-80 westbound west of SR. 193, regarding a reported vehicle stopped on the roadway in the passing lane. Dispatch further advised the caller had stated there was someone in the vehicle slumped over the wheel.

I was on the far east end of the Interstate, so it took me only a couple minutes to arrive. Traffic was light because of the early hour, being just after 2a.m. I activated my overhead lights and high beams and pulled in directly behind the vehicle which was blocking the left lane.

"199 Warren Signal 3 (On scene) with this vehicle Paul William John 244 a blue Ford Taurus," I said into the mike.

"OK 199," the Post answered.

I stepped out of my vehicle quickly and started up the left side of the stopped vehicle. I noticed it was running, and as I got near the driver's window, I could see it was down and I could smell that familiar odor of stale beer. The driver had slumped over partially on his right side exposing my view to the steering wheel and gear shift. I realized the vehicle was in drive and the driver's foot was resting on the brake pedal.

I don't want to try and wake him until I get this car in park, I thought to myself. I reached in and shut the car off first then put the shifter in park.

145

OK, good. Wow, this guy is huge I thought as I reached in again through the window and grabbed his shoulder and started to shake him.

"Hey buddy, are you alright?" I shouted. "Hey, wake up, wake up," I said as I continued to shake him.

"Uhggh. Ughh. Ugahhhhaaaa," responded the driver. "Leave me alone," he mumbled, obviously not aware of what was going on.

"You have to wake up buddy," I said loudly and with a sense of urgency. "You've got the whole lane of the Interstate blocked and I don't want us to get run over. Wake up, now!" I demanded in a loud tone as I shook him more.

He raised his head slightly just enough to open his eyes and squint at me. He then dropped his head back where it was and said slurring his words, "F- you (garbled words). Go away."

I took a half step back to look at the surroundings and assess my next move. This guy is so drunk, I thought, he has no idea where he is or what he's doing or who he's talking to.

I realized to expedite matters I had to get this guy out of the car now and get it off the road before some other drunk smashes into us.

I opened the driver's door, and when I did, he slowly sat up.

"Hey State Patrol," I said firmly. "Your stopped on the roadway. You need to get out of the car," I said as he turned his head and was looking directly into my eyes.

"Come on," I yelled as I grabbed his collar and started to pull him towards me and the open door.

"F-you, you pussy," he said as he grabbed my right wrist and started pulling me towards him.

"No, you're coming out now," I said as I pulled my arm back and slipped my right arm around his neck and twisted him to my right, so his back was flush against my chest.

I pulled backwards as hard as I could but was barely budging the guy. I knew if I wanted him to come out, I'd have to make him angry enough at me to want to come out after me.

I still wasn't convinced this guy knew who I was, but it didn't matter now because mission number one was to get this car moved. There was no time for negotiations.

I remembered Trooper Stillman from the Academy showing us some extricating methods. One of them was in this similar situation where he showed us how to burry a knuckle just behind the ear, where there's a painful pressure point.

With my left hand I made a fist and used my index finger knuckle and jammed it as hard as I could behind his left ear while I pulled hard.

He let out a yell that sounded like an Indian Comanche war cry. I had heard something similar years ago watching Saturday afternoon movies of the Lone Ranger and the Rifleman at my house when I was a kid. He let go of the steering wheel as I continued to grind my knuckle behind his ear. As I was pulling, he started yelling profanities and slid his torso out and off the seat, and somehow had the strength to stand up with me on his back. He reached back and grabbed the back of my head, and with one motion bent slightly forward and catapulted me skyward. I did a half somersault before hitting the ground tailbone first. I landed in the median with my back to him.

Flash back to the OSP Academy PT class. Tpr. Bellinger standing over us while we were trying to do that last sit-up. I Had a vivid picture of him and what he was yelling at us. "Are you going to let some drunk sit on your chest and cave in your face and take your life?"

I started to get up and spin around so I could see him, and I could feel like an electric shock, and then a blast of pain shoot down my left leg.

At the same moment I noticed a silhouette come from behind my suspect holding a flashlight. My suspect for some reason didn't charge at me. He turned towards the person with the flashlight yelling and screaming, and then started to lunge at the person. I charged my suspect and attempted to tackle him with my shoulder hitting him in the stomach and wrapping my arms around his torso. I didn't budge him much.

He then turned his attention back to me and was trying to pick me up by my waist. At the same time, I heard a couple loud cracking sounds.

I thought, what the hell is that? And then I heard it again. "Crack, crack." I heard a voice command, "Get down."

I couldn't see because I was bent over holding on to the guy at his

147

waist. I could only hear again, "Crack, get down now, get down."

Suddenly I felt the guy shift his weight forward and down to the ground on his stomach.

"Don't hit me anymore. Don't hit me mother #@$#," yelled the suspect.

I let go of him and put my knee in the middle of his back and looked to my left. It was one of the best sights I had ever seen. It was Sgt. Al Marks from Liberty Township P.D.

"Sarge!" I said excitedly. "Thanks," I said as I was trying to get the handcuff on the driver's wrist.

Just then an ambulance pulled up. They were on a return trip from the hospital and pulled over to see what was going on. Two attendants got out and helped me and Sgt. Marks handcuff this guy. He wasn't fighting anymore, but just holding his hands underneath his body so we couldn't handcuff him. It took all four of us to pry his arms out from underneath him and get him handcuffed from behind. I could only get my cuffs to click one time. That's how big his wrists were, and I had to use two sets of handcuffs together because his shoulders were so broad.

After squeezing him into the back of my patrol car, I shut the door and leaned up against the rear passenger glass. I was a mess. Torn uniform, grass stained pants, out of breath, sweating and slightly injured. This guy could have killed me. Maybe I should be dead right now?

I walked over to Sgt. Marks' cruiser where he had sat down. "Thanks Sarge, you saved my ass," I said.

"Yeah I saw your lights when I went by the underpass and I knew you had been there for a while. So I thought I'd swing up on the Interstate to see what was up," he explained, as a big smile broke across his face.

"Shit, I'm so happy you did," I exclaimed and chuckled outload. "He's a big fish eh Sarge?"

"Oh yeah," said Sarge." I forget his name, but he used to play for the Hardhats years ago."

"Hardhats?" I asked.

"Yeah the Youngstown Hardhats semi pro football team. He played tackle for them for a while. I think he's the same guy I'm thinking of had a pro look, but it didn't pan out for him."

"Wow," I said. That's the biggest guy I ever had to tangle with. Again thanks, I definitely owe you one sir."

I walked away after shaking his hand and got in the car. I looked in the rear-view mirror and noticed he was nodding off. I couldn't help but think where would this guy be if he would have caught a break and been able to stay with an NFL team? Here he sits drunked up in the back of a police car.

After I got finished locking the guy up and getting all the right paperwork filed it was almost 6am. I was driving across the bypass on the way to the Post to gas up and get ready to go home. The sun was just coming up and it was a beautiful sunrise. Traffic was starting to pick up and everybody was going about their routine.

Routine? I thought. These people have no idea what goes on while their sleeping. Routine? I'll never know what routine is like as long as I have this job, ever.

I also thought how things could have gone last night. What if Sarge had never shown up? What if the guy would have hurt me bad or killed me? What if I would have killed him? Maybe shot him? Would I have been justified? Only God knows, I thought. Only God has that in His control. Did God help me last night? Was He there?

CHAPTER **28**

"Signal 30"

AFTER NIGHT SHIFT my four-day weekend rolled around. As usual we loaded up the Ford and drove to Erie. Cindy stayed at her parents and I stayed at mine. In the evenings I got the chance to sit with my Dad and spend time together. It's funny how when your growing up you love your parents, but as far as Dad went, I tried to avoid him sometimes. He was my Dad, and not my best friend. He was going to call me out if I did something wrong or if he had advice I didn't want to hear. I loved him dearly, but I would duck him now and then.

Since getting married and moving away I regret I didn't spend more time with him. At least now I had the chance to talk with him more in a man to man setting. It was something I looked forward to because he was pretty cool.

Dad obviously had a great interest in my job. He'd ask me continually how the job was going and wanted to know every detail. I thought back to the times I'd bug him to tell me his war stories, and how reluctant he was to talk about them. Now I was kind of understanding why he didn't expand on his stories. It was because if you didn't experience it in the moment, it was hard to get a grip on the emotional side of the story. I was feeling the same way. I'd tell him about my most exciting calls and encounters but didn't expand on what I was thinking or feeling at the time. He wouldn't understand just like I wouldn't be able to understand what he went through. Plus, I didn't want to worry him much. If I told him some of the things he really didn't need to know it would be more for him to worry about. When I'd be leaving to go back to Warren he'd always say, "Don't turn your back on those yeahoo's." And I'd say, "No, don't worry Dad, they can't outsmart me." Haa. Whatever a yeahoo was?

We got back to Champion on the usual Monday night which gave me until Tuesday afternoon to report for work. Cindy's battery was always recharged, and she had grown close to the Marshalls next door and missed them when we were away.

Tuesday afternoon at 4pm started the week. Afternoon shift was always the busiest. I was on IS-80 near the Pennsylvania line and was westbound approaching the US 62 exit to Hubbard. I had the CB on scan which monitored emergency channel 9, and I always listened to Ch.19 which is the trucker talk channel. You could pick up a lot of info listing to the truckers go about their day. They were quite a bunch, and they certainly didn't like "Smokey."

I heard some unusually loud chatter and turned up the volume to listen closely. They were talking about some traffic tie up on 80 around the Belmont Ave. exit. I was headed in that direction and didn't give it much credence because of all the crazy people on that channel.

Then I heard the channel 9 squawk and a report of an accident near the Belmont exit.

I picked up my speed a bit and traveled a few miles westbound when the Post called.

"Warren to 199."

"Go ahead Warren, I'm 80 westbound, east of Hubbard," I responded.

"Signal 31A possible Signal 30 on 80 westbound just east of 193.

Awww. Did I just hear that right? Possible 30? Shit, a fatal? They just set me to a fatal! I hadn't seen a dead person yet.

My heart kicked into near spasm. I could feel it in my chest and the blood busting through my neck thumping, thump, thump. I took a couple of deep breaths, but I had learned not to get too excited about anything until you saw it for yourself. But just in case, I took more deep breaths. Dennis had taught me to oxygenate prior to arriving at stressful calls.

Here we go, I thought. I'm about 5 miles away. Time to run hard. I hit the toggle for the overheads and hit the switch for the siren and I was off. It was just 5pm. and traffic was crazy. Most people got out of my way and I got in the area in about 4 minutes. As I approached from the east, I got within a half mile and traffic westbound was at a standstill. I drove up the left side of the stopped traffic driving mostly in the median to get closer. The closest I could get initially was about 50 yards. I parked sideways in the lanes and got out and jogged towards what appeared to be the center of the melee. There were probably 10 semi-trucks and 6 or seven cars blocking the access to the lanes, and about 25 people standing in the immediate area.

As I got within 20 ft. or so I could see about 8 or 9 people huddled around something laying in the right lane. A couple of the people saw me and stepped aside so I could walk into their circle. I got to them and looked down at what was drawing their attention. I saw what appeared to be a human body half clothed lying on its back. Its torso was twisted so the persons bare buttocks was positioned in the front. The back was completely broken because the back of the torso was lying flat on the ground. The subjects head was severed just above the upper lip and the nose, eyes, and forehead were detached laying partially in the left lane about six feet from the head.

I wasn't sure what to do, but I knelt and put my hand on the neck of the subject. It really wasn't registering what I was seeing. It was like being in a dream and everything around me was hazy.

"Smokey that dude is dead," a voice came from behind me.

"No need to feel for a pulse on that mother #%&# Smokey," a different voice said.

Then within a few seconds everything got clear and vivid, and very intense. My senses were extremely keen. I could smell the raw body parts and diesel fuel. My vision and hearing were precise. It was a total adrenaline overload.

I stood up and turned to the direction of where the voices came from. "Somebody get me a sheet or blanket to cover this guy up," I spouted. "Are there any witnesses?" I asked the crowd.

"Yes sir, I'm the driver of the first rig. He was driving the second rig," said the man directly in front of me as he pointed to the man standing next to him.

"What happened?" I asked the first driver.

"I think the guy internationally ran out in front of me," the first driver said. "I cut it to the left and missed him, but the guy driving the semi behind me hit him."

Then the second driver said, "Yeah, he swerved, and I saw the guy all of a sudden, and I swerved, but my trailer caught him. The ribbing on the side of the trailer caught the side of his face and ripped it off, and it spun him around I guess," he said. "Then when he fell my rear tandems ran him over. I saw that looking back in my side mirror. That's why his back is broke, and his clothes got torn off. I saw his clothes fly off."

"OK, I'm eventually going to need to get statements from you as soon as I get some help here. Don't go anywhere," I said in an ordering tone.

I keyed up my portable and confirmed to the Post we had a Signal 30 and to send anybody they could. I heard Jack key up. He had been working an overtime speed enforcement program on the west side of the county. He was about 25 miles away. When I heard him key up and tell the Post he was headed my way, in the background I could hear the four-barrel on his Plymouth kicking in. It was an awesome feeling knowing he was coming.

He'll burn the paint off his engine getting here I thought. He had been worried I hadn't handled a fatal and would screw it up. Not going to happen, I said to myself.

I called off any ambulances and asked for the coroner. The main priority is to tend to the injured. That wasn't a problem. The second priority of the Highway Patrol is to open the road.

It took me about fifteen minutes to get one of the lanes open. I was having trouble getting the guy covered up because whoever had the Patrol car I was driving last used the first aid kit and didn't replace the blanket. Unfortunately for about 15 minutes this guy laid in the driving lane all busted up. I was able to funnel vehicles around him in the passing lane.

I knew if I didn't have the road open by the time Jack got there, I would have caught hell for it. What I didn't plan for was that Mr. and Mrs. J.Q. Public driving by the victim and getting an eyeful of that. I was stuck with that situation until I could get him covered. I was able to move my car at an angle that somewhat obstructed the view of the body, so I didn't have to listen to anymore screams that I had been hearing from the passing motorists. I had help from a couple volunteers directing the cars around the corpse, but I never imagined something as simple as not having a blanket would cause such a fiasco.

Finally, one of the truck drivers came up with a blanket and got the poor bastard covered. I was angry about not having that blanket in the first aid sack.

I had gotten my photos taken and was starting my field sketch when Jack arrived.

"Junior why is your car on the berm?" Jack asked. "You should have it in front of the guy so nobody runs him over again."

"Geeze Jack," I responded. "He's already dead. I've got it coned off and flared. You always preached to me about keeping the patrol car off the roadway and on the berm," I answered. "I had it parked protecting him because I didn't get him covered right away, and people were freakin out. After I got him covered, I pulled back on the berm."

"OK, well, pull in front of him. If somebody re-runs him over we'd be hard pressed explaining that one," Jack said with a smirk.

It took about an hour before we got the body loaded and the coroner on his way out of there. For some reason coroners rarely get to you in a hurry. Why should they? The corpse isn't going anywhere.

Jack and I finished taking statements and I finished up the field sketch. Jack stayed on scene while the fire dept. hosed down the blood and pieces of tissue off the road, and I left for the hospital.

I had to meet the coroner at St. Elizabeth's Hospital for a blood draw. Every fatal accident that OSP investigates we are required to take blood from the victim and send it to Columbus GHQ for analysis.

I arrived at the hospital and was instructed to meet one of the deputy coroners in the morgue.

I entered the morgue and noticed our victim lying bagged on a gurney in the middle of the exam room. The room smelled like a meat locker and it was cold.

A few seconds later this beautiful female stepped into the room. She was gorgeous. Auburn hair, very pretty with blue eyes and a big smile. She was wearing a tightly fit blue hospital style smock. She introduced herself and stated she was the deputy coroner and would be doing the exam.

"Exam?" I asked. "Really? What's to examine? I'm supposed to just have you take blood so I can send if off to Columbus," I stated.

"Oh, I know" she said. "Your Sgt. called, and he wants me to examine him and you witness it."

"Oh, fine," I reluctantly said. "If that's what he wants, then fine."

I wasn't really happy about that. I didn't know what to expect. Again, all this was so surreal. She had me walk over to the exam table as she unzipped the bag. Ugh, the smell is very unique. Like ring baloney I thought. That's it, that's the smell I concluded. Smells like the ring baloney we used to eat when we were kids.

I watched this beautiful woman put on a pair of elbow length gloves and pick a few pieces of skull away from the back of this guy's head. She had to make a hole large enough to put her hand through. She entered the skull from the back of the head and was speaking doctor language into a small tape recorder.

The scene was very bizarre for me. Her hand extended down the inside of what face was left, and she stuck her fingers out through the guys mouth. She continued speaking into her tape recorder. She pulled her arm out of his head and started examining the bones that were broken and protruding in the back area.

I thought, that just about does it for me. Ohhhh yea, I've seen enough to know what killed this guy. She can play around for hours for all I care, but I'm leaving.

"Can you take that blood for me now?" I asked.

"Sure, I'm almost done," she replied. "In a hurry?"

"To be honest, I'm not feeling too good. So, I'll be out in the outer office when you're done, and I can take the blood sample with me," I said as I was walking backwards and turning to step quickly to the office.

I think it was two things that bothered me during that exam. Number one is the overall smell. Like a cold old meat locker. The mind goes to strange places sometimes. Secondly was this beautiful woman doing a job like that. It didn't look normal. I really don't know if I could be interested in a woman that did that for a living. She'd be hugging you, and who knows what she'd be thinking about? My inside skull diameter? Yea, not a match for me and my preferences in a woman.

I cleared the hospital and immediately Sarge called me.

"199?" said Sarges voice over the radio.

"Go ahead," I answered.

"Meet me on Belmont north of the city for Signal 38," (Lunch/Dinner) he stated.

That's Denny's I thought. Dinner? What? He wants to eat? Aww, man I don't know if I'm up for that, although it was after 7:00 pm. and I had missed dinner.

"OK, in route," I answered.

I pulled into Denny's and Sarge was parked in the rear of the lot. I pulled up beside him and he had this huge smile on his face.

"Something funny?" I asked and smiled back.

"Your Daddy was worried about you and drove all the way across the county to see if you were OK," he said chuckling.

"Yea, that was nice of him. I needed the help. Where were you?" I asked.

"I was there observing from a far. I saw everything that was going on. I'd a helped you if I thought you needed it," he said chuckling.

" Oh, I was so busy I never saw you. I guess I got everything done I was supposed to?"

"That was a bad fatal. Good one for you to have for your first one," said Sarge.

"So officially now 199, welcome to the Highway Patrol," sarge said loudly. "You popped your cherry today."

"Did you call the coroner and request the doctor give me an up-close look at the postmortem exam? I figured you did when she took her time and started playing with the guys face."

"Well I wanted to make sure you experienced everything concerning a fatal," he answered with a smirk. We also got a call from an acquaintance of your victim. He had just been released from Youngstown South and had been in psychiatric care. It looks more like a suicide."

"Yea, the lead driver said it looked like he just hopped right out in front of him intentionally," I advised Sarge.

"Too bad," remarked Sarge. "Let's eat Freddie. You must be hungry right?" asked Sarge smiling.

"Maybe a little. I could choke something down, I think."

We went in and ordered. Sarge ordered two burgers, I ordered one. I couldn't get that smell out of my mind. My burger smelled like ring baloney. Admittedly I nearly gagged a couple times and felt a little nauseous after I got back in the car. The burger didn't settle well.

CHAPTER 29

Broken heart

FALL CAME AND went. So did the Holidays. I was lucky to have Christmas Eve and Christmas day off and spent them in Erie. Cindy was happy about that, and Angela had been a good girl and Santa was good to her. We were looking forward to the new year and 1980. We had a baby due in May, and I had an adequate handle on the job by then. It was an exciting time.

It was February 8th and I was working day shift. I had left the house at 7:15 and arrived on Post for the start of the workday.

When I left the house that morning all was well. Cindy was up and waiting for Angela to wake up. Nothing out of the ordinary.

I was working the west county area. The weather was cold and clear. It was a busy morning and I had handled a couple minor accidents. I got a call from the Post advising me to call or come on station. I was near so I pulled into the back lot and was walking towards the rear door.

Sarge met me at the door and told me that my wife had called. She had some cramping and pain and the Marshall's took her down to St. Joes hospital.

Sarge told me to go ahead to the hospital.

I drove to the hospital and when I got there I was led to a standard hospital room. I walked in and Cindy was laying there by herself in bed and I could tell she had been crying.

"What's wrong? What happened?" I asked as I laid my hand on her shoulder.

"I lost the baby," she exclaimed as she started to cry.

"What? Why? Are you OK? My God what happened?" I asked as I hugged her.

"I don't know. About eight o clock I got a couple shooting pains in my lower stomach and felt wetness, so I called Larry next door. Ruth watched Angela and Larry took me down here. They put me in this room and said a doctor would look at me soon. I was laying here only about ten minutes and I lost it right here. I yelled for the nurse and she came. Then they took the baby away," she explained.

"Oh my God are you OK?" I'm so sorry you had to go through that alone," I said as I hugged her tighter.

"We can have another, don't worry please," I said as I tried to console her.

Over the next hour a couple of nurses came in and out and Cindy was feeling better physically. I tried to act like it didn't crush me, and keep a positive face while we waited for the doctor.

I knew little about miscarriages. I knew my grandmother had seven kids and five miscarriages. I had a couple friends over the years that their mothers had miscarriages. All I knew was that they weren't rare, and women usually recovered physically easily, but it was the emotional healing that varied.

Then the bombshell happened for me.

Cindy while still lying down turned her head towards me. She looked at me like she was looking straight through me. "It was a boy," she said.

"What?" I was stunned. "What did you say? It was a boy?" I asked.

"Yes, it was a boy."

I felt that familiar blood rush sensation to my neck and face. "Really? I guess I didn't know you could tell at this stage?" I said to her.

"Fred, their fully formed at 6 months. Their just very tiny and their lungs aren't developed or their eyes," she said.

"Oh God, I'm sorry I'm so ignorant when it comes to this stuff," I responded.

I had to sit there for a few minutes and gather myself. The more I thought about it the more emotion was churning inside me.

"Did they baptize him?" I asked.

"I think so," Cindy responded.

I got up and started down the hallway. I had to find a nurse, and I had to know if he was baptized.

"Nurse," I called out as one came out of one of the rooms. "Did our baby get baptized?"

"Oh yes. This is a Catholic hospital," she answered. "Did you want to see him?"

"What? He's still alive?" I mumbled. I could feel my eyes start to well up.

"Yes, at his birthweight of about a pound they survive for only a short time. Usually an hour or two."

I was looking straight ahead but not really seeing anything. My mind was racing, and my legs were weak. I could feel my lower lip quivering.

"Did you want to see him?" again she asked.

I heard what she said. I just couldn't form the words right away. "Yes, yes I do. I have to," I stammered.

I followed the nurse to the nursery, and she escorted me into a small room that had an incubator on a table. The nurse asked me if I wanted to sit down but I declined. I looked at the baby who was not even the size of my hand. I couldn't really tell if he was breathing. My mind was totally blank. I turned to the nurse and asked, "I guess it's not practical to hold him, right?"

"Oh no honey. He's too fragile. Not a good idea," she said.

"Yes, but he's just all by himself," I said as I could feel a tear run down the side of my face, and my chin starting to quiver.

"Com'on," she said as I could see she also was having difficulty keeping her composure. She touched my arm. "Your wife needs you to be with her right now."

I walked back to Cindy's room with the nurse and asked her not to mention I had seen the baby. I didn't want to upset her any more than she was. I told Cindy I had talked to the nurse who Baptized him. Fortunately, she didn't ask me anything else. I was having a hard time not to show any emotion in front of her.

The doctor eventually came in and explained that Cindy's cervix had opened prematurely, and it was something we would have to address before trying to have another child. He also explained the baby was far enough along where the State requires naming the child and burial. This was just so overwhelming, I thought. Why did God permit this to happen? I was angry. I just didn't know who to be angry at.

The doctor also suggested Cindy spend the rest of the day and night at the hospital. We agreed and I decided to go back to the house and get a few things she needed. I called the Post from the hospital and asked for the rest of the day off. Sergeant Pacer was on Post and advised me he'd meet me at my house to pick up the car.

I arrived home about 20 minutes later and Sarge was there waiting for me. He came in and we were standing in the kitchen.

The Highway Patrol I had learned is one big family. When one hurts we all feel the pain. A real family-oriented brotherhood.

Sgt. Pacer wanted to know how Cindy was doing and what had happened. I started to explain what had transpired but was having trouble spitting it out. He could see it had emotionally messed me up, and when he reached out and put his hand on my shoulder and said he was sorry, I lost it. I started sobbing and had to sit down. I tried to get the words out that the baby was a boy, and how much I wanted a son.

"Go ahead Fred. Let it all out. Nothing wrong with showing emotion at a time like this," he said.

He stood beside me patting me on the back as I sat in the chair. I explained the baby was far enough along where it had to be named and buried.

"Is it OK for me to tell the Lieutenant and let the guys know what's happened?" he asked.

"Yeah Sarge, and thanks for being here with me," I said while still choking back tears.

"I'm sure all the guys are going to want to chip in to help with your expenses, so I'll let them all know," said Sarge.

I took the next few days off and tended to Cindy. Within a few days she seemed back to normal.

We named the baby Jason William, and we buried him in Erie that week.

A couple weeks later I got some more bad news. A Trooper I graduated with was killed while on duty investigating an accident. He was stationed on the west side of the state. He was out of his car directing traffic. The roadway was slippery, and a vehicle lost control and apparently spun out striking him. Troopers who were at the funeral, which our whole Class attended together, said he had pushed another person out of the way of that vehicle but was struck himself. He was a very quiet, unselfish, confident kid. Such a young life to give up. Only a little over a year on the job, but I know it was a job he loved.

CHAPTER **30**

Bad Pinch

TIME PASSED AND things got better emotionally for me and Cindy. The doctors had cleared her to try for another child. They thought her cervix opening was a fluke.

So, towards the end of June of 80'Cindy announced she was expecting. I was thrilled as usual. Our families were excited. I asked God to keep everyone healthy and for a normal pregnancy. It was hard for me to accept I had buried a son. He had no chance at life. All I could think of that gave me some peace of mind, was that this life is meaningless and unimportant compared to what's to come, and Jason is happy in the arms of the Almighty. I just wish I could truly believe that.

I worked OASIS (Ohioans Against Speed In our State) which was a government subsidized overtime program that was available to us. We could work one extra shift a week for the overtime, so I continually worked the extra day. Without that extra shift I would have had to work a second job. The economy was in the tank and had been for a few years. I had been raised in a Democratic household, but Jimmy Carter was doing a good job of changing my mind and I was looking hard at the Republican party. I think the abortion issue steered me away from the Democrats the most. I also started to develop a negative attitude towards people that didn't work. I had to go to work. Entitlements for the lazy was a hard concept for me to swallow, and the Dem's were quick to find excuses for these people. I'm all for helping people who need a boost in life, but I was seeing that some made their living off the government.

One morning while working OASIS I stopped a car near the end of the shift. It was an unwritten policy that in order to maintain acceptable productivity and keep the grant people happy, we were to try and write one HP-7 (ticket) per hour. If you worked eight hours that day it was expected for you to write at least eight tickets. It wasn't a written quota, but it was a realistic goal.

Depending on traffic volume and weather, sometimes that's very easy, and sometimes the fish aren't biting, and it can be difficult.

On this day I had worked over from a nightshift for two hours from 8am to 10am. I had been running radar on Rt. 5 and hadn't checked any speeds that justified a ticket, and there was only about twenty minutes left before I had to secure. I had never come in from an overtime detail empty handed, although it had happened to a couple other guys.

Then coming westbound towards Cleveland, I checked a speed on a car for a consistent 66 mph. Ten over the speed limit was the unwritten minimum speed to write tickets for. At least I had gotten one, I thought, as I turned my car around to pursuit the violator.

I stopped the vehicle and upon speaking with the driver advised him I was issuing him a citation for the violation and I'd be with him in a few minutes. I went back to my car and wrote the ticket. When I walked back up to the car, I spoke to him briefly and explained the procedure for mailing in the fine, or how to plead not guilty if he so chose.

He thanked me and asked me if he was on the right road to the Cleveland Clinic. I said he was, and then I made a huge mistake. I asked him why he was going up to the clinic, because they had a small child in the car, and I was hoping it wasn't the baby.

"The baby has cancer," was his response to my stupid question.

I was totally stunned and lost for words. A few uncomfortable seconds went by. Can I void this ticket? I asked myself. I should take it back from him. He'd be so happy.

"I'm sorry," I finally blurted out, and turned and walked back to the car.

I wanted so much to reach in and pull that ticket back out of his hands, but I knew I couldn't. Those tickets are numbered, and each are accounted for. Once those tickets are written they can only be voided by you presenting it to a supervisor with what better be a good excuse. And feeling sorry for somebody isn't enough.

I sat in the car and fell into my stare over the dash mode. Those people didn't need me to add more grief to their lives. How did I help them? I thought. Maybe stopping them saved their lives because he was driving so fast? Yea-maybe. But I didn't need to write the ticket. No- but what about the last guy I wrote for 66 in a 55mph. Would it be fair to him for me to let these people go?

Com'on man, you have to get a grip on this job as far as feeling sorry for people. He was speeding and putting his family at risk. You're just doing your job. Remember what Jack said, "Just do your job an let the courts decide." Let him plead not guilty and tell the judge his kid has cancer. Let the judge throw it out. Quit being a sissy. Yea -but I'm a human being. I have feelings. Don't I? Well- be a social worker then. Quit!

Quit? If I was having doubts, this wouldn't be the time to consider it. I've had too many emotional setbacks happening lately to make an objective decision.

Then one morning after arriving on Post for day shift, I was told Trooper Kraft had resigned. It was strange because of the timing. I had developed a few doubts, and now someone that was a peer, and I respected, had decided this wasn't for him.

Later that week I got a chance to talk to his Coach. He wasn't surprised by the resignation because he had been having issues regarding writing tickets. For him it was emotionally too much stress. Times were tough and it hurt him to be a part of a system that punishes your wallet. Kraft's heart was just too big. That's how I rationalized the whole thing. And if it wasn't for Jack's talk to me months before about just doing your job and let the courts decide on punishment, I may have thought about it also.

And there was a big part of me that took satisfaction in writing someone who had total disregard for the safety of others. Case in point for which I would think back to, was a guy I had stopped on SR.11 a few months before. I had him on the radar for 112 mph. It took me miles to catch up to him, and when I finally stopped him his excuse was that he was a professional stock car driver, and he was good at driving that fast. A pinch like that keeps things fresh and reminds me there are people out here that have to be policed to prevent them from hurting themselves or others.

CHAPTER 31

Big Day

THE REST OF the year flew by. It was a very busy summer and fall. The Holidays came and went. For the second straight year I was able to spend Christmas in Erie which made the wife happy.

1981 came fast. Cindy was due in March and her pregnancy had gone well. We were getting close to her due date. The job was going well. I had learned enough to keep myself viable and productive.

I had registered at our local church so the new baby could be baptized. I had even started going to church most Sundays when I wasn't working day shift. My attitude towards going to church was at an all-time high. I even started back to saying prayers when the mood struck me. Mainly prayers of thanks and asking forgiveness. So, in going to church I wanted to set example for my kids like my parents had instilled in me. Angela was getting old enough to start to understand, and I wanted her to see us going together as a family. I figured God had blessed me with a good job and family, and even though we had lost a baby recently I wasn't mad at God. I'm not sure why I wasn't, but my mother would say everything is under His control, and everything good and bad happens for a reason. I couldn't figure what good came from losing the baby, but I'm just a spec of sand on a large beach, so who am I to ask why? And still, I wasn't sure that He even existed. Deep in my heart I had to admit I wasn't sure. I was a doubting Thomas and that still bothered me.

Then the big day came. I had taken Cindy to the doctor for her final visit and we were in that "anytime now" mode. It was about 5:30 in the morning on March 10th and Cindy announced it was time to go. I called work and told them I wouldn't be in, and I called the Marshall's who immediately came to the house to watch Angela. I drove Cindy to the hospital with plenty of time to spare.

They set her up in the labor room, and she and I went through her breathing techniques we had learned. The doctor came in and checked her dilation and announced that it was time. I hugged Cindy and then walked across the hall into the fathers waiting area and sat down. Fathers were still not allowed in delivery rooms.

Time to pray, I thought, as I made the sign of the cross and closed my eyes to meditate and focus. There was one other fellow in there who was sleeping on one of the couches. I looked at the clock and it read 6:50am.

Within about a half hour I saw the doctor coming down the hall. I got very scared because he was walking very slowly, and I thought it was too soon to have delivered. I stepped into the hallway and looked him straight in the face.

"What happened?" I asked in a worried perplexed tone.

"You have a little boy Mr. Munch, and everyone is fine."

"Oh, Doc," I spouted, and grabbed his upper torso and pulled him into me and squeezed and hugged him. "A Boy! Are you sure?"

"Oh, let go! Yes! A boy!" he repeated.

"Thanks Doc. Thanks man! Can I go back and see them?"

Doc walked me back to Cindy's room. I don't remember much else other than looking into the nursery and seeing him in the warming in-cubator. Wow a son. A healthy son, I thought as my thoughts turned to my Dad. I have to call my Dad.

I walked into the lobby and called my parents' house collect. It was about 7:20 and my Dad hadn't left for work yet. My Mom answered and I gave her and my Dad the news.

"Frederick William Munch is born," I stated firmly as I fought back tears so I could speak. My Mom was ecstatic, and my Dad cried. It was a great day!

CHAPTER **32**

"Not Above the Law"

THE SPRING OF 1981 came and so did a couple crazy stressful situations. I'd be asking God for a lot of direction in the upcoming weeks.

It was one of those things where you try and meet all your neighbors, but the guy next door I never had gotten a chance, and actually never saw him. With the weather, and his and my work schedule, it just hadn't happened. I had gone over and knocked on his door a couple times but could never catch him at home. I knew he was a younger single guy who was gone a lot. That's all I had heard about him from the neighbors. I didn't even know his name.

While working the afternoon 4-12 shift I was driving north on Rt.5 into the town of Cortland which is north of Warren. My radar was reading the oncoming car at 70. That part of Rt.5 turns into a two-lane posted 45mph.

As the car went past, I got turned around and stopped the vehicle. I approached, and upon speaking with the driver I could smell the odor of an alcoholic beverage. I asked the driver how much he had to drink. He admitted he drank a few beers. I asked him to step from the vehicle and perform coordination tests.

I initially had looked at his license after he handed it to me, but I didn't read the address. After he flunked the majority of tests I asked him to perform, I advised him he was under arrest for D.U.I, handcuffed him, and placed him in my car. I had moved his vehicle off the roadway so I wouldn't have to tow it. That saved me time and him money.

I sat down in the car and started running his license. To my dismay the address on the license indicated he was my next door neighbor.

"Do you still live at this address sir?" I asked.

"Yes," he answered.

Could this really be happening? Can I be this unlucky? I have a family I like to think is safe when I'm at work, and now I'm going to have to worry about this guy seeking revenge. I tried to think of a way around this. It doesn't make much difference because I've already placed him under arrest. He's going to have to go with me because I'm not risking my job to cut this guy a break. We don't give breaks for drunk driving. They would fire me in a second if I got caught taking him home. I'm sure he'd tell everybody he knew about how the nice policeman cut him a break and I couldn't trust him not to.

"Yea my new neighbor moved in months ago. He's a State Trooper," said the subject. "Do you know him?" he asked. "His last name is Munch."

I turned my head looking forward and gave it the out the windshield and over the hood stare. After several seconds and without looking back towards him I blurted out, "Yep, I know him. That's me," I said, and then looked at him to see his reaction.

"Your Munch? Oh, not cool, I guess we finally meet," he mumbled.

"Yea looks that way," I said. "Looks that way."

My neighbor was taken to the Patrol Post and processed. I did call a relative for him so he could be picked up, which was protocol for drunks that cooperate. Charges were filed the following day.

Of course, I had to tell Cindy the whole story so she was aware that the neighbor might not be very friendly in the upcoming years.

Summer came and it was a very busy time. Again, the 4p-12a shift proved to be challenging.

It was around 9pm. and the weather was hot and muggy. I was working the east county when I was dispatched to the Belmont Ave. area south of the Interstate just north of the Youngstown city limits. There was a multiple vehicle accident with the report of an ongoing disturbance. I hustled to get there and upon pulling up I noticed two Liberty Twp. police cars blocking the southbound lanes.

Before I could get out of the car a Liberty P.D. officer walked up to my window. "This one is a real cluster," he stated.

"Why, what's up?" I asked.

The Liberty unit explained an off duty local police officer was drunk and smashed into the rear of a stopped car containing five people, and all were injured and being transported. That vehicle stuck the vehicle in front of it, and three people in that car were also going in the ambulance.

As he was telling me all this I had begun to get out of my car and now was standing facing the Liberty officer.

"I know the cop. He's not a bad guy," the Officer stated.

"Yeah. You know what has to happen," I responded. "If he's 19 he's going with me. You guys know that- right?"

"Well you might have some trouble. He's still armed and he's popping off asking about why we called the Staties."

"He's a good friend of yours?" I asked.

"Kinda. Yeah."

"OK. Then while I start my pictures, you get his gun and get him in the back seat of my car. You tell him if he doesn't give you his gun, then I'll have to take it from him, however he wants it to go, but he's giving up that gun." I explained.

As I started to open my trunk for my camera equipment the Liberty officer walked over to the area where this off-duty officer was standing. The intersection is extremely busy and there were about 25-30 onlookers walking around. Plus, several ambulances, the fire department, two wreckers, and several witnesses on scene. It was controlled chaos I thought, as I continued to snap my photo's.

It was hard for me to keep an eye on the subject and the Liberty officer due to all the people and confusion on scene. I could see them conversing, and the subject seemed to be quite animated. He started pacing and flailing his arms in the air while the Liberty officer continued to talk with him. After about five minutes the Liberty officer walked the subject over to my car and had him sit down. The Liberty officer then walked over to me and told me he had the driver's gun but couldn't promise any good behavior forthcoming.

"I've got some measurements to take and I'll be over to talk with him. If you don't mind, make sure he doesn't wander off."

I got some quick measurements and jotted them down on my clipboard pad. About ten more minutes had passed and I could finally go over and deal with this guy. I was hoping for the best, but if it was going to get ugly, I had decided I wasn't going to hold anything back. I'm not going to get hurt trying to be gentle. If this guy is dumb enough to resist, then that's on him.

I opened the rear door of my car and bent over at the waist and looked in and saw the subject seated. Before I could get a word out of my mouth the subject said, "I'm a cop. And you're not going to burn me, are you?"

"I want you to step out. I'm going to pat you down to make sure you don't have any other weapons on you, and I'm going to give you some field tests," I stated.

"You're going to burn another cop? You're a piece of shit," he mumbled and then got louder repeating what he just said.

"You just put eight people in the hospital. I don't care if you're a cop or not," I answered.

I had reached in and grabbed his arm and assisted him out of my vehicle. We were standing face to face. The Liberty Twp. Officer and one of his co-workers were standing towards the front of my car on the opposite side.

"Turn around and put your hands on the car so I can pat you down," I said.

He complied but continued to banter about how I was burning a fellow cop. I patted him down thoroughly and was confident he had no other weapons on him.

"I'm going to ask you to do some coordination tests," I stated as he turned back around and faced me.

"F#** that. I know better. I'm not doing any of your f#**ed-up tests," he said in a raised and angry tone.

"Then you're under arrest for DWI," I stated, as I put my hands on him and turned him around with his back towards me. As I was putting the handcuffs on him, I glanced over and made eye contact with the Liberty unit. I couldn't help but wonder how he would have responded if my drunk would have fought.

I secured him in the back seat by belting him in and we were off to Howland Twp. Police Dept. We took drunks there for Intoxilyzer testing. I knew I would have to contact my Sergeant and let him know what transpired. I was pretty certain that he would back me up on my actions, but I hadn't dealt with anything like this, nor had I heard of any recent arrests of police officers. I remember Jack touching on the subject once, and that no one is above the law. I certainly took no pleasure in what was happening.

The subject whined, whimpered, and threatened the entire 15-minute ride to Howland PD. He asked me where I lived and how many kids I had, all in an attempt to get me angry enough to crack him a couple times. I wasn't going to fall for that one, although he didn't directly threaten my family. If he had, I'm not sure I could have maintained control of myself, and not gotten physical with him like I would have liked to. They were all vailed threats. The more he talked, the better I felt about arresting him.

I had notified the Post to request an officer from Howland PD be on station to serve as a witness to everything that was going on. I wanted to protect myself civilly, and from any lawsuit this guy might decide to suit me for whatever he might dream up. I certainly wasn't going to trust the actions and motives of a drunk cop.

Upon arrival I called Sgt. Carnival the officer in charge and laid it all out to him. Sarge stated he was going to have to call the Post Lieutenant and let him know what was going on. Sarge said he would get back to me shortly.

There wasn't any doubt in my mind that everything I had done was by the book. The Highway Patrol does not play those types of games regardless of who you are. I know years prior to my hiring one of our Troops arrested an Ohio State Senator for DWI. I guess we didn't get a raise for several years after that incident. (Ha) Oh well. If your wrong, you pay the piper. That's all there is to it. It's pretty simple.

Within ten minutes Sarge called me back. The phone chain went all the way to Columbus and back. Sarge knew it went as far up the chain as the Operations Major.

"You got the Lieutenant, Captain, and Major out of bed Bud," stated Sarge as he chuckled.

"They didn't wake up the Colonel?" I asked jokingly.

"They might of Bud. It wasn't a need to know basis for me. I'm just a Sergeant, so I didn't ask, and they didn't say other than the Major was notified. Now if he's still being an asshole, you can go ahead and lock him up. But it would probably be best for inner departmental relations if you can get somebody to pick him up."

"OK Sarge. Will do. Thanks for the support."

The subject refused to take the Intoxilyzer test. He was a bit calmer over the next half hour, and I told him he could call for a ride home for which he did.

I ran into Jack the following day at the Post before work. He looked at me with that crazy grin and just shook his head. "Well Junior your making quite a splash since you been out on your own. You just keep doing what you're doing," he said almost proudly.

"Thanks Coach. Coming from you means a lot to me."

For about six months I was updated by a friend of a friend who was privy to the goings on at the police department my subject was employed by. I was updated on the subject's behavior, and I was extra vigilant in my day to day routine. I had told Cindy bits and pieces of what had happened because I didn't want her to be naïve to the threats made on Officers in their course of duties, but I didn't want her walking around scared either

CHAPTER **33**

"Re-Tread"

THE REMAINDER OF 1981 and into 1982 proved a very difficult time for our marriage. Cindy just couldn't seem to adapt to our new life. It was lonely for her. She just couldn't accept the living away from home.

I was understanding, but I felt she had to realize her mother, father and friends weren't the center of her life. It was Angela, Freddie and me. It seemed no matter how many times I drove her to Erie to visit, or how many times her folks came here, it wasn't enough. I became admittedly bitter. I was trying to keep focused on my job and keep her content, and that wasn't the easiest in the world to accomplish. I didn't go out after work. If I wasn't working, I was always home.

Cindy had left on two occasions for a couple of weeks at a time. Once in January and again in May. Each time I hoped it would recharge her and change her attitude. Visiting certainly helped the situation but she would fall back into what seemed to be a mild depression.

I talked to Jack about the matter. He was my confidant. I was considering divorce and even counseled with an attorney. Both said I should just gut it out. There wasn't much else I could do. I adored those kids and I couldn't imagine not being with them every day.

During those two periods that she left I missed the kids terribly. It was gut wrenching for me. I had to weigh which was more important to me, the job or those kids. There wasn't much of a decision to make. I was going to give up the job and move back to Erie. I talked to my Dad about the whole thing. He got angry with me when I told him I was considering moving back. He always liked Cindy but there wasn't much room for discussion as far as my Dad was concerned. He told me he didn't want to give me the wrong advice, but I knew what he wanted me to do, and that was send her packing.

I decided to talk to my new Post Commander Lt. Nielson about the whole thing. I explained that I felt I had to do everything I could to keep the marriage solvent even if it meant leaving the Patrol. I asked him about possible re-instatement if I left and things didn't work out back in Erie, would I be able to be re-hired? I knew there were a couple of instances where guys had left and came back. They were labeled as "re-treads."

The Lt. stated he couldn't make any promises and I would have to contact him when the time came. He did say he personally would recommend I be considered for reinstatement.

After leaving the Lt.'s office it kind of hit me as to what I was considering doing. Giving up a dream. But I had to feel years from now, if my marriage and my relationship with my kids all turned out to be a failure, I had done everything I could to prevent that. I decided I was going to contact my old boss back home and leave if I could get my job back.

I told Cindy of my decision. She was happy, and I guess I wanted her to sound reluctant, or maybe a bit hesitant, but she wasn't. That made me mad I guess. Was she thinking of herself only? Was this all something God gave me and now I was throwing it away? Or was He taking it from me? Does God do that? Does He take things away from people, or was He giving me this opportunity to keep my family together by moving back to Erie? I was totally lost and confused when I tried to put God into the equation. I continued to wrestle with my spirituality.

I contacted my old boss and explained everything in detail. He contacted the franchise owner who at the time owned all ten of the McDonalds in Erie. Within a couple hours I had an answer and a new position offered. The owner had been wanting to hire a Training Consultant to specifically work with and train the mid and upper management staff. He felt that I would be an asset in that position due to my experience. He was offering more money than I was making when I left in 1978, and substantially more than I was currently.

I put in my two week notice with the Patrol. I was sick. Physically sick to my stomach every time I thought about the Academy and the guys that had become my brothers. But I had to give this an honest effort. I wanted to be able to look in the mirror twenty years from now and say I did all that I could have done.

The next couple of weeks were a blur. Moving, finding a place, meeting my staff, and settling into the new job. It was stressful and I was not happy. I was thankful to have a nice job that paid well, but not happy.

Cindy had gotten her old job back she had since high school. It was a small shop she worked at that made diodes and crystals for electrical components. It didn't pay very well but it was steady employment.

Ironically the Millcreek Police Dept. had announced they would be testing, and I had signed up and took the written test. After all, that was the department I had done my internship with in college. I guess at one time it would have been my first choice. It offered the work I loved and in my hometown. What more could I ask for?

A few weeks had gone by and Cindy and her family were happy we were home. My family also was happy, but I think my parents held a little animosity towards Cindy. I didn't want that. I didn't want to look like a martyr, so whenever I was around my parents I put on a happy face, but they weren't stupid.

My job was challenging and fun. I had about 40 mid and upper management people to train and keep evaluations on. I was busy all the time. The owner was a great guy, and I considered my boss one of my good friends. I felt it wasn't the end of the world, but I knew a big part of me was back in Ohio and would always be there.

It was in late May 82' and I had been at the new job for about six weeks. One night while watching TV with the wife, she turned to me and stated, "I don't know if we made the right decision?"

"What?" I responded as I felt my stomach tighten.

Cindy stammered, "I don't know. It's not the same. It's not like it used to be, home I mean."

"Home is never the same once you leave and come back. People change. Priorities change. I think that's normal," I said, as I wanted to

177

not make it look like her statement just kicked me in the gut.

"Is it working full time and the kids too much?" I asked.

"No, it's not that. I just miss a few things about the life we had there, and I miss seeing you happy," she said.

"Is it that obvious? I can be happy here," I responded.

"It's obvious to me. After experiencing some of the things you've done the last couple years, how could you ever be happy doing what you're doing now?"

I could feel myself starting to get angry and frustrated. I had to slowly take a couple of deep breaths.

"Well that's something I wish you might of thought of before we left."

"I know. It's easy to look back and say could have or should have," Cindy said, as I could see her eyes welling up trying to hold back tears.

"OK. We don't look back. Remember, forward only. No rear-view mirror in our car," I said.

"Well what do you want to do?" she asked.

"Seriously? I'd go back in a second, but God knows where they'd send me. It could be Cincinnati eight hours from Erie," I explained. "You can't handle being an hour and a half away from your mommy. How would you be able to deal with eight hours?" I said sarcastically.

"I don't care. We made a mistake. I mean, I made a mistake. It doesn't matter where. No one here is the same. Everyone has changed."

"Well did you ever consider maybe it's me and you that have changed and not everyone else?" I asked. "We've matured. We have a bigger family. Our priorities are different than they were a few years ago. That's why you don't feel the same being back home," I tried to explain.

I actually felt sorry for her. But all I knew, I was "bustin." I could barely control the intense glee I was feeling, along with being angry, and trying to sit still on the couch. I didn't want her to see how happy I was because I had done a pretty damn good job of acting kind of happy the last couple months, or so I thought.

"Here's the issue for me Cindy," I said as gently but intensely as I knew how. "If we go back to Ohio, and after some time you decide you want to move back to Erie again, you're going to be going back by yourself. That's it for me. I've given this my best shot."

My mind was racing. I was trying to rationalize it all. Cindy had hugged me and gone to bed. I'll call the Lieutenant tomorrow. How long have I been gone? Six weeks, I think. Will I have to go back through and wait for another Academy class? No, I don't think so. I think it's just a refresher couple of weeks at the Academy just for liability reasons. I wonder where they will send me? Wait, what if they don't take me back? I wonder if I'd have a chance to go back to Warren? That would be great. I sure do miss it.

I sat there for over an hour speechless with all these thoughts scampering through my head. I was staring straight ahead like I had done so many times from the front seat of my patrol car. High anxiety I thought. I'll call the Lieutenant because there's no decision to make here. It's a done deal if they'll take me back.

It was kind of a sleepless night. Morning came and I had gone to work and waited until 9 am. I called the Lieutenant from my office. The conversation was positive. He genuinely seemed happy that I wanted to come back, although his biggest concern was, had I given it enough time back in Erie? I didn't know how to respond to that other than to tell him I was just going with my gut. I summed up what the wife had said. I told him I was confident I was making the right decision. He stated he would contact the Captain and go from there.

Later that afternoon the Lieutenant called. He instructed me to call the Captain first thing in the morning.

I called the Captain, the District 4 Commander the next morning. We had a short positive talk. His concern was the same as the Lieutenant's. He stated he was going to call the personnel Major in Columbus and would get back to me sometime soon.

The following morning the Captain called and told me the Major and Colonel were optimistic about having me come back but wanted to interview me. The Captain had made arrangements for me to report to the Academy the upcoming Monday at 8am for retraining. Depending on how I performed he thought I would be there for about a week. At the end of the week I would interview with the Colonel and receive my duty assignment.

The next few days dragged by. I had told my boss I'd be leaving. It was hard to do considering how well they had treated me, and it was only a few days' notice.

The following Monday I drove to Columbus early in the morning and arrived at the Academy. It was a glorious feeling, and I knew I was where I belonged.

The week went fast with reviewing case law updates, firearms qualification, and yes, a physical agility test, but no, no car push. It was the usual torture test, a timed mile and a half run, pushups and sit-ups.

I arrived at GHQ on Friday morning in full uniform and had an interview with the Colonel. It was almost a father to son advise exchange on marriage and life in general. He was a guy that I'd take a bullet for. A man's man for sure. Wow, I thought, five years has gone by in an eyeblink, and so much has changed in my life. Somebody has been watching over me.

"Munch were going to send you to Ashtabula," the Colonel stated. "Is that too close to home, or would it be better to send you farther away?"

Ashtabula is the closest Patrol Post to Erie. It's about a 35-minute drive to my in-laws' home.

"I don't know the answer to that sir," I responded. "The wife knows that wherever I'm stationed, I'll be staying. I'm sure she'll be happy that you chose to send me to Ashtabula."

With that the interview ended and I was sworn in. I left Columbus that afternoon and drove home a happy guy.

For the next month I commuted to work from Erie to Ashtabula until we found a place in Jefferson, which is few miles south of the Post.

CHAPTER **34**

"Post-4 Ashtabula"

THE ASHTABULA POST is one of the six Posts in District 4. Ashtabula's manpower was substantially less than a Post like Warren's due to call volume. Warren had 22 uniformed officers; Ashtabula had 16. There were many shifts worked at Ashtabula where there were only two Troop's out to cover the entire county.

The summer of 1982 was challenging in leaning the new area. It's the largest county in the state. Back-up and getting help in tough situations in a hurry, was kind of a crap shoot. Help could be as far as 30 miles away. We depended quite a bit on backup coming from the Sherriff's Department.

Ashtabula was a fun area to patrol. It had everything Warren had but on a little smaller scale. I can honestly say there wasn't anyone I worked with, or worked for, that I didn't like. There were a few guys where personalities may have clashed and a couple of men had strange senses of humor, but for the most part there was general respect and admiration between officers.

There were a couple older Troops that should have been promoted long ago in my opinion. These guys were really dedicated to their jobs and their life's work. They were good people to be around and excellent role models for me.

1983 started off with great news. In March my wife informed me she was expecting sometime in November. We were both very excited and had decided three was going to be our limit.

Activity on the job got pretty intense. I had two instances where I was assaulted attempting to make DWI arrests. One was no big deal because I had backup arrive after a short wrestling match. The subject was pretty drunk and decided he didn't want to come with me. The second was a bit more involved.

I had stopped a car on Myers Rd. just east of Geneva, about 2 am for weaving. Upon talking to the lone occupant, I determined he had been drinking and exhibited all the classic signs of someone that was under the influence. I had asked him to step out of his vehicle to perform coordination tests. He was verbally abusive but complied with my request. Once at the rear of his vehicle while standing in between our vehicles he stated he wasn't taking any tests. He stated that I should get back in my patrol car and drive away, otherwise "I'm going to kick your ass."

Flashbacks popped into my head of Jack telling me how we had to let people vent, until the venting became threatening or disrespectful to the uniform. I considered that statement to be both. I advised the subject he was under arrest and to turn around and put his hands on the car. He started to turn but then threw a straight right. I ducked and the punch hit the top of my Stetson which smashed it down over my eyes. As I was trying to pull it off my head so I could see, he continued to punch, but I was able to block punches and return a right hook that landed on his lower left jaw. It knocked him backwards and up on the trunk of his vehicle. He rolled off the right side of the trunk and landed headfirst on the asphalt splitting open his left eye above the eyebrow. Blood spurted wildly as I sat on him and got him handcuffed. I called the Post for an ambulance and my Sergeant in charge.

Once at the hospital the subject took twelve stitches to close the cut over his eye, and I took two stitches to close the laceration on my right hand.

The driver was from Tennessee and appeared to be a self-proclaimed red neck. Or at least that's what he wanted me to think with his southern drawl and threat to kick my ass if I didn't let him go when I stopped him. I wondered later how many times he had pulled the same thing on officers in the past and got away with it. I'm guessing it had worked for him before. Unfortunately for him he ran into someone that has always believed that you only have to be a coward one time to be a coward for the rest of your life.

In the morning, the Ashtabula newspaper got wind of what happened, and they read my report. They printed the incident on the front page of the local section. The headline in the newspaper read, "Munch punch lands, one suspect in jail." There was a detailed account of what had transpired.

I had these two assaults happen fairly close together and I was worried when my Lieutenant called me in to ask me if I was having trouble reasoning with people. My Lieutenant at the time was kind of a laid-back type guy, and I think he thought I might be too aggressive. I assured him that I wasn't some rogue officer out beating up the general public. It was my first experience with working for someone that I wasn't sure if he'd stand behind me in the future.

The summer of 1983 was busy. The area draws a lot of tourism because of Lake Erie. Traffic on Interstate 90 is always busy, especially commercial traffic being a main trucking route between Detroit, Cleveland and New York. I learned that Ashtabula County was a busy place to work.

There are also a lot of motorcycle clubs and gangs in the area, mainly around Geneva and Geneva on the Lake. Motorcycle accidents weren't uncommon. And usually it involved driving off the roadway and striking a pole, tree, or ditch.

One night while working the Geneva area I was southbound on Rt. 534 south of Geneva on the Lake. My radar went off and I checked the oncoming northbound vehicle well in excess of the speed limit. The vehicle was a motorcycle and it was going so fast my radar flashed and the bike went past me in just a couple seconds. I didn't have time to lock in the speed on the radar, although I saw the initial flash on the screen was upward of 80mph. I looked in my rear-view mirror as I slowed to attempt to turn around and pursue the bike. I could see it's taillight as it went past, and it was already at quite a distance. By the time I got turned around the bike was nowhere to be seen. It seemed strange to me that it had just kind of vanished. It's a pretty long straightaway in that area prior to a slight curve to the left, and I thought I'd be able to keep an eye on the taillight, but it was gone.

I drove northbound quickly in an attempt to possibly close the distance and try and catch up, but I figured he either turned somewhere or just drove out of sight. When I got to the city limits, I turned around to go back southbound. I was driving slower, and as I passed by the first slight curve in the road something caught my eye in the darkness off to my left. I slowed down and stopped, then backed up and used my spotlight to light up the area off the east side of the road. The glimmer that caught my eye looked to be a piece of a fender or chrome lying about 30 ft. off the road in a field east of the ditch that runs adjacent to the roadway. I pulled off the roadway and activated my overhead lights. I exited my car and walked across the ditch and started up the slight bank on that side. As I continued, I walked up on a large tree that sits off to the right of the curve. As I got closer and shined my light on the base of the tree, I saw a person who appeared to be sitting upright. I hurried forward and got around the tree so I could see exactly what was happening. There I found a large white male sitting up with his back leaning on the base of the tree. He was big and burly and had leathers on and was obviously a biker. He was barely breathing, and his eyes were open. I realized he had hit the tree and kind of just stuck to it.

I used my portable radio and advised the Post I had come upon a motorcycle accident and to send a squad immediately. I knelt down beside him and shined the flashlight in his face. He blinked as I said, "You're going to be ok. I have an ambulance coming."

He moaned in an attempt to speak but he couldn't. It was apparent he hit the tree with his chest and torso and just slid down the tree. His chest was seriously damaged because it appeared to be caved in a couple of inches. His breathing was labored and there was blood seeping out of the corner of his mouth and had soaked his beard.

"Can you hear me? You're going to be ok. I have an ambulance coming. Hang on. Try and breath. Keep breathing," I said, as I could feel the emotions welling up inside me. I thought, this poor guy has a family, but I don't think they're ever going to talk to him again. It was very sad.

I kept telling him to hang on, but it was obvious he was dying, and I felt so helpless. I got closer to him and put my arm across the back of his shoulders in an attempt to hug and console him a bit.

A couple more minutes went by. "Just a couple more minutes and we'll have you out of here. You're going to be ok," was the last thing I said to him as I patted his shoulder and held his hand.

He blinked again and ever so slightly shook his head as if to say, no. Then his jaw dropped slightly, and his breathing stopped.

I could do nothing for him. CPR wasn't possible because of the condition of the bones in his chest. All I could do was hold him. Comfort was all I could offer. The ambulance arrived and I was relieved.

The crazy thing about it all was while taking the photographs after he was transported, I walked up on the gas tank that had separated from the chassis and landed about 150 ft. from the tree he struck. In English style Gothic writing, the inscription painted on the tank read "Until Death Do Us Part."

There was a dark humid haze like fog in the air, almost a wetness in the air as I breathed, and it was the eeriest feeling I had ever experienced. I knew there was nothing for me to fear standing out in that field, but for some reason I felt nervous. As a slight wind blew across the field the fog started shifting ever so slowly. It swirled up and around me and I felt a presence that I could not explain, and my mind played tricks on my eyes, and I saw a silhouette of a large man about 30 ft away, and it appeared he was holding his hand up as to be waving goodbye.

"Holy shit!" I said right out loud, as I seriously felt all the hair on my head and body stand straight up as I pivoted and started a slow sprint towards the roadway. I got in my car and turned on the dome light and looked at myself in my rear-view mirror to see if my hair was still dark brown. I wouldn't have been surprised if I would have seen all my hair turned white. Wow.

I later spoke to one of the ambulance attendants who told me they were pretty sure he was dead when they loaded him. There wasn't any doubt in my mind he died in my arms. As worthless as I felt for not being able to help him, at least he didn't die alone.

Another notable crash that summer was again on SR. 534 in the same area south of Geneva on the Lake.

One of the new Troopers who was going through coach/pupil

training was assigned to me for the shift. His coach had called off sick, so Trooper Keith Patterson rode shotgun with me for the evening.

It was the 3-11 shift around 9:30 pm., and again while driving south on SR. 534 I checked the speed of a northbound vehicle well in excess of the posted limit. As the vehicle passed me, I activated my overhead lights and started to turn around to catch up to the vehicle. Apparently, the driver saw me turning around and sped up in an attempt to get away. I got turned around and had closed the distance between our vehicles, but the vehicle was still way out in front of me. As I got within a few hundred feet of the vehicle it swerved sharply to the right and then left. The driver then lost control and slid right again, and off the right side of the roadway striking a driveway culvert. Upon hitting the culvert, it caused the vehicle to shoot up in the air and simultaneously roll while airborne. At about 18 ft in the air the vehicle struck a tree head-on which literally tore the vehicle in two. The front half dropped almost immediately straight down landing in the ditch. The rear half landed directly in front of me on the roadway in the northbound lane. Upon striking the pavement there were three females that were ejected in different directions.

In order to avoid striking the rear half of the vehicle and/or any of the occupants that were lying on the road, I had to lock up my brakes and steer left, fanning the brakes and changing direction as I slid past it all.

Somehow, I missed the vehicle and all occupants and came to rest with my front wheels off the left side of the roadway into the ditch about 200 ft. past the wreckage. I backed up and got out of the ditch quickly and drove my vehicle in reverse past the whole mess and stopped. I blocked the road so no other vehicles could get past, so none of the victims would be run over. It was quite a driving experience, and quite a traumatic thing to witness. Once we came to a stop I looked over to my right at Keith. I noted his fingers had been dug into the dash, his mouth was somewhat hanging open, and he was staring straight ahead.

"Keith, get the first aid kit while I call for a squad," I said loudly. Keith never moved.

"Keith, get the first aid kit," again I repeated. Again a few seconds went by, but he stared straight ahead.

"Keith!" I yelled loudly.

Finally, he turned his head towards me and said very softly and slowly, "That was quite a piece of driving. How did we miss everything?"

"Shit, I don't know, but we did. I'm going to see how many people we have here," I advised Keith as I exited the car. He got the first aid kit and we attempted to help the three injured females lying on the road.

Ambulances arrived quickly and saved all the females. All three front seat passengers were males and were in the front half of the vehicle that landed in the ditch. All were seriously injured, and the driver eventually died from his injuries.

I kept God very busy that summer. There was no logical explanation for me missing those injured people. If I would have plowed into the back half of that vehicle, I would have faced manslaughter charges if anyone died.

I felt that some higher power was there for me that night. And I felt the same way the night the motorcyclist died. God didn't want him to die alone.

CHAPTER **35**

Miracle Baby

IN AUGUST I was selected to work the Ohio State Fair. Each Post across the state selects one or two Troopers to travel to Columbus and work the State Fair for a two-week period. It is an honor to be selected and I was a bit surprised because I had only been at the Ashtabula Post for a year, and I knew there were other people wanting to go.

I drove to the Academy and arrived the afternoon of August 5.th The Academy is where all the working Troopers stay during the Fair. The Fair started the following day. The schedule calls for work shifts of twelve hours on and twelve hours off.

On the morning of the second day I was notified by my supervisor that my wife had been taken to Ashtabula General Hospital and was experiencing cramping pertaining to the pregnancy. She wasn't due until November, so she was only about six months along.

I was told the Major didn't want me driving, and to expedite matters had arranged for me to be flown up to Ashtabula in one of our fixed wing aircraft. The Patrol has an aviation section assigned to various tasks in areas of the state. The pilots are Troopers assigned to that Division.

We took off that morning and arrived shortly before noon. Upon arriving a nurse met me in the lobby and explained Cindy had experienced cramping, and her father drove her to Ashtabula so she could be seen by her doctor. Cindy and the kids were staying at her father's house in Erie while I was in Columbus. My parents had been notified by Cindy's dad, and both my parents had driven in from Erie to Ashtabula to be with Cindy.

I was still in uniform from the trip because I didn't have a car to go home and change. As I pushed the button on the elevator to go upstairs a million thoughts were bouncing around in my overloaded brain.

I hate those small single engine planes, I thought, as the elevator door closed. That stressed me out bouncing around in that little plane, but the Patrol is a first-class organization to fly me up here. They didn't want me driving knowing my mind would be somewhere else. What an awesome outfit I work for. I continued to think to myself; I hope this isn't a repeat of the baby we lost. Cindy's pregnancy with Freddie was so perfect. Why is she having trouble again now? "Com'on God," I said out loud. Be with us now please sir, I thought to myself. Don't let this happen again please, not again.

The elevator doors opened, and I exited and walked down the hallway towards her room. This is a Sunday, I reminded myself. Not too many staff people here.

I entered Cindy's room. She was lying on the bed just like the last time. I couldn't help having that memory. My Mom and Dad were seated on either side of the bed. I hugged them all. Cindy explained the same symptoms had occurred earlier this morning except her water didn't break like before. She had felt no wetness but was scared enough to get to the hospital.

"Good Hun," I'm glad you got here. Has the doctor been in?"

"No. The nurse said the doctor wants me to rest and he'd see me first thing tomorrow morning," Cindy explained.

"What? He's not coming in to examine you now?" I asked.

"No. The nurse said she talked to him and as long as I'm comfortable and stay off my feet that's all they want to do today."

"Did you tell them about losing a baby before?" I asked.

"Yes, I told them," Cindy answered, with her voice trembling from her fear.

"That's Bullshit, that friggin doctor is going to come in here now," I bantered as my Dad looked at me with that "Oh shit," expression.

"What Dad? You don't think the doctor should have examined her?" I said to my Dad in an emotional tone. "I'm pissed. Just because it's

189

Sunday he's decided he's not coming in. That's bullshit incompetence."

"Well yeah, but being Sunday, you know they're not going to come in unless they think there's an emergency," Dad said.

'"This is an emergency as far as I'm concerned," I said as I turned and continued to pace. "I'm going to get the nurse."

I walked down to the nurse's station. I explained my concern and how I felt the doctor should have examined her by now. I asked her to call him. She was polite but initially refused. I persisted and after a lot of coaxing she finally agreed. She called him and asked if I could speak with him.

He agreed to speak with me. I was very polite and apologetic for "bothering" him. I explained I felt he had to understand my concern considering losing a baby in the past. He assured me he felt confident she would be fine since she was not spotting. For today he would like her to rest and be monitored, and he'd see her in the morning.

I told him I disagreed with his opinion, and I would speak to Cindy about transferring her to St. Vincent's hospital in Erie if he wasn't going to come in. With that our conversation ended.

I thanked the nurse and started walking back to Cindy's room. I was angry and getting more frustrated and worried.

I got back to the room and Cindy had begun to cry. She was scared, and I felt helpless. I told her about my call to the doctor, and I was considering moving her to St. Vincent's. My Dad asked if I thought the doctor would release her? I told him it didn't matter. I didn't care if he wouldn't.

"Well you can't just take her out of here," my Dad said in an almost joking tone.

"I can't? Watch me," I responded. "I have a couple calls to make and if I can arrange a transport that just might happen."

"Oh, no. You're not going to take her against the doctors' recommendations, can you?"

"I don't care Dad. I've been through this before and I'll never go through it again."

Cindy continued to cry. My heart was breaking but the anger in me kept me focused and functional. I prayed, and I asked the Almighty if I was doing the right thing. I mumbled to myself, "I know I haven't always been a believer Lord, but if I'm doing something wrong here please stop me somehow."

I went downstairs and used a hospital phone and called a friend who owned an ambulance service in the southern part of the county. I explained everything to him. He was reluctant to move any patient without a doctor's order or approval. I asked him if he could provide a nurse or an EMT. He told me he would have the appropriate personnel available but was indecisive as to whether he was going to assist me. He tried to talk me out of it, but he knew how serious I was, and after a few minutes agreed to the transport. I explained I'd call him back when I was sure on what time.

I went back to Cindy's room and filled everyone in on my plan. My Mother was silent. I think she was praying. (Ha) My Dad sat down and just looked at me with those cold steel blue eyes and said, "Whatever you decide I'll support." Cindy didn't say much. She always trusted my decisions, but on this one I wasn't sure.

I decided I'd call the doctor one more time and ask him to come in. If he refuses, then we're going to Erie, plain and simple with no other decision to be made.

I went back to the nurse's station. About 40 minutes had passed since calling the doctor. I told the nurse I wanted to call him again. She refused, but I told her that if the doctor refuses to come in, or if she refuses to call him, I was going to have my wife moved to Erie.

She called him, but this time he wasn't so accommodating. He explained again since there was no spotting, he wasn't exceptionally worried. Then he admitted he had company and was having dinner.

That was it for me. "Doc, your fired. My wife is going to be seen in Erie today," I spouted and hung up the phone.

I turned to the nurse who had been standing off to my right listening to the conversation. "Please get my wife ready to leave," I said.

"Oh, Mr. Munch you have to think this through. I can't remove her IV without the doctor requesting it."

"I just fired the doctor. If you don't remove it and do whatever is needed, then I'm going to do it myself," I stated.

Almost with a smirk and a challenging tone she said," Oh, you can't remove an IV."

"I'm going to," I said, as I started walking back to Cindy's room.

Then I remembered I had to call my friend to tell him when to be here for transport. I stuck my head in the room and told Cindy we would be leaving. I then walked downstairs and called. I told him the doctor refused to examine her and Erie was our only option.

I walked back upstairs and into Cindy's room. The nurse along with two other nurses were talking to Cindy. I asked the nurse to remove the IV. She refused. I asked the second nurse and she also refused. I didn't bother to ask the third. I walked over to the left side of the bed and slowly began tearing the tape off Cindy's arm. I put my fingers on the plastic part of the syringe that was stuck in her arm.

"Wait," the nurse said. "I'll do it."

She stepped around to my side as I stepped back, and she removed the IV.

"Thank you," I said.

"I can't help you move her," she said.

"That's ok. I'll wheel the whole bed down," I said as I started to push and steer the bed through the doorway.

Down the hall I pushed her and into the elevator. There was room for all of us as we squeezed in.

I looked over at my Dad as the elevator doors closed and the downward motion began. He had a look of exasperated disbelief on his face.

The doors opened and we were on the ground floor. As I pushed the bed out through the front lobby doors, I could see the ambulance coming up the driveway. The ambulance pulled up and the EMT helped me move Cindy to the gurney, and we lifted her into the squad. I jumped in the back and we were off to Erie.

I had asked my friend to call ahead to let staff at St. Vincent's know we were in route. Upon arrival Cindy was admitted and examined immediately by a doctor. After the initial exam the doctor explained he was afraid of internal bleeding, and he was going to continually check her.

When we arrived at St. Vincent's we had requested Cindy be put in Dr. Palmer's care. He was our pediatrician for Angela. It had gotten very late in the evening, and we were told Dr. Palmer had arrived. Cindy was so happy to see him.

Dr. Palmer advised us that he wanted to check the placenta for blood because he felt this could be more serious than first thought. He asked me to step out of the room while he and a nurse did the exam.

I stepped out in the hall and after only a couple minutes he came out and put his hand on my shoulder. He had a long probe in his hand, and I could see the tip had blood on it. He looked very concerned.

"She's been bleeding inside. We're going to do an emergency caesarian Fred. I don't think the baby will survive, but we have to act quickly in order to save your wife," he said, and started running away from me to the back-hall stairwell to get to the OR.

I was in total disbelief. I went totally numb. All I remember is a nurse walked up beside me and grabbed my hand and started pulling me down the hall. I could see Cindy's bed being wheeled out and going in the other direction with two nurses and an orderly heading for the elevator.

"What the hell is going on?" I asked the nurse who was leading me by the hand.

"They're taking her to the OR and I'm going to get you prepped so you can be there," she said.

"Ok," I responded. I wasn't sure what she just said. I was having trouble processing all of what was happening. Was this real? I gripped the nurse's hand and followed her into a prep area that looked like a small kitchen with several sinks.

"Here put this on, quickly," she said as she lifted the gown over my head and pulled it down over my torso. "Hold this mask while I tie it in the back," she stated.

I don't think five minutes went by from the time the doctor told me what was happening until the time the nurse pushed me through the OR doors. Directly in front of me was a gurney with Cindy lying on it. There were several people scurrying around her, and Dr. Palmer appeared from my left peripheral view. He had a scalpel in his hand, and in one motion sliced Cindy's lower abdomen from hip to hip. I saw him reach in as blood ran over the side of Cindy's torso. He said something to one of the other doctors and pulled the fetus out and handed it to him. The whole thing took less than 10 seconds. I watched the other doctor run over to a sink and start to work on the baby. I looked back at Cindy as Dr. Palmer was pulling at something, and intensely speaking to the nurses giving them direction.

The nurse that had been standing beside me the entire time asked me if I was ok and if I needed to sit down. I didn't respond. I just shook my head as the other doctor announced from the sink area that the baby was breathing. I don't know if he said that for my benefit, but those words made me very hopeful.

My nurse then said it was time to leave the OR as she led me by the hand again back into a waiting room where I took off the gown and sat down.

As I sat there by myself, I was trying to put everything I just witnessed in perspective. I could feel my eyes welling up and then tears started running down the side of my face.

What just happened, I thought? Was the baby alive? Is Cindy OK?

I couldn't sit. I stood up but immediately had to sit back down. I felt dizzy. The stress of the last 24 hrs. was catching up to me.

As I was wiping the tears from my face, I felt a sense of calmness come over me. God must be here with me, I thought. There's no way to deal with all of this and not feel that God is in control. He must be watching.

Then at that moment Dr. Palmer stepped into the room. His worried expression I had seen before was gone. He was all business. He explained Cindy's condition as satisfactory and going to the ICU for now. "The baby we'll monitor closely, but for a 6-month fetus he's doing ok," he said.

"Thank you so much Doc. You saved them both. And I have another little boy," I said as the tears started again.

"Well, I'm glad you got her here when you did, or it would have been a much different outcome. She's lost a lot of blood," he explained. "If we would have waited another hour or two the baby would have been lost, and likely your wife too."

"So, she's been bleeding all along?" I asked.

"Yes, the placenta was torn and was slowly hemorrhaging. That's why she was cramping. It's a miracle the baby didn't drown in all that blood. It's really a miracle, it truly is," he said, as he turned and left the room.

I dropped to my knees. I could feel the back of my legs quivering. "My God," I spoke out loud. "My God, thank you. Thank you," I whispered.

I sat back down in the chair for a few minutes to rest and compose myself. Within a short time, I was able to see Cindy and the little one.

After seeing Cindy, I walked over to the nursery. I could see the baby in the incubator. Thoughts of the day we lost Jason racked my mind. This baby was substantially larger than Jason but still very small I thought to myself. This one is in God's hands now for Him to stay healthy.

I left the hospital and drove to my mother's house and crashed. I hadn't gotten much sleep since Saturday. It felt good to lay down, and the feeling that all worked out well was amazing. I prayed myself to sleep.

I woke up late morning and drove to the hospital to see Cindy. I walked into the room and I could see she'd been crying. "What's wrong?'" I asked.

"The pediatrician was in. He said the baby won't hold anything down. He keeps throwing everything up," Cindy explained.

"Well that could be anything," I said. "I had colic when I was a baby," I said trying to make her feel better.

"He said they're going to run some tests right now and they should know more soon," Cindy said.

"Ok. Well as my Dad always says; "Let's stay in the buggy. No one needs to jump out yet."

I wanted to be positive because after all that's happened nothing more could go wrong, could it?

Several hours passed and it was now late afternoon around 4 pm. Cindy was physically feeling better and we were hoping they'd bring the baby in soon for us to feed and hold.

Surprisingly Dr. Palmer stepped into the room. He had that look I saw before prior to the emergency cesarean. He didn't have to say a word before I asked, "What's wrong?"

"The tests show the baby has a malformation of its esophagus. It's not attached to the stomach. That's why he throws everything up because the food has no place to go," he explained with concern in his voice.

Again, I could feel the numbness start at the top of my head and slowly start to travel down my body.

"What the hell else can happen?" I exclaimed. "Can they fix it somehow Doc?"

"Not here. He'd have to go to Pittsburgh. It's experimental surgery when it's on a child this small. Three pounds, the survival rate isn't good. At Children's Hospital I know they have been successful in some stomach malformations, but this one is very rare. You may want to consider the financial devastation this is going to have on your family if your insurance won't cover it," Doc explained.

"You mean just let him go? Let him die?" I asked with my voice cracking.

"I'm just giving you all options. I'm concerned for you. You have two other children you're going to have to provide for, and this could ruin you financially, if it even works at all. I just want you aware, that's all," he said.

"I appreciate that sir, but if there is any chance to save this kid then that's what we're going to do. I don't care if we have to live in a cardboard box. Please make whatever arrangements need to be made," I said as I looked at Cindy for her approval.

She just nodded, and that meant for me to do whatever. The nod was good.

Dr. Palmer set up the helicopter ride to Pittsburgh and had one of the hospital staff come up and give me driving directions to Pittsburgh Children's Hospital. By 7:30 pm I was driving south on IS-79 and the helicopter was landing on the roof of St. Vincents to pick the baby up when I left.

I drove to Pittsburgh and arrived there just before 10 pm. I was instructed to meet the attending surgeon in the ER upon my arrival.

I met the doctor as scheduled. He was a very distinguished older man, almost old enough to retire I thought, which raised my level of confidence due to his experience. He explained he had viewed the CAT scan and felt guardedly confident he could perform the attachment successfully. He stated they hadn't done anything exactly like this but had several experiences with similar problems on infants. He explained this type of malformation is extremely rare and requires microsurgery in repairing the esophagus and attaching it after making an opening at the top of the stomach. The doctor escorted me to an overnight waiting room that had a few cot's set up. He suggested I try and rest as he was going to start the surgery within the hour. He said when the surgery was over, probably around 4 to 5 hours, he would come back and brief me.

There were a couple other people already asleep in the waiting area. I lied down and tried to doze off, but I don't think I did for more than twenty minutes at a time. Of course, I prayed on and off throughout the night.

Around 4:30 am. I saw the doctor standing in the doorway of the waiting room. I jumped off the cot and walked over to him. He had a smile on his face.

"All went as well as it could have," he stated.

"Oh, great Doc. Everything got put back together, so he won't have any problems?" I asked.

"If all goes well, he'll be very normal. Healing is the key. If everything heals correctly there should be no immediate issues."

"How long will he be here in the hospital?" I asked.

"That all depends on his weight gain. I'd like to think he'll be out of here in a few weeks," he said. "He needs to get up to 5 or 6 lbs. before we'd consider letting him go home."

I thanked him several times and gave him a hug. I was so relieved and happy that his chances of survival were promising.

I had gone back to work, and on my days off drove to Pittsburgh to see baby Robert and Cindy. She had driven back and forth from Erie while staying at her Dad's house. When I would visit, I'd meet Cindy at the hospital, and we'd spend the day together. Just the three of us.

Three weeks later he was released, and it was a great day. We finally were all together back home in Ashtabula.

CHAPTER 36

"Trooper of the Year"

THANKSGIVING OF 1983 was very special for me. I had a lot to be thankful for! The Holidays came and went and we entered 1984.

A Highway Patrol tradition is for the Trooper's at each Post to vote for whom they felt should be recognized as being exceptional in their work throughout the previous year. The "Trooper of the Year" at the Post then competes with the Troopers who were selected at the additional five remaining Posts in each District for the "District Trooper of the Year Award." Then the 10 District award winners compete for the "State Trooper of the Year."

At the end of January, a secret ballot vote is taken and submitted to the Post Commander. Sometime in February it is announced as to who was selected by his/her peers. I was very surprised and so very honored to have been selected for Post Trooper of the year for 1983. It was quite an honor considering I had been stationed at Ashtabula for only about a year and a half. I felt there was one or two other guys that were more deserving. I was then in contention for the District Trooper of the Year which was announced in March. The award went to a Trooper at the Chardon Post who I knew to be a really good guy, and I was happy for him.

In April while stopping a vehicle on the Interstate for speeding, I met a man who identified himself as a Secret Service Agent assigned to Cleveland. We struck up a short conversation and he requested I call him if I was interested in applying to his agency. He stated the Secret

Service likes to hire in service policemen that have several years of experience, and he felt I would have a good chance of being hired.

Wow, the Secret Service, I thought. That would really be reaching the top of the Law Enforcement field. I don't know if I would like that type of duty, but I felt it was worth exploring.

About two weeks went by and I had decided I was happy where I was and maybe in the future I would reconsider. Then I received a call from the Agent. He wanted to come to my residence and talk with me and my wife about the possibilities. I thought why not?

He arrived a few days later and we spoke at the house for about an hour. He had me basically convinced to submit my application until I asked him about the starting pay and subsequent duty stations. He explained the starting pay was slightly above 13 thousand a year, and you are required to live in one of the "Big 7" cities for your first two-year duty assignment.

I couldn't believe the starting pay was so low. And the cost of living in these areas is way higher than most places. I told him I couldn't put my family through that kind of lifestyle. He understood but wanted me to realize after the first two years the pay jumps are more significant. I ended up deciding I didn't think I'd be interested unless the pay was at least what I was making here on the Highway Patrol. I labored over that decision for about another month, but I finally called the Agent and advised him I was going to pass on the offer.

In May I received a call one evening from my Dad. He wanted to let me know that a Sergeant from the Millcreek Police Department called him and was looking for me. He said the Sergeant explained my name had come up on their list and they would be hiring soon. He requested I call him.

The following day I called the Department and spoke to Sgt. Bill Stanton. I had met Bill during my internship there while attending Mercyhurst College. It was kind of surreal for me. All had been going so well in my life the past few months and I had given leaving the Patrol a lot of thought when I was approached by the Secret Service agent. I basically decided I was pretty happy where I was even though I knew if I wanted to advance my career and take promotions, I'd be doing a lot of moving. That was the way the Patrol handled their promotions. It was very rare to be promoted and stay where you were.

Then I looked at it from a different perspective. Had my newfound faith and belief actually started to reward me? Had all these good things been happening because I had become so much more of a believer? Was this new job possibility a gift? After all, Millcreek police department had been one of the primary goals from day one. The number one family benefit was I would never have to move again. My career advancement wouldn't require any relocations. Wasn't that the big issue in 1982 when I left the Patrol was that Cindy missed home? This would be a trip home and satisfy my career goals all in one.

Sgt. Stanton asked that I take a few days to think about it because if I was interested, he would like to set up an interview with me and the Chief of Police. I thanked him and told him I'd let him know soon after speaking with my family.

I guess I was happy but guarded. I knew leaving the Patrol again was definitely burning a bridge. There would be no chance of ever going back after leaving a second time. I really had grown to love OSP. There was no better organization in the Country as far as I was concerned. And look at all they had done for me. The next couple of days was very stressful and emotional for me in trying to decide. It was like contemplating the loss of a loved one.

I called Sgt. Stanton and advised him I'd like to interview for the position. I felt I should at least go ahead with an interview and decide later if the position is offered. Sarge set the interview up and I was to come in a few days later.

The day of the interview came, and I drove to Erie and met with Sgt. Stanton and the Chief. The interview was much more informal than I thought it would be, and as the interview ended, I was offered the job. I was kind of caught off guard because I thought they were interviewing several candidates for the one position, and it would take time for them to decide on who they would hire.

The Chief explained I had come up on the list, and with my prior internship and my almost six years of experience they felt confident in offering me the job now. I was somewhat stunned, but I didn't want to show any indecisiveness, so I accepted. They shook my hand and told me I'd be starting sometime during the first week of July.

It was a long drive home. I was torn to say the least. I was thrilled to be accomplishing a lifetime goal of being a member of such a progressive and highly regarded Department serving my home community, and sick to my stomach that I was leaving an organization I so much respected and cared about, and had treated me like a family member.

Was this a gift from the Almighty? I pondered. I felt it had to be. I couldn't ignore an offer for an opportunity to satisfy everything I had ever asked God for. I felt I had to accept this new job.

CHAPTER **37**

Millcreek Township Police

AS I DROVE home I continued to think, should I give my notice now? What if something falls through or something changes? I'm not giving notice until the week before. I can't risk quitting a job and have to wait two weeks before I leave. If something did fall through, and I stayed, it would not fare well for me.

When I got home, I told Cindy what was going on and asked if there was any reason for us not to take the Millcreek job. She smiled and just shook her head.

I called my Dad and told him I had the interview, but I didn't tell him I committed to taking the job. I wanted his honest input, and if he knew I had already decided, he wouldn't say anything negative about it if he thought there was something I was overlooking.

I called him; "Yeah they offered me the job Dad," I said while taking a deep breath in anticipation of his response.

"Oh. Well I guess that's good then, right?" he stated. "You'd be going from a state organization to a local outfit. Does that matter much to you?" he asked.

"I don't know that it matters. Some people might consider it a step down, but I know what Millcreek offers. It's one of the best police departments in the state as far as FBI UCR reporting goes. I don't look at it as a step back at all. Plus, the main reason for the move would be the stability in having my family living in one place. It's a trip home," I explained.

We talked for a few more minutes and I told him I was leaning towards taking the new job. I know he was a little disappointed because he had grown very fond of the Patrol. He always wore a white OSP ball cap I bought for him, and I knew he wore it proudly.

A week went by at work and it was difficult to concentrate. I was still wrestling with the idea and the option of backing out. I knew once I gave my Lieutenant the weeks' notice there was no turning back.

A couple days later I got called in to the Lieutenants office. He informed me I had been chosen to teach at the Academy for a weeklong driving school. The students would be police officers from outside agencies. The school would start the first week in June for five working days.

I really should tell the Lieutenant, I thought as I sat there listening to him explain the details. It's an honor to be selected as a driving instructor. Knowing I'm leaving I think I should be honest because someone else would love to go. But I can't risk giving the notice so far away. Anything could happen and then what?

But where's my faith? If I have this improved faith I'm telling myself about, then what's the worry? I'm being a hypocrite.

"That's great lieutenant, thanks. I'll look forward to going," I said.

I went home and labored over the whole situation. If someone would have told me six years ago that I was indecisive about taking a job with Millcreek P.D. I would have thought they were crazy. This is the opportunity I've always wanted, so I should be happy.

I went to the Academy in June and taught the driving course. It was great to spend time there because it always brought back fond memories. When I pulled out of the Academy parking lot to drive home at the end of the week, I had a sick feeling because I knew it was the last time I'd ever be there.

The week before my scheduled start date with Millcreek I advised the Lieutenant I'd be leaving. Walking into his office that morning to tell him was one of the hardest things I had ever done.

The date came quickly. I was sworn in during a Township board meeting on my thirtieth birthday, July 5th, 1984.

I immediately learned the difference between a state-run organization and a local one. With a state agency, politics doesn't play as big a role in lower management decisions as it does in a local agency.

It did not take long to hear from some of the guys how politics had started to filter into the Departments promotions. The Dept. had historically promoted with seniority being a big consideration. Just recently there were a few promotions that had political overtones and senior members were passed over. To say the least the members moral was at an all-time low, and the first few months were more than difficult adjusting to a variety of do's and do nots.

Millcreek was no different than any other agency, although some of the stories I heard and things I observed led me to believe there were departments far more infected with politics than Millcreek's. I think that is why we got the respect we did from the general public. And that's the most important thing in community policing is support from the citizens.

From 1984 until 1999 my life was generally rewarding. I was assigned to the Patrol Division and was a genuine street cop. I had been promoted to Corporal in 1991 and was a first line street level supervisor. I minded my own business for the most part and just did my job. I had earned a general respect from my fellow officers. I was on the SWAT team which I enjoyed, and eventually became the Assistant Commander. I was a Technical Accident Investigator and was deemed an Expert during a jury trial in Erie County Court. Most importantly I was a Training Officer, and broke in many good men, which was my most rewarding duty. Being a training officer made me realize that Tpr. Jack Martin was one of the best things that ever happened to me. He was a true blessing. In looking back at my time with him, I now realized how much he taught me.

I also had been assigned to the Detective Division where I was promoted to Sergeant and spent my last four years. Career wise I was satisfied when looking back at my decision to leave OSP. Although many times I thought and wondered what might have been if I had stayed.

Christ teaches us to never look back and forget the past, so for me I have been satisfied with the decision I made. It all had worked out for my family, and that was by far the most important thing.

My kids were amazing, and it was my greatest pleasure in life was being their Dad. Raising a family is challenging to say the least, and Cindy and I did a pretty good job of it.

My faith in the Almighty remained stable, but witnessing the things you see in police work can breed indifference and doubt as to whether there is a higher power. If there is a God, why do bad things happen to good people? That is the question that has haunted "wan a be" believers since the beginning of time.

I also lost my Dad to cancer in 1991. It changed me and I became more cynical. He was only 64 and had only been retired only for a year when he got sick. That made me angry and fueled my cynicism. Not so much from his death alone, but from witnessing all the death and sorrow the job brings with it. And the reality that it all ends regardless of how good you try and be in life, death brings it all full circle.

I think what affected me the most during this time were suicides. I never realized how many there are in an average community. There were some years I was present on scene at only two or three. Then there were years I was on scene at eight or nine. One of our officers was unlucky enough to be dispatched to seventeen in one year. We nicknamed him Dr. Death.

A violent crime scene, homicide, or suicide are memories that never go away. Depending on how you deal with the memories depends on each person individually. Some guys are able to laugh it off. Others it effects their outlook on life in varying degrees of negativity.

They talk about PTSD soldiers suffer after combat. I can assure you PTSD effects policeman just as much, only its spread out over a long career of witnessing bad things. Some guys can deal with it and some cannot. That is why the suicide rate for policemen is so high.

I always felt I handled it adequately and put myself somewhere in the middle as far as being able to keep my sanity, and not bring the job home with me. I never talked about the job to my wife unless it was something positive or pleasant. She understood what was really going on. She knew the profession had changed me. It is nearly impossible to maintain a positive outlook on life, but I always did my best not to let it show in front of my kids. They deserved stability in their relationship with their parents.

As the 90's came to a close two things happened that affected me greatly. In 1999 I lost my brother to brain cancer. He was only 42 years old. He had a great job, a nice wife, and two adorable children ages eight and five. I was at his side when he took his last breath. It was the worst day of my life. Why God? Why? That's all I could think as I paced around his bed looking at him after he passed. Again, anger, confusion, and for the first-time bitterness towards God.

Now I was starting to regress, or already had regressed concerning God's existence. And if He did exist, He wasn't listening to any of my requests.

The second setback came in 2000. During a SWAT training scenario, I injured my tailbone and damaged two vertebra in my lower back from a fall. I was off work for a couple weeks, but my back never fully healed, and after months of discomfort and pain I consulted with a surgeon. His advice was to strengthen the muscles through rehab and weightlifting. He was honest enough to admit back surgery isn't usually a fix all. He also suggested I consult with a pain management specialist and hang in there until I could give it time, and things might improve.

By the middle of 2001 I couldn't manage the pain any longer without medication. I went to a pain management doctor who started prescribing me a cocktail of various drugs for pain relief. All of them were addictive opiates, but he felt with my background and self-discipline that I should not have any issues with taking the medication.

After six months of being on the medication daily I noted a change in my personality and drive. I had become lethargic and lazy. I complained to the doctor and advised him I felt a need to take the medication even when I didn't hurt too much. I felt I had become addicted.

I learned the doctor had a reputation of being a liberal prescription writer. I frequently would run out of my medication, and for the first two years he never gave me much of a hard time in refilling when I needed them.

To add to the chaos my son Freddie had a scholarship to Mercyhurst College to play football. His sophomore year which was the 2000-2001 football season he suffered a career ending concussion. He finished the academic year but that summer he wrestled with the idea of joining the military. After much discussion he decided to enlist in the Army. He was in bootcamp about to graduate when the Twin Towers were attacked. On top of that he decided to join the Airborne and got assigned to the 82nd Airborne Division. That is one of the Army's ass kicking units. His unit was one of the first to deploy to Afghanistan. Within days of being there he called on a STAR phone from Khost Afghanistan which was the forward outpost looking into Pakistan. He described his first taste of combat and what transpired the first few days. I was certainly a proud Pop, but the next four years I can say were the worst of my life contending with my drug addiction and the hand wringing daily worry of having a son in a combat zone. He deployed twice in that four-year period, once to Afghanistan and once to Iraq, and it literally almost killed me. I found out how strong his mother was. She handled it much better than I did.

I can say I prayed a lot during those four years even though my faith had regressed, and the day he was finally discharged I wept thanking God for bringing him home to us. I can say the whole experience made me cry out to God for his help in protecting my son. I guess I became more of a believer, but I became the type prayer warrior that only prays when there is something going wrong. It fueled a lot of guilt.

By the beginning of 2004 I was a full-blown pill head. My work suffered. My attendance at work was sporadic, and I had lost a lot of confidence in my ability to perform my job. I had been assigned to the Detective Division in 2003 and I had a substantial case load as all of us assigned there did. It took a lot of mental focus to do that job, and eventually I was promoted to Det. Sergeant. I never took the medication prior to working, but I knew I couldn't continue to maintain the quality of work I was used to putting out, and I looked at the possibility of retiring. The narcotics had destroyed who I was and stole my soul. The addiction had also made it harder for me to focus on the good things and the life God had given me.

When I thought about God, I thought about the fifty plus suicides I had been present at over the years. Images of decapitated heads removed by shotgun blasts were always just a thought away. I remembered the thirteen-year-old who pulled the trigger on a shotgun while

207

he had the barrel tucked under his chin as he sat on his mother's couch while she was in the next room cooking dinner. He had stated earlier in the day that he was mad at his father. Why would God permit those parents to go through that horror?

Why would God permit a guy to blow his head off in his basement on a Sunday morning when his wife and ten-year-old son were at church. They came home to find him and called 911.

After arriving there I was taking pictures of the body in the basement. The boy had come down the stairs without me seeing him. He walked up behind me, and I felt a tug on my coat. When I turned, he was standing there looking up at me. He looked so much like my ten-year-old son I had at home. Then he asked the big bad policeman a question with tears running down his face. "Did I do something to make my Dad mad at me?" I instantly began weeping about as hard as I ever had. I scooped the boy and ran him up the stairs and asked his mother to watch him, so he does not come back downstairs. I was angry at her for not making sure the boy stayed upstairs. As I walked back down the stairs and was wiping the tears from my face, all I could think of was how much I'd like to punch this guy in the mouth for doing that to his little boy. Why did God let that happen? Visions of that little boy haunted me for years. I often wondered how he coped with such a tragic event, and did he grow up normally?

Or when a local physician stuffed his wife in a plastic bag and buried her in a hole he dug in the basement of a new house he had just purchased. He concreted over her and built a bookcase over top of her. What a nice guy. When we broke up the concrete floor the decomposition fumes seeped through the cracks and the stink caused us all to run for breathing apparatus which we got from the local fire department. When we got her out of the hole the good doctor had dug, she was wet and shrunken up. Her skin had rotted off, and her tissues had turned bright green. One of the guys remarked, "How do you go from loving someone, to doing this to them?" Especially someone you had exchanged vows with before God. What was God's purpose in permitting such evil?

With the narcotic addiction I had become a different person. My only goal was to get enough pills to get me through the day so I would feel normal and not sick. That was it. I knew it was time to change course.

I had 23 years of service with Millcreek by this time. I had almost six with OSP for a grand total of twenty-nine years. Maybe I had done this job long enough, I thought? Cindy and I talked about what I had accomplished, and how I had met most of my goals. I had helped my community, and up until now I was looked at by my peers as a good cop. That's all I ever wanted was to be was a good cop. I never needed to be the big boss. I enjoyed serving the good cops above me. We talked about the goals she and I had accomplished together. We had a successful marriage and raised three good kids. We were both very proud of our kids.

I talked over the options with Cindy and family, and on April 17, 2007 I retired from the glorious field of police work. My pension was adequate, and if I worked somewhere part time pushing a broom or cutting a lawn, financially we would be fine. I never believed in full retirement. I don't think that's a healthy thing. I have always dreamed about a part time job where I could just park my brain somewhere and push a broom, or something with little responsibility. I didn't want to worry anymore about other people's lives like I had to do for so many years. That was incredibly stressful, and It takes its toll.

Now that I was retired and responsible to no one, I decided I had the time and fortitude to stop using the narcotics. The idea of going to rehab became a reality, and in February of 2008 I entered a thirty day in house rehab facility.

I left after three days. I walked out. It was the first time in my life I quit something. I was in there with a bunch of heroin addicts, and I rationalized I did not belong with them, but I was so wrong. I was as screwed up as they were, but I could not admit that to myself.

I gave up the pills then on my own. It took months and I decided to start drinking in the afternoons to relieve the horrible withdrawals. I was never much of a drinker. Mainly just social events and occasional nights out with friends. I soon realized I had to increase the drinking to stay off the pills, and that was turning me into a drunk. Those two years from late 2007 until mid-2009 were torture for my wife. I was always a mess, and I don't know what kept her from leaving. Finally, at the beginning of 2010 I had cut the alcohol out of my life.

I still was dealing with a lot of pain and changed doctors. The new doctor's specialty was injection therapy, and I was getting some relief and started to feel better about life. He didn't hesitate to allow me to use pain medication, but I was able to stay away from them for the most part. The only time I would use pain medication was the day after an injection.

By the beginning of summer of 2010, I was on a strict regimen of exercise and therapy. I was able to maintain an acceptable pain level. Things were starting to get better.

CHAPTER 38

The Accident

AUGUST 8 TH 2010 was a tragic day that words cannot describe. It was my youngest son Robert's birthday who lived in Mentor Ohio. We decided to have a family birthday get together at my daughter's house who lived in Girard. Pa., only about seven miles from my home. The birthday party started later than planned, and I got to my daughter's house around 8:30 pm. Cindy was not feeling well and decided to stay home.

I don't know what prompted me to do so other than I was in a great mood seeing family, I decided to sip on a bottle of beer. It was more than stupid. One beer led to another, and another. I do not offer any excuses other than being weak and stupid.

From arrival at the party until the time I left at around 10:30 pm, I would guess I had five or six beers. Not a large quantity, but over a short time period it was not a good decision to drive home.

I was angry for letting myself give in to the temptation to drink, but I felt tomorrow is another day, and I'll go back to my sobriety. It was a family get together and not a night planned to party it up, so I rationalized it as not being so bad of a thing.

On the way home while turning left on to a road which is within a mile or so from my home, the right-side passenger window of my pickup truck shattered inward. It startled me. The only thing that immediately entered my mind was I'd been shot at. I ducked down and pulled off the road and waited hunched over for a minute or so.

I was confused. There was a woman who had come out of her house and was in the front yard. She was yelling at me about something. As I was opening the door to my vehicle, I could hear her yell something about a motorcycle.

When I got out, I saw a motorcycle laying in the roadway. I quickly realized I must have turned left in front of him. There had been two occupants, and within minutes there were ambulance personnel on scene treating the injured.

The State Police arrived, and gave me field sobriety tests, and had me blow into a field-testing implement. The Trooper stated the test was a .11 which is over the legal limit of .08.

I was numb with fear. Fear for the people that were injured and fear for what I knew was forthcoming. I was arrested and transported to one of the local hospitals where blood was drawn. I was then taken to the county prison where I spent the night. I was released in the morning on a ROR bond.

I spent the next few days thinking about how many times I had locked someone up for DUI. I knew better. I didn't feel like I was a bad person, but the hypocrisy and guilt were overwhelming me. How did I not see that motorcycle?

The following days were a blur. I could not believe I was dumb enough to let something like this happen. I was embarrassed and sick with worry for those passengers.

Seventeen days after the accident the male driver succumbed to his injuries. Words cannot come anywhere close to describing how I felt about myself, especially someone like me that spent a lifetime helping others. It all seemed like none of this could possibly happen. I prayed a lot, but I guess it didn't help. The man died and I am responsible. I did not plan anything sinister, but I was reckless in my choice to drink and drive. I knew there was a mandatory minimum three-year prison sentence forthcoming.

I consulted with an attorney and decided to take responsibility for my actions and accept whatever the Court deemed as punishment.

In mid-September my attorney suggested I go to a 30-day rehab. I went to an in-house facility and got home in late-October. The studies are faith based and some of the religious speakers there made a lot of sense. God did not do this to me, I did this to me. I chose to drink. God gives us free will to make choices, and then we live with those choices. Surprisingly, I was starting to feel better about myself. I had told Cindy that I felt this was something we were going to get through, and knowing I was facing a potentially long prison term, I tried to keep a positive outlook. Cindy was a great supporter, and as long as I had her to back me up, I was going to be OK.

My friends disappeared. I had only one come to the house to see how I was doing. I know I made a huge mistake, but aren't friends supposed to help you through times of trouble? I found out that true friends are extremely rare. Cindy had told me many times throughout the years that I took my friendships too seriously. Of all the "brothers" I worked with and thought I'd die for, only one was there for support.

After all that happened, I couldn't imagine it getting much worse, but it did. I lost my true best friend.

On Dec. 22, 2010 Cindy died suddenly of a brain aneurism. She was gone in an instant. She had gone shopping that afternoon. I had said goodbye as she backed out of the garage. She was excited about Christmas and spending time with our 2 1/2-yr. old granddaughter Maddie. As she backed out of the garage and pulled away, I had no idea that I would never talk to her again.

My family was more than devastated. She was the anchor everyone looked to. She was my heart and soul. The sorrow and then the anger were more than I can describe.

As soon as I heard the words from the doctor that she had passed the first thing I thought about was God. Why? I learned in rehab we are not to ask God why? He has his reasons. We are to accept things as they are and go on.

Go On? I pondered. For what? Hey, I'm not wasting my time any longer wondering about this God bullshit. After the last few months and now this, why would I ever think there was a loving God watching over me. I was more than sick. I was walking dead, and I was done wondering if there was a God or not.

The services for her I barely got through. A couple of my friends showed up at her viewing and one at the funeral Mass. I was walking around in a coma. My heart ached for my kids. Losing a Mom is such a terrible thing.

I was having trouble dealing with the guilt of putting the added stress on Cindy with the accident, and I thought it may have contributed to her death. So much so I had to ask the doctor in Pittsburgh if stress plays any role in causing aneurisms. He said it did not, and aneurisms are caused by malformations of the vein walls from as early as birth. I guess that made me feel a little better, but it didn't matter much at this point. All I wanted to do was for this life I was living to end somehow and take the pain away.

As December of 2010 ended, I was living alone. It had been the worst year of my life. I began drinking again and used her death as an excuse. My son decided he would sell his home and move in with me and then live in my house while I was in prison. I knew I'd be leaving sometime in June, and it gave us time to get him settled.

I felt better having my son, his wife, and my granddaughter living with me. But by May my daughter in law was so stressed with my drinking she had to leave. They moved out and temporarily stayed at her father's house until I was gone, and then move back in.

So, when April came, I was alone again. I was doing nothing now but drinking and hoping I'd drop dead before my sentencing. I had thoughts of suicide, but I had been so critical of people who took their own lives as being weak. Suicide was for those who did not have the courage to pull yourself up after getting knocked down.

The worst thing I did was wait for the sentencing. I should have had my attorney request the court sentence me months before. It did me no good sitting around the house by myself month after month. Then the sentencing got pushed back which was even worse for me. When I told my son the sentencing had been pushed back a month, he said sarcastically, "Oh, wonderful." He was sick of me too. That moment was the lowest point of my entire life.

Finally, I was to be sentenced July 7th, 2011. Almost a year since the accident. On sentencing day my attorney picked me up at my home. I said goodbye to my two dogs which were the only loyal beings I knew, or now cared about. I was not sure if I would ever see them again because they were both getting old. I looked back at my house as we pulled away. I wasn't sure if I'd ever be back. I knew cops do not fare well in prison and felt there was a good chance I wasn't going to live through it all.

We arrived at the courthouse and walked into the courtroom. The deceased's family was there. The Judge came out as we all stood. He read the charges and asked if I had anything to say. I looked over at the family members and apologized for my actions. I don't have a vivid recollection of the proceeding. I knew I deserved whatever sentence the Judge gave me.

"You will be remanded to state prison to serve a sentence of no less than three and a half years to seven years," the Judge said firmly.

I heard what he said, but as I was led away, I turned and asked the Deputy what the Judge had said. "You got 3 ½ to 7," the Deputy said. I knew now my minimum sentence would be three and a half years. In Pennsylvania you must serve all of your minimum sentence before being considered for parole.

The Deputy walked me downstairs for processing. My case had drawn quite a bit of publicity and I knew when I got in there, I would have to be vigilant because cops usually don't survive incarceration, at least not in general population.

I spent the first few days in a cell with a glass front. It's called "suicide watch." All prisoners in jail for the first time are initially held in that type of cell. It's very uncomfortable because you're being watched constantly.

The first eight days I went through intense alcohol withdrawals. I was miserable, but it was a unique never felt before type of emotion I can't describe that came over me. The more miserable I felt, the more my life felt worth living. I was there to be punished. That was the mission- to be punished. Take my punishment and get on with life. If I do not survive it then so be it. If I do get through it, then the debt is complete, and the slate is clean. I knew some will argue that the time I'll spend in prison will never be enough, but that's not anything I have any control over. Society sets the standards, and I am required to comply. For the first time in a long time I felt some sense of purpose, and that was a good feeling. As miserable as I was, it felt positive. It sounds crazy, but maybe I was going crazy after all that had happened in the last couple years? I really had to think about that possibility. Maybe I was losing my mind, but whatever it was, it motivated me to get through the day.

On the twelfth day I was told I was leaving the county prison, and the following morning I was transported to Pittsburgh to begin the process.

CHAPTER 39

"Western Penn"

I ARRIVED AT Western Penn also known as SCI Pittsburgh on the 19th of July 2011. The prison was built in the late 1800's. It's old and dirty. It was closed for a few years in the early 2000's because it was too hard to maintain. It had to be reopened due to overcrowding across the state.

I know prison isn't supposed to be a nice place, but this was close to being uninhabitable. I know no one feels sorry for anyone who ends up in prison, but rats and mice and bugs of all variety in the cells is really pushing the definition of humane.

I was told I was supposed to be there a week and then transfer to SCI Camp Hill for final processing and Classification. For some reason six weeks had gone by and I was still there. I wrote the Unit Manager of the Block I was on, asking him why I was still there along with several other guys that had come in with me. I guess he didn't think much of my letter and he transferred me to isolation. (the Hole).

It was a good thing for me because I had been in a cell on the third floor of a five-story tier system Block. The temperature was a constant 105-115 degrees because there is no ventilation in those old blocks. When he sent me to the hole it had been remodeled and updated years prior and had a partially working air conditioning system. So, it was the "Hole," but it was much more tolerable if you don't mind not seeing or talking to anyone. I was there for 13 days and never left the cell other than to take a shower every third day. The showers are only several feet from the cell doors so that was the extent of any exercise for me. I asked about the hour per day that is supposed to be afforded to isolation inmates, but the guard just laughed.

On the morning of the 14th day I was transferred to Camp Hill. It was a three-hour bus ride, and I was handcuffed and tethered sitting next to a guy that was so big he filled both of our seats. He smelled like he had skipped a couple showers. The windows on the bus are blacked out so there was no seeing any landscape. Upon arrival we were assigned to a Block housing unit.

Camp Hill is unique in that all the inmates processing and getting Classified are there temporarily. Therefore, the guards have no reason to be decent to you because they don't have to work with or around you for any length of time. They have no need to build any rapport with inmates. Subsequently, they are very mean spirited and can be at the least verbally abusive. And if you were to talk back in a negative manner you would certainly risk more than verbal abuse.

Camp Hill was supposed to be a three to six month stop prior to being assigned a permanent prison, which is called your "Home" prison. After being at Camp Hill for a few weeks I dreaded the thought of having to be there for possibly six months.

When I arrived at Camp Hill I was Classified quickly because I had stayed so long at Western. I was Classified a Level 2 non-violent low risk inmate. I was also told I would likely be sent to a Level 2 prison, or possibly Level 3.

Level 5 is the most violent because it houses inmates that have committed the most heinous crimes. The counselor I spoke with mentioned I would fit nicely at SCI Mercer which is a Level 2 prison. Mercer is only about an hour drive from Erie. Level 2 inmates usually are of the non-violent nature and have committed property or drug crimes. I was anxious to get to my "Home" prison and get settled into some type of routine. In listening to inmates talk over the last month, I learned it takes about a year for a person to settle in, and the time supposedly goes much faster.

I also learned that if you're an older white male the majority of the inmates assume, you're a pedophile. Most pedophiles are older white males.

When you get Classified your given a Classification sheet which lists your crimes and sentence, and other information etc. I made it a point to show mine to every new cell mate (celly) I got assigned to so they knew, and the word would spread, that I was not a pedophile. I had seen two guys get beat up bad at Western who were accused of being pedophiles.

My biggest concern throughout my time in prison was it being revealed that I was a retired policeman. Other than being a pedophile, I think being a cop or x-cop is just as dangerous. There was a policeman that came into one of the blocks adjacent to mine soon after I arrived. It was known he was a policeman because he lived in the area and had been in the news often. I heard he had arrived and was beaten up the first week he was there. I heard he had been put in isolation for his protection.

Along with all the problems prison presents I also had an ongoing medical Issue. In 2009 while undergoing an MRI to check the condition of my back the doctors found I had an Aortal Aneurism. That is an enlarging of the main artery that leads from the bottom of the heart to the groin leading to the Femoral Artery. The size of the bulge was at 2.5 cm. I was told if this artery were to rupture there is no surviving it. Death would occur within 20-30 seconds due to the amount of blood lost in a short time period. They explained the cause is usually hereditary, and I later found out I had an uncle that had his repaired after it had grown to 5.5 cm. This was a condition that had to be monitored every six months. They would not repair the artery unless it grew over 5 cm. due to the complexity and risk of the surgery.

My attorney was concerned that I would not get an opportunity to have this monitored while incarcerated.

Upon my arrival at Camp Hill I advised the medical staff there of the condition. They assured me they would monitor it, but only on a yearly basis.

I guess I had to avoid being punched in the stomach during my prison stay, and hopefully keep monitoring the problem hoping I parole in time, and have it repaired upon my release.

CHAPTER **40**

"SCI Forest"

IT WAS LATE October and I had been at Camp Hill for about five weeks. I was notified by the afternoon guard to pack my things because I was being transferred out of Camp Hill at 4am the next morning. I was happy because I had planned on being there well past Christmas. I felt if I could get assigned to my home prison, I might be able to receive a visit from family during the Holidays.

The following morning, I was escorted to the departure area. There was about forty of us in the waiting area. We were eventually all handcuffed and tethered and led on to the bus.

The windows are blacked out so there is no way of knowing where you are once its moving. The driver was not allowed to announce where we were going.

During my final Classification interview the counselor asked me if I had any requests as to which prison I wanted to go to. I told her I had no idea, but I explained the first counselor I spoke with suggested I might fit well at SCI Mercer. If not Mercer, then my only request would be to do my time on the west end of the state so I could get visits from family on occasion. I was happy with Mercer because it's only an hour from Erie.

As the bus made its way off the Camp Hill grounds, I could see out a crack above the metal window ledge. After a short ride I noticed we had turned on to a ramp leading up to the Interstate. As we drove past the end of the entrance ramp, I could barely make out a sign that read

80 WB. I was happy to see we were traveling west and not east towards Harrisburg or Philadelphia.

Knowing we were westbound I tried thinking of all the prisons west of Camp Hill. I was only familiar with Pittsburgh, Mercer, Albion, and Houtzdale. I was pretty convinced we were headed to Mercer.

After about an hour and a half suddenly the bus slowed, and we exited the Interstate. We were all surprised and were wondering where we were headed. After about an hour of driving along what seemed to be two lane roads the bus slowed and pulled off into a large receiving area. The driver and guard announced we had arrived at our destination, being SCI Forest.

Forest? I thought to myself. I've never heard of that one before? There were a lot of guys complaining aloud as the guard warned everyone to keep the noise down.

The guy next to me said, "It's a Level 5 jail man. This place a lot of people don't go home from."

"What do you mean?" I asked.

"People get killed here. It's a Supermax. Bad people. Locked down a lot," he answered. "Most of the people here are from Philly and the east side of the state. A lot of lifers. They send the bad ones here, so they won't get many visits because their people have to drive to far to see them."

I tried not to show the fear I was feeling. What am I doing at a Supermax? The counselor told me she was going to try and get me to Mercer. This is the exact opposite. A level 5 prison? I think out of the 20 some prisons in the state there's only six Supermax's. Great, just great.

The bus doors opened, and we all stood up and shuffled down the stairs and out into the secured yard area. I don't think I ever saw so much razor wire and fences. We stood in single file and made our way into the Receiving Block.

It looks to be a newer prison, I thought, as I looked around the outer building and once inside could see the newer style lighting fixtures. It's definitely much cleaner than Western or Camp Hill.

The guards were yelling at one of the guys at the front of the line about him not paying attention. I figured the guards couldn't be any meaner than the guards at Camp Hill. Those guys were nasty. If I hated a job as much as it appeared they did, I'd have to go do something else. There were a lot of guards here, I pondered, as my turn came up to get my clothing issue. It must be because of the Level 5 rating. A lot of gates, fences, razor wire, and guards.

It was getting close to 3pm and finally we were told to go to our Blocks. I was assigned to 'A' Block. We were escorted by several guards as I walked carrying everything I owned, which wasn't much. I had my clothing issue, a box full of paperwork I had accumulated, and some toiletries. We walked what seemed to be quite a way. As we walked, I heard one of the inmates in line talking about the prison. This is his "Home" prison, and he is always sent here when he re-offends or violates parole. He said this jail (jail is the preferred word used by inmates) was built in the late 1990's. It holds around 2500 inmates. It's a level 5 Classification although at every jail there is a mix of inmates concerning their Levels. He said that's because a lot of lifers and Level 5 inmates refuse to work. If you refuse to work, you won't make parole. So, they mix the population with inmates that are expected to eventually be going home, like Level's 2 and 3. Somebody has to work the kitchen duties, cooking, cleaning, maintenance etc., so it's a mixed batch of people. Then he started talking about the guards. He said for the most part they are pretty decent, but this prison led the state the last few years in assaults on guards and prison employees. It also leads in inmate on inmate assaults most years. The only prison in the state that compares to Forest as far as being the most violent is SCI Graterford located near Philly.

In the ten minute or so walk from the Receiving Block to the main hub of blocks, we passed through three gates manned with guards. Also, there are two towers strategically located for maximum viewing of the grounds. "Those guards in the towers are armed with rifles," said the fellow we were walking with. "Don't get any ideas about escaping this hell hole. It's impossible," he said.

As we walked into an outer waiting area outside the blocks there were four separate gates. Each gate led you to a specific block. The blocks are set up in a round hub type fashion. This hub contained four blocks, A, B, C, and D, and was referred to as the West Side of the prison. There's another hub with four blocks on the other side of the prison E, F, G and H. There is also "I" Block, which is a dormitory style setup, and "J" and "K" Blocks which are Isolation Unit's (the hole).

The gate for 'A' block opened and me and one other guy along with the guard walked into the outer concrete yard. That yard is about half the size of a football field and is fenced in. After walking through that concrete yard, we approached the outside entrance door and were buzzed in by one of the guards that was inside.

I was assigned to AB. Each block has two sides to it once inside the front entrance. 'A' side and 'B' side. Each side contains 124 inmates. The door on the 'B' side buzzed open and the guard motioned for me to enter and approach the "Bubble." The Bubble is a glass enclosure that sits off the ground and separates the two sides of each block. One guard and sometimes two, man the Bubble and are operating and controlling movement on each side.

I walked up the two steps in front of the Bubble and handed the guard my paperwork through the glass window. "Your assigned 17 Cell," the guard stated. I heard a cell door pop and as I turned I saw the door opening to a cell on the first floor right in front center. I stepped down from the Bubble and started to walk towards the cell. As I got closer, I could see the number 17 on the cell, and the guy inside stood up and moved to the doorway.

As I got close, I saw a very large black man standing in the doorway. He didn't look too friendly. As he was looking at me, he said, "You com'in here "Oldhead?" (a prison name for an older inmate but complimentary)

I stuttered, "Yeah, I think so if this is 17?"

He didn't say anything and stepped back into the cell as I stepped in. This dude is at least 6'4" and has to be near 300 lbs., I thought to myself. The door closed behind me. I was scared and wasn't sure if this guy was going to beat on me or welcome me. He had a blank look on his face.

"This your first time in prison?" he asked.

"Yeah," I answered. "Is it that obvious?"

He didn't answer but asked, "You a pedophile?"

I was prepared for that question and reached down and pulled my Classification sheet out and handed it to him. "No," I answered.

He looked it over intensely. "OK," he said. "Then we can be cool. Pedophiles don't make it in this block. They be gone," he said, as he motioned his finger across his throat.

"I'm cool with that," I said. "Pedophiles need stabbed up for sure."

"Yea, for sure," he responded.

"Hey, I hate to ask but are we allowed to smoke in this jail? I'm just coming from Camp Hill and there ain't no cigarettes to be had any-where in that jail. I haven't had a smoke in weeks."

"No, we ain't allowed to smoke in the block. Outside is cool, but inside they might write you up or hassle ya," he said. "You want one?"

"Really! You'll loan me one?" I said enthusiastically.

"Yea. Fire away," he said as he handed me his tobacco pouch and papers.

"Aww man I don't know how to roll. Can you roll it for me?" I asked with a sheepish grin.

"Man, you lost aint you? You a lost motherfu***r," he said, as he took the pouch back and started rolling a smoke.

"Yeah for sure," I said. "This is all new to me. At 58 years old com-ing to prison for the first time. Yeah I'm pretty lost."

"You don't belong here for that charge. First time, and you too old for this shit in here. They should be sending people like you to a local halfway gig for a couple years," he said.

"Yeah, a guard at Camp Hill told me the same thing. Maybe be committed to a halfway center for a few years. Like a long rehab place," I said.

My new celly then handed me a rolled smoke. I can say that might have been the best smoke I ever had, until the guard came to the door and asked who was smoking.

In response to the guard's question, we both answered at the same time. I didn't want my celly to get written up because of me, so I said," Yeah I was sir."

Simultaneously my celly said, "No, nobody in here."

The guard looked at me through the glass window and just shook his head and walked off. My celly kind of yelled at me. "Don't be admittin' to shit around here Oldhead! Fuck these guards! They all piece's a shit cops! I ain't never going home, so I don't listen to anything I don't have to," he said.

"Yeah, well thanks for the advice. I'm sorry you're not ever going home. I can't say I know how you feel. It must be hard," I said, as I swallowed hard after hearing his opinion on cops.

"It ain't hard. I get by. I'll be all right," he said.

"My name is Fred by the way," I said as I extended my right hand.

"Mel," he said as he shook my hand.

Lots of things were flying through my brain. My fear had subsided a bit. I felt I might have made a friend here with Mel. He's so young, I thought to myself. And he's doing life. He can't be much over 30, if that.

Mel went on to tell me his story. I hadn't asked because I had learned it's a prison insult to ask how much time somebody is doing unless they tell you. When he was 23 years old and selling drugs, he got into a shootout and killed another dealer. He got convicted, but somehow it got thrown out and he was released and not re-tried. He didn't get into the details of the case. A few years later he again shot someone and killed them, but he wouldn't elaborate on that crime. He got sentenced to life on that charge.

Mel for some reason put up with me and some pretty stupid questions I had for him. During meals for a couple days I walked with him and many of his friends back and forth to the chow hall. No one talked to me, and I was happy with that. One of the first days in line at the chow hall I counted 73 guys in line. Only 7 white guys. That's a 10-1 ratio I thought. That's about the ratio in this prison. I'd say 70% Black, 20% Hispanic, and 10% White. `

As it turned out Mel was the block "boss" for lack of a better word. He OK'd things that went on between inmates on our side of the block. If there was bad blood between a couple guys Mel would decide how it was to be handled. Kind of like the local judge. It seemed every block had at least one "boss." So, for me it worked out because everyone knew Mel had no issues with me, so no one else did either. Although after a few days I was moved to a different cell, the few days I spent with him kind of worked out good for me.

My new celly was a white guy in his mid-thirties from DuBois named Brian. He was easy to get along with after he read my Classification sheet. He was in for four years for multiple burglary convictions and had made parole two years ago. Then he got arrested while on parole for a bank robbery and was currently a year into an eight-year sentence. So, basically, he'd been locked up for a total of five years with about six remaining.

Brian kind of took me under his wing and taught me things about surviving prison life. I had no idea how much I didn't know. There are a lot of unwritten rules to know if you want to stay out of trouble with other inmates. Rule #1 don't be a snitch. Rule #2 don't borrow money. Rule #3 don't lend money. Rule #4 don't disrespect anybody. Rule #5 don't gamble. Those are the top five of a long list of do and do nots. It is basically a mini society in each block. Guys have their jobs within the prison. Some guys don't or won't work because they have their own little hustle, like opening a store. Stocking your cell with saleable foods, toiletries, tobacco, extra clothing, etc. The prison staff frowns on these stores but during cell inspections usually look the other way.

There was usually a store per each side of the block. Everything the guy running the store sold he would get back two-fold. Within a certain time period, I repay him back two, and in some cases like candy bars its three to one. Depending on his inventory and demand he sets the payback rate. If you don't payback then you're going to have major issues with the person you borrowed from. That means it's not uncommon for a guy to get stabbed because he owed somebody a dollar and had refused to pay. (A dollars' worth of food. There is no monetary exchange.) It's not the dollar owed that gets you beat up or stabbed, it's the disrespect you show the guy that loaned you the item by ignoring the loan.

The Commissary carries just about anything you would need to get through life. Clothing, batteries, food, candy, cigarettes, chips, soups, cookies, peanuts, TV's, radios, etc. It's a five-page single spaced order form. People on the outside put monies on your account and you purchase these items weekly through the Commissary. Guys who worked got paid an hourly rate, and on pay day the prison puts it on your account. I eventually had a job in outdoor maintenance and was paid 17 cents an hour. Tuesdays were big days on "A" block because that was our Commissary day. That is when you went and picked up your order you submitted from the previous week. And once you got your stuff it was time to pay your bills if you owed anyone anything.

I faired Ok because I put monies on my prison account from my personal outside account once a month. Plus, I had my job that netted me a few dollars a month. Then weekly I'd order what I needed. I learned not to go to the Commissary too often because the word spreads quickly as to who has money and who doesn't. Those that had money became targets for paying for protection and giving money away. You were called a "Pic," which is somebody with money that's weak, and easy to pick on to get things.

I stayed to a strict self-policy about loaning out things. If you were hurting and needed a shot of coffee or a cigarette and you had treated me with respect, I didn't hesitate to help. There were times that I said no because they were habitual beggars or were only nice to you when they wanted something. There were many times when I ran short on something and people helped me out.

It was getting near the Holidays and I was getting anxious to see my family. It had taken five months to get to this point where all my paperwork had been submitted and family members had been approved for visits and were entered on my list.

Then came December 16, th 2011. It was my first scheduled visit. My son brought his family and my granddaughter Maddie. They also brought the new baby that was born in August. Jenny was only three months old and I got to hold her and play with Maddie. It was one of the best moments of my life seeing her and the others after five months. They stayed for a couple hours which was great, but when they left and I was walking back to my block, I can't describe the emotion and despair that numbed me.

CHAPTER **41**

"Barry- the Angel"

THE FIRST OF the year came and went and we were into 2012. I had been locked up 6 months as of January 7.[th.] I thought about my release date being exactly 3 years away if I made parole on time. This last 6 months seemed like it had been 6 years.

My Mom was continually on my mind because prior to my sentencing she had been diagnosed with Dementia/Alzheimer's. My sister Marianne had visited a couple times, once in late 2011, and in the summer of 2012, and brought my Mom with her. It was extremely hard and sad because I could see her slipping.

During the visit in the summer 2012, I had an eerie feeling that this would be the last time I would see her. I think she realized what had happened as far as me being incarcerated, but it was apparent she was not sure of her surroundings.

We said our goodbyes as her and my sister left the visiting room. On the long walk back to my block my eyes welled up and I knew. Within a couple months Mom passed. The worst part of the entire prison experience was I could not be with her during her last moments here in this life. I can't put the despair I felt in words, but that's what prison is all about. It takes you to a place psychologically that you had no idea existed, and for good reason, because if you are sorry for your crimes, you have no placed to go but up.

I met a guy in the Day Room (Rec area inside the block) one evening at Block Out. (The time designated each evening or afternoon

228

allowed out of the cells). We were as opposite as you can be. He was a black guy from Philadelphia with no money and no family to speak of. He was my age, and that was all we had in common. I was a white guy from the opposite end of the state. I had a job my entire life and had a large family.

For some reason while watching TV we struck up a conversation. Blacks usually hung with blacks and whites with whites. So, it wasn't unusual to speak to one another but the interest in one another's lives was unique. We were seated in the fixed chairs at the far end of the Day Room. There was the usually loud background noise of guys talking and playing cards, so we had to sit close to hear one another. He had an attitude and ora about him that raised my curiosity. Here we were two guys who grew up at the same time but totally different lives. I guess I wanted to learn about his world. We ended up hanging out together often and spent most of our evenings talking.

He had introduced himself as Barry. We had some pretty in-depth conversation's about life, race, and politics. Barry was a very smart knowledgeable man. Very articulate and street savvy. He could talk informed on just about any topic. He never once mentioned what he was in prison for, and I never asked. He knew I was in for the DUI manslaughter, and he too had the opinion that state prison isn't the answer for a crime like mine. I explained to him that the punishment has to fit the crime, and I felt a sense of purpose enduring my punishment for what I did.

Barry felt the state's responsibility is to deal out punishment but also should focus on rehabilitation for which in my case being locked up in a Level 5 jail, gave me little formal rehab counseling. He suggested I sign up for the AA classes offered some evenings, the religious classes offered one night a week, and church on Sundays. I told Barry I'd sign up for the AA classes but the religion stuff I could do without.

Barry showed his dissatisfaction with my answer by handing me a Bible. He had been mentioning the Bible for several weeks and had been trying to get me to take one back to my cell.

"Barry, whats this for? You know I don't believe anymore after my wife died. I can't even think of God without getting mad," I said.

"I know, but your injured. Your heart is injured, but it's time to repair things. You are lucky enough to be getting out someday. There are guys in here that aren't getting out, but they have discovered the truth," Barry responded.

"Barry, com'on, everybody who comes to prison says they find God and make excuses for their crimes. Then they fall back on that God still loves them. It helps them get through the day, and it makes them feel better about themselves. I don't want that. If there is a God, he hasn't been there for me lately," I said.

"Please brother, just take this Bible and read it like it's just a history book. A book of stories from ancient times. It's a history book, and you said you like history. Just start to read it," he pleaded.

"Ok. For you I'll start to read it before bed for a half hour or so. If it shuts you up, I'll do it," I said as we both laughed.

Barry was very cool. Here was a guy who just held odd jobs and trudged through life but had a great attitude towards his fellow man. Many times, I saw Barry counseling some of the younger inmates. Younger guys were drawn to him like a father figure that most of them never had. He had a general concern for everybody. I felt good when I was around him and I felt I could learn so much from him. You cannot trust anyone in prison, but Barry was different.

Barry told me to start reading Matthew in the New Testament. So begrudgingly before bed, I would sit down and read for a half hour.

"Celly, why are you reading a Bible?" Brian asked.

"Barry has been bugging me day and night to read it, so to shut him up I'm going to read it before bed."

"I've read the New Testament three times," Brian said.

"You have?" I asked.

" Yeah, nothing else to do at night with no TV sometimes and nothing else to read."

"And what did you get out of it?" I asked.

"Nothing. It's a nice story book but I don't believe any of it," he said.

"Huh, Ernie said to believe and receive. If you don't want to believe, then reading it is just a waste of time. But he said meditate prior to reading it asking God to come over you and understand His words,"

I explained. He said it's a magical book.

"Whatever," Brian answered. "It didn't do anything magical for me."

A couple weeks went by and I continued to read almost every night for a half hour or so. I enjoyed some of the stories, and some brought back memories of my childhood when my grandmother would read a passage or two around Christmas time concerning the birth in Bethlehem and the Magi.

Then usually in the mornings I'd run into Barry at breakfast and without fail he'd ask me what I read the night before. His tenacity impressed me. He was genuinely trying to get me back on the road to being a believer. He had something special he wanted to share with me. He told many stories about times in his life when he had no one to turn to for help and would get on his knees and pray. He really opened up and told me personal stories I can't imagine I would ever tell anyone. When I'd see him in the mornings he'd ask, "Has it happened yet?" And I'd reply, "No Barry, not yet."

Along with reading the Bible Barry talked me into sitting in on a couple of his prayer groups in the evenings when he and four or five of his friends would sit around at Block Out and have prayer and Bible Study.

I think what started to get to me was the genuine passion a couple of the guys had for the Bible, and how they broke down and interpreted some of the scripture. I had never studied any of what was being explained, and some of it really spiked my interest in the meaning of what was written. I realized these passages can be interpreted in many different ways, and the detective in me wanted to find out which meaning was the right meaning. What I came to realize was there are some very smart people in the world that are true believers and have been studying for lifetimes without finding the answers. I believed it was important to go back to previous writers and make comparisons of the way it was being told by writers Matthew, Mark and Luke. John was more of a poetry writer I thought, and left the meanings more inconclusive. So, for me it was interesting comparing what each writer said about the same happening or incident.

I also eventually attended a one night per week Bible study hosted by the prison. We were allowed to leave the block and walk over to the Chapel. They had a retired clergyman and his wife come each week, and we would study writings by modern day writers that were scholars, and doctors. They also brought in doctors and clergy from the community to speak. Very intelligent educated men who were passionate believers. It made a huge impression on me to see them and listen to their messages.

I always thought religion was a crutch for the weak of mind, the poor, the lost, people who were confused etc. It was a feel-good solution for their problems. I was seeing for the first time these people we were studying were so much more educated than the average person, and they were believers. They're so much smarter than me. Maybe I've been the dummy all along? Maybe I've ignored what's been right in front of me my entire life? Maybe all those times in my career I walked away unharmed from a dangerous call or something where I shouldn't have, and then wondered how, that it _was_ God that was there for me?

As we got into mid-year, right around my one-year anniversary, I began looking forward to my nights before bed. A half hour a night reading scripture had turned into an hour, and then an hour and a half. Then I wasn't getting to bed until one or two am. I began to develop a sense of contentment with the whole prison experience. I actually felt that there were parts of the day I enjoyed, and I could see how people survived long prison sentences. Maybe Barry is right about scripture being magical and will change a person.

I began wondering if I was getting caught up in exactly what I had told Barry months before, about how everybody in prison thinks they find God because we're taught that God forgives, and it's a crutch.

No. I told myself _NO!_ This transformation for me is real. Yes, I know God loves me when no one else will, and that is a feel-good crutch to believe, but that doesn't matter to me. I don't need anybody to love me except my family, and they haven't abandoned me. I'd be just fine walking out of here some day with no friends or a thousand friends, it makes no difference as long as I know who I am, my family knows who I am, and maybe I wouldn't need God. So I'm not in here trying to be a believer, or have God show me he loves me. It is happening on its own.

I'm taking the time to look and search for the first time in my life. I have continually had questions about faith, but I never searched?

They teach that God does not punish. He gives man free will and lets things play out from people's decisions. That is why bad things happen to good people. They make poor decisions and God cannot accept sin, _so He steps back_, and lets it play out. God does not want to see us suffer and always wants the best for us, but we have to pay for our sins if we want eternal life. God hung His own son on a cross to pay for mankind's sins.

My favorite scripture passage is Romans 8:28. "And we know that all things work together for the good, for those who truly love God, and are called according to His purpose."

It says _all_ things. That three-letter word is so, so powerful. All things good _and bad_ that happen to you eventually work for your good, but only if you're a believer and you truly love God, and you've turned over your life to God, then even the bad things that will happen in life will come out for your good. He puts people He loves in the fire. He wants them to be strong and refined like tempered gold. Accept the bad as part of God's plan to make you ready for the Kingdom. He put His own son on a cross, which there is probably not a more arduous death in existence. What makes you think you can go untested? Unrefined? Adversity builds character of soul. And most important in scripture He says he will never abandon you or forsake you if you truly believe. What more do we need to know if we believe that scripture? Many, many times Christ says in the Bible, "Do not be afraid." The unknown can be terrifying, but if you believe the Lord is with you then fear is manageable.

The last line of that Romans scripture says, "and are called according to His purpose." That means you must do more than just believe. You have to be called to work for His purpose. Work for Gods mission of teaching the Word and bringing people to Christ. Love is the main mission. Spreading that love to all is His purpose. Our families should be our first priority in accomplishing this.

CHAPTER **42**

"Houtzdale"

PRISON IS A very daunting place. It was a unique experience to meet and study with inmates and Clergy staff, who truly were good people. But those people represented a very minute percentage of people who were incarcerated. The large percentage were bad people who intentionally hurt others and would do so again if given the opportunity. There are a lot of people locked up that society must make sure they stay locked up. They are predators not of true human value. They do not have consciences and they don't feel guilt. Yes, God wants us to love all His children, but He doesn't want us to be hurt in trying to do so. Some are absolutely evil and willingly not going to change. I never really knew anyone that I would define as evil prior to going to prison. That certainly was a revelation even to a 29-year law enforcement guy like me. I thought I had dealt with evil people in my work and maybe there were a couple, but nothing of the magnitude I got to see in prison.

Being sent to a Level 5 prison I certainly expected to live around bad people, but without experiencing it firsthand I would have never believed that human beings could be so animalistic. It is one thing to watch it on the evening news, it's quite a different feeling being there.

I witnessed many fights over nothing but someone saying that someone else disrespected them. Maiming type assaults and stabbings all without any remorse. Prison is truly a jungle. You can feel the hate spilling from some, and you did not always know who you were sitting beside at the lunch table, or who they were going to assign you a cellmate.

I had 18 different celly's over a 42-month period.

In August of 2013 I was assigned to the TC Block. It is a requirement for parole that all inmates convicted of alcohol related crimes attend Therapeutic Community. It is a four to six-month program conducted in a Block where all participants live together and share community duties and learn different responsibilities within a team concept setting.

It is a very difficult program to get through. A lot of people get kicked out and must start over months later. Quite a few people quit and forgo their parole and do their maximum sentence just to avoid having to participate. It is the best program the state offers in my opinion.

There I learned why a lot of these people think the way they do. Unfortunately, without good family structure growing up these people never learned values and social skills. They learned everything on their own in a culture they grew up in without structure or accountability. Their whole concept of self-worth revolves around how much respect they earn amongst their peers. It is instilled in them from an early age, and in most cases, they had no good male role models to show them how to be a righteous person. And if you add drug and alcohol addiction to that lifestyle can you expect any good outcome? Can you expect them to change? Can you expect them to want to change?

I'm afraid we have lost a large portion of our society with little chance to rehabilitate the majority of them.

I graduated TC in January of 2014 with less than a year to go to my minimum and parole.

The reason I express my thoughts on this is because I too got caught up in the dog eat dog mentalities of prison life. I stated earlier I helped people whenever I could and even some who I knew had no appreciation for anything done for them. I had only one red-line in the sand where I was not willing to negotiate for, and that was assigned phone use. The only thing I had to look forward to each day was calling home. In the mornings on the way to breakfast, staff had a daily signup sheet for the days phone use. If you were fortunate enough to get on the sheet before it was full you could sign up for a 15 minute collect call. I usually got on the phone signup sheet successfully about four out of seven days.

At the prescribed time you signed up for, you would ask to leave your cell and go to one of the six phones in the Day Room. Usually everything would go reasonably well once you made your way and stood in line at the phone. Usually at the fifteen-minute mark the guy on the phone in front of you hung up so you could step up and make your call.

The first few attempts at this I didn't have much trouble, but there is always some buffoon that when it's time to hang up wont, and if you let him stay on through your time you lose it.

The first few days I was on the Block all went well. I was a new guy, and everyone knew it. It didn't take long before I got a moron in front of me who refused to give it up.

My celly Brian had warned me that it would eventually happen, and if I wanted to show everyone I was an easy target, then I should just walk away when the buffoon refused to leave. I knew I was not going to let that happen regardless of who it was.

During the second week as my time came up, I had a younger, large in stature guy give me the shaking of the head when his time expired, which meant for me to go away. I admit I had to swallow hard and take a couple deep breaths because I got so pissed, and I knew I wasn't likely to come out of this the victor.

I took the five or six steps to the phone and simultaneously asked him if he was going to hang up. He pulled the phone from his ear and tucked it to his chest. I then reached up and clicked his receiver closed and said, "Looks like you and me are going," and that's all I got out of my mouth as he shoved me into the phone. I got him in a head lock and down to the hard floor we went.

Now sometimes you can take a beating for a long time before a guard or somebody pulls your attacker off. And sometimes a guard never gets there.

What saved me was the age difference. There were a couple guys on the other phones that saw the mismatch and started pulling at the both of us. I was able to hang on to this headlock long enough as to not be dealt any real blows, and I hadn't really hit him because I was holding on to the headlock with both arms. I knew if I lost that grip, I was going to get the worst of it.

Yes, I made an enemy. No, I didn't get to make my phone call. But everyone on the Block knew not to mess with me during my phone time. The guard never wrote us up because nobody got hurt, and all ended well for the moment.

Although I did get in a few altercations during my time at Forest, I never had to fight for a phone again because people knew that even though I probably wasn't going to kick their ass if they took my phone time, they knew they were going to have to fight me for it and risk punishment by staff.

Point of all this being is we are a product of our environment and we become a part of the chaos. So, can we really judge these predators for who they are? I don't think we can, but we should give them the opportunity to change, and for some, that's not possible.

After getting out of TC, I got assigned to "I" Block. It's the only Block in the prison that is dormitory style. It's a reward block for long timers that are older and have decades of time accumulated, and a reward for lower level inmates who are within a year of parole. It's like a military barracks setup with two dorms housing 75 inmates each. It's a welcome relief from the standard Blocks and all are on their best behavior so they don't get bounced out. There are no cell lockdowns for long periods of time. There still are altercations, but not anywhere near as many as in a standard block.

In the normal blocks every time there is an assault or stabbing usually the entire prison is locked down, which means you do not leave your cell for any reason. Since I had been at Forest, we had been locked down 22 times for periods averaging 3-4 days, and the longest lockdown I experienced was 8 days. That's a long time to be in a 9'x11' cell 24-7 which is basically a concrete toilet room with a bunk bed in one corner. And to be in there with someone you might not like or do not get along with is hell.

On 'I' Block your allowed out of your dorm from 8:30 am until 9 pm. if you follow the rules. A lot of guys aren't there for long because they get paroled, and there are guys that have long sentences and have been there for years. It is a real easy way to do time.

I only had 10 months to go when I got assigned to 'I' Block and I was elated. It was a sign for me that I was over the hump, and I could finally see a big light at the end of the tunnel. I had several people in the dorm I knew and trusted them to some degree. Basically, I was on the downhill slide. My counselor on 'I' Block knew me well and was handling my parole paperwork. It was just ticks on the clock to get to go home.

I had been out of TC and in the dorm for about two weeks when I got called in by my counselor.

"You're not going to like what I'm about to tell you Munch," he said.

"Aww. What?" I responded.

"You're getting transferred to Houtzdale. There was nothing I could do about it. They randomly transfer people from Forest to there, and your name came up on the transfer list."

I was stunned. I couldn't say a word. I just sat there. I kept looking at him straight in the eyes believing I didn't hear what he just said.

"You alright?" He asked.

"I only have 10 months to go and I'm gone. That's all new people. It'll be just like my first six months here. It's hell proving yourself all over again," I said.

"Yea I know. Nothing I can say. It's going to happen day after tomorrow. I'll get in touch tomorrow and let you know what time to be over at Receiving."

I stood up and just walked out of his office. I didn't know much about Houtzdale. I knew it was south of Forest, south of IS-80 near Clarion. It's adding an hour for my family's drive for a visit. I know it's a Level 3 jail. Probably should have been put there in the first place and I wouldn't have to go through what I know I'm about to go through.

Moving to a different prison is like transferring to a different high school. All unfamiliar inmates. You don't know anybody. You can't trust anybody. You automatically become a potential "pic" until you prove you're not. "This really sucks," I said out loud as I walked into my dorm.

A couple of my acquaintances asked me what was wrong, and I filled them in. They wished me the best and thought it was pretty low because of my short time left.

I laid on my bed for about an hour staring at the ceiling. I started thinking about how I learned the Almighty doesn't let His good people rest for very long. Back in "the fire" for more refinement I guess is all I could think this meant. Another test of faith. I'm a true believer now so I must accept it as His plan. "All things work for the good for those who love God and work for his purpose." So this transfer is going to somehow work for my good. There must be a reason he wants me there.

The next day my counselor stopped by the dorm and told me the bus was leaving the next morning at 5:30. All my parole paperwork would be forwarded to the counselor at Houtzdale.

The following morning, I got strip searched, shackled up, and bussed to SCI Houtzdale. Built the same year as Forest. The geography of the grounds was completely different. It wasn't set up in a circular spoke type Block system like Forest. It was really wide open, and you could stand at the north end of the complex and see each individual block in two long rows, one row across from the other. Not as many gates and checkpoints, no towers, less razor wire. A lot more grass and landscape with much less concrete.

I was assigned to "C" Block for the first three weeks. It's a Receiving Block and home to a few inmates that couldn't blend into the other blocks. My celly was an older guy who kept to himself and chose to have no contact with anyone. He basically stayed in his cell and left only to walk to chow three times a day. I knew he had to be a pedophile because of his behavior. I treated him fine. I didn't ask him about his crimes. I guess I didn't want to know.

I then got moved to "D" Block at the far end of the complex. It was a long walk to the north end where the chow hall, commissary, and office buildings were located. It was mid-May and the weather was nice, so a ten-minute walk was fine with me.

Houtzdale was a Level 3 jail. That sounds safer than a Level 5 jail, but it was far from it. It had about the same number of inmates as Forest but fewer guards, or at least it always seemed they were shorthanded there. There was less physical control of inmates because of fewer gates and security fencing and wires. For some reason the guards seemed more apathetic or slower to respond than the guards at Forest. Houtzdale had all levels of inmates up to and including Level 5 guys. It seemed there were more lifers at Houtzdale, but that can be a good thing for safety because the older the inmate gets the less chance of them acting out. In my humble opinion I felt less safe at Houtzdale than I did at Forest. I think mainly because all movement at Forest is totally controlled, and where there are more freedoms at Houtzdale with much less control. Case in point:

One sunny afternoon while in the outside Yard I was working out with another guy on the flat bench. There were a couple hundred guys out in the yard, some on the baseball field, some on the handball court, mostly men walking the track, and a lot just milling around.

While I was in the middle of a set on the bench, I heard multiple cracking sounds like someone getting hit with a stick. My friend yelled out for me to look over to my left. About 30 ft away I saw four individuals striking one single guy on top of the head and neck with shanks. (homemade knives) I'd seen blood spurt from a head wound before but not like this. In less than ten seconds these four guys stabbed him 38 times and killed him right in front of me and about 50 other eyewitnesses. It took the guards at least five minutes to get to his aid. That's a long time. It didn't matter because he was obviously dead, but my point is Houtzdale was not a safer place to be. I saw a stabbing at Forest also. I wasn't as close to that one but there were many more guards out at Forest and response was quick.

My first celly in "D" Block was a black guy from Philly doing life for killing a guy in a botched robbery. By far the worst celly I had ever had. We bumped chests many times over a two-month period. We just could not get along. I think he prided himself on how many celly's he had throughout his prison tenure. He was in for life and he knew I was going home in a few months. I got believing he was going to try and get me to assault him or him plant something in my bunk and get me jammed up, so I'd lose my parole. I had seen that happen to a guy at Forest.

One Saturday morning I was standing in line during Day Room getting hot water for a coffee and one of the Sergeants walked by and asked me how things were going. That didn't happen too often, but this Sgt. was a real decent human being. I hesitated to tell him the truth because if he ignored my request to move and it got out that I went to staff with a problem, I'd be risking a serious ass beating, or worse, and be considered a snitch.

I had to whisper and be very quick about it because it's not cool to be seen talking extended conversations with staff.

"I'm supposed to be paroling in about 7 months and my lifer celly is going to try and prevent that," I said. "If I don't get moved, he or me is going to end up on the slab." (dead).

"Oh. Ok, I know him. He's a piece of shit. I'll move you this afternoon," Sarge responded.

"Won't they wonder why?" I whispered.

"I'll make something good up. Trust me."

"Thanks, Sarge. I hope your right," I said.

My hands were shaking as I tried to hold my cup under the hot water dispenser. "Shit," I said under my breath. If this goes wrong, I'm going to have to do the next seven months in the hole in PC, I thought. (protective custody). Am I a snitch? If this were to get out, I'm going to get jumped on the way to chow by three or four guys for sure.

I walked back up to my cell on the second tier and just sat on the edge of my bed thinking, while my celly was out in the Day Room playing cards.

Lunch time came and went, and it was around 1:15 pm and we were waiting for afternoon yard to begin. (outside rec area) Our door popped and in walked Sarge with another guard.

"Munch, pack your shit. I have a note here from the Unit manager. He wants you moved to the other side of the block. Your counselor got changed and his office is over on that side," Sarge said forcefully.

"They don't move no body on Saturdays! What you got going on here? You know they don't do nothin on the weekend, Ha!" said my celly with an accusatory tone.

"I got the note right here in my hand if it's any of your business anyway. Is it? Is it your business?" Sarge spouted. "Now get your shit packed Munch and I'll be back in fifteen minutes."

Sarge walked out and the door closed. "What the fuck, thays' don't move on Saturdays. Sometin' happened. Somebody said somehtin," spouted my celly.

"Maybe the guys in the next cell complained about us screaming at

241

one another and keeping everybody awake," I said half-jokingly with a chuckle.

'Yeah. Maybe Munch. Maybe," he said with a grin.

Sarge came back and I walked over to the other side of the block with him. I thanked him about ten times. "I just didn't want to risk him setting me up to blow my parole," I said to Sarge.

"I don't blame you a bit. A guy like him has no conscience," Sarge answered.

My new celly was a black guy about five years younger than me. He was a decent person. He was doing life for the three-felony rule violations, and they were all robberies. He said he never hurt any of his victims, but it got to where after spending 38 months in prison, I didn't believe anything anybody told me.

This guy had nothing. He had never worked or paid any income taxes in his entire life. He sold drugs and robbed people to survive. He kind of sounded proud of his past. He had a job in prison in maintenance, and that netted him a few dollars.

When I would go to commissary, I'd order him a couple candy bars. You'd think I gave him a million dollars. He was a very appreciative person but was not motivated to do much of anything other than lay around.

He was the first celly I had that constructed a still. (Homemade alcohol) He would steal oranges from the kitchen and ferment them in vinegar. (I think it was vinegar) He'd cover it up and let it sit for seven days under his bunk. He had a large plastic trash can liner he took from the kitchen and taped it inside a box he got from somewhere. At the end of the week he'd drink the majority of it and get totally wasted. We underwent cell inspections periodically, but he always seemed to know when they were going to take place, and he'd have his still apart. I think one of the guards he was friends with would tip him off.

One Saturday morning he started drinking and I went out to yard for two hours. When I got back in the block one of the guys in the cell next to ours met me at the front entrance and told me my celly was laying on the floor outside the cell with the door open. It took three of us to get him awake and into bed. He always offered me some, but I had to explain to him more than once that I was in for DUI, and I didn't think It would make the Parole Office very happy if I got caught drinking. Ha!

In mid-November they moved me to a different cell and different celly. I had a couple gay celly's at Forest, but they were kind of closet type, and not fully outed with their preferences. They would admit they were gay if you asked them, but they didn't go around flaunting it. I made sure from day one with any gay celly I had, I'd warn them to keep their gayness to themselves. I didn't want to see it, and I didn't want to hear any talk about it.

This new celly was a flaunter. He was only twenty years old and very confused as to who he was and where he wanted to be in life. After spending a week with him I realized why the Almighty had sent me to Houtzdale. He needed a father figure in his life even if it were just a short while. He admitted he had not ever spoken to any male adult since he was an adolescent. He had lived with his mother and she had no brothers or a husband. He had never gotten any direction from an older male and admitted he didn't know why he liked men over women, because he never had a girlfriend.

I didn't know where to begin with this kid. We had six weeks together and had many long conversations about morals and ethics, right from wrong etc. He was in jail because he was primarily a burglar and had admitted to many, many, burglaries in his hometown, and was serving a two to four-year sentence.

I didn't try to change his sexual preference, but I think I may have helped him focus on the future and formulated a plan for him to concentrate on once he paroled. He was one of those inmates that wasn't going to participate in the TC program which enables you to parole at your minimum. He said he didn't have the self-confidence to go through it. I explained the whole program to him, and I told him I thought it would teach him a lot of the things he hadn't learned and needed to know to move forward with his life outside of prison. So, he did sign up to go, but I paroled prior to him going to the program so I'm not sure if he ever went.

CHAPTER **43**

"Goodbye"

FOUR CHRISTMAS'S, FOUR Thanksgiving's, and three birthdays locked up. It was coming to an end. Just as I had prayed so hard for, I was going to be a free man again, free to be with my family. I cannot forget about the victim in my accident. He'll never be with his family again. He was on my mind every day in prison and has been every day since the day it happened. I have taken full responsibility for my actions, and have paid a price, some of whom say it wasn't enough. Maybe it hasn't been.

Regardless of what some people told me about my crime not deserving a state prison sentence I have to say I disagree. It wouldn't have had the same shock value going to a halfway house for a couple of years.

That's what I needed, and most people need, is to be taken to the deepest darkest place society offers, and experience true apathy, depression and total despair. It is punishment in its purest form, and it's a great deterrent for someone who might think about re-offending.

There are people who have great difficulty getting through prison. Usually because they don't accept the responsibility of committing their crimes. A lot of people in prison won't admit their guilt. When I woke up every morning and my feet hit the cold concrete floor, I knew I belonged where I was. I accepted my fate.

That's what we have to focus on while going through life's bad times is looking forward and not back. Christ said many times to "forget the past." I learned to just remove the rear-view mirror and let Christ drive

244

the car. All we need to do is sit in the back seat and enjoy the ride.

On January 6th 2015, the day before parole, a lot of crazy memories ran through my head all day. It seemed like a whole lifetime of emotions were jammed into that 42-month period. Through the night I slept intermittently. My biggest concern was having a heart attack before I could get out.

On January 7th at 8 am. my door popped, and I made the long walk from "D" Block to the Receiving Block. I walked it very slowly, and looked around at the sunlit morning, and every step I took had meaning. It was a glorious moment, and I could feel the Almighty and the Archangel Michael walking beside me. The hair stood up on every part of my body, and my biggest fear was I was going to wake up, and the moment be a dream.

My two sons were waiting in the lobby when the guard walked me to the outer door.

"Take care," he said.

"Thanks. You be safe also," I responded, and turned and walked out into the lobby and hugged my two sons.

From the memories of my early life to now there is a drawerful of unforgettable photographs in my mind. They only have meaning and trigger emotions in me. Some of those pictures are disturbing and gruesome, and some are bright and very beautiful. How do you share the experiences for the good of others so they don't make the same mistakes, or how can they enjoy the gloriousness of the many victories?

That is the mission now is to let my family know about God's love for them, and hopefully to touch as many lives as I can with what I have learned.

It took a lot of time for me to realize what Christ meant when He said, "Friends will come and go, family is forever." Loyalty and love are synonymous when it comes to friendships. Loyalty is rare to find, and that is a hard lesson to learn.

Most importantly I learned that God continues to love us even though He is hurt by our sin. And rather than punish, He'll step back and let the bad things happen, which can turn out for our good, if we eventually cry out and surrender it all to Him. We must give Him all the glory and become true believers.

I will never be timid or afraid to profess my learned faith. It came at too high a price for me to ignore or suppress it. Those that want to be cynical, let them be. Christ called them "Hypocrites" and "Mockers" many times in Scripture. Those are the people that are definitely going to lose in the end.

It took a lifetime journey to finally realize that Christ has been with me every moment, and He is conscious of every breath I take. Our purpose here is to love and be loved.

I surrendered my life to Christ. I handed Him the keys to my car. I'm just going to shut up and sit in the back seat and go wherever He takes me. He's going to drive the rest of the way home. Praise God.

CPSIA information can be obtained
at www.ICGtesting.com
Printed in the USA
BVHW041050220221
600778BV00009B/1165